The Life and Times of Gardiner Spring
VOLUME 1

AUDUBON PRESS
2601 Audubon Drive / P.O. Box 8055
Laurel, MS 39441-8000   USA

Orders: 800-405-3788
Inquiries: 601-649-8572
Voice: 601-649-8570 / Fax: 601-649-8571
E-mail: buybooks@audubonpress.com
Web Page: www.audubonpress.com

© 2008 Audubon Press edition
All rights reserved.
Printed in the United States
Cover design by Crisp Graphics

ISBN # 978-09820731-3-1

Original Publication:

In Two Volumes

Volume 1

New York:
Charles Scribner & Co., 124 Grand Street
1866

Original Publication Layout and Typography:
John F. Trow & Co.,
Printers, Stereotypers, & Electrotypers,
50 Green Street, N.Y.

CONTENTS OF VOLUME I.

CHAPTER I.
PAGE
PRELIMINARY CONSIDERATIONS, ... 5

CHAPTER II.
MY PARENTS, ... 10

CHAPTER III.
MY MOTHER, ... 35

CHAPTER IV.
MY EARLY LIFE UP TO MY ENTERING THE MINISTRY, 74

CHAPTER V.
MY ORDINATION AND MY MINISTRY, ... 104

CHAPTER VI.
THE EMBARRASSMENTS AND ENCOURAGEMENTS OF MY EARLY MINISTRY, ... 119

CHAPTER VII.
PRINCIPLE AND EXERCISE, ... 142

CHAPTER VIII.

REVIVALS, ... 160

CHAPTER IX.

AFFECTING INCIDENTS, ... 179

CHAPTER X.

FANATICISM IN REVIVALS, ... 215

CHAPTER XI.

DOMESTIC MISSIONS, ... 239

CHAPTER XII.

FOREIGN MISSIONS, ... 277

CHAPTER XIII.

THE ANDOVER THEOLOGICAL SEMINARY, . . . 306

CHAPTER XIV.

AMERICAN BIBLE SOCIETY 326

CHAPTER I.

PRELIMINARY CONSIDERATIONS.

ADAM FERGUSON, in his "Essay on the History of Civil Society," relates an anecdote, the spirit of which was the first impulse to the present volume. "It is said of Spinola, a famous commander in the service of Spain, in the sixteenth century, on being told that Sir Francis De Vere, who served under Leicester in the expedition to Holland, *died of having nothing to do*, replied 'that was enough to *kill a general.*'" Nature, not less in the intellectual and moral than the physical world, "abhors a vacuum." I have never aimed at cessation from labor, but rather at incentives to action. While I retain my relation as the senior pastor of the church whose pulpit I have been permitted so long to occupy, I have, at my own request, been released from the more weighty responsibilities of the pulpit and the pastorate, and am exposed to the depression of *having nothing to do*. Fourscore years of my pilgrimage have passed away: not without many a struggle I have, for the most part, relinquished a ministry which has been my joy, and am disposed to feel that my work is done. It is indeed a sad hour. To resort to unemployed repose neither suits my habits nor my taste. My intellect and my affections require stimulus. There is not even embellishment in listlessness. The inventive powers are unstrung; the imagination has lost its promptitude, and is slow and hesitating; and there is no quickness of apprehension, where the mind has nothing upon which to exercise itself, or where there are few, if any, subjects that interest it. Though descended from a vigorous and long-lived stock, I have never anticipated old age; I have never looked for it. But I realize it now, and am contemplating it, not so much with sadness, as with the apprehension that I shall be a cumberer of the ground. This is just the state of mind in which I commence these personal reminiscences. Now that the wintry blast of age has come upon me, I have ventured to summon memory and reflection, to compensate me for the ardor of youth and the vigor of riper years. Yet, at the best, it is but the mournful swell of the night-wind, the solemn wail of days that are with the "years beyond the flood."

If these pages have any interest, it is because they combine biography with history, and advert to those public affairs from which the individual life of the writer cannot well be separated. If they contain some discussions upon theological subjects, in which there is now less interest than there was fifty years ago, it is because historical verity requires some such discussion. If they contain the remarks of others, it is because my younger days had the advantage of intercourse with men of eminence in the theological world, and whose remarks are deeply imprinted on my memory.

I never thought much of a man's writing memoirs of himself; nor do I now think of it without embarrassment. The subject itself is a most humiliating one; and were it not inwoven with so many sweet memories of others, and so many important events, and, above all, with so many delightful recollections of that almighty and invisible hand that brings "the blind by a way that they knew not," and leads "them in paths that they have not known," and whose grace abounds more than my sin abounds, the discouragement and mortification of such a review would be absolutely forbidding.

In the course of writing these pages, I have often felt that I may be accused of egotism, perhaps justly. Yet if I know myself, it is not a conscious self-conceit that has prompted my pen, but the love of labor, and a desire to furnish an unvarnished, unaffected statement of facts. As I am no "noun of multitude," but a single individual, speaking of what he himself has seen and heard, there would be no modesty in arrogating to myself the royal style. After taking counsel of judicious friends, I have come to the conclusion that not to use, in this narrative, the first person singular, would be mere affectation. The relation in which the writer stands to the reader, and to the persons and events of which he speaks, requires this directness. Richard Baxter, John Bunyan, Jonathan Edwards, Andrew Fuller, Samuel Hopkins, Nathaniel Emmons, William Jay, and a host of others, were at no loss to speak of themselves; had they not done so, their biography would have lost its charms. No small part of the Old and New Testaments, so rich in characters and events, is made up of the autobiography of the sacred writers. Moses was no egotist, neither was David, nor Samuel, nor Ezra, nor Nehemiah, nor Ezekiel, nor Daniel, when they were directed by the Spirit of God to give *themselves* so prominent a place in the sacred narrative. The Apostle Paul was no egotist when he addressed his farewell sermon to the elders at Ephesus; nor when he made his defence before Agrippa; nor when he wrote his Epistle to the Corinthians; nor when he said, "Whereinsoever any is bold, *I am bold also;* Are they Hebrews? *so am I.* Are they Israelites? *so am I.* Are they the seed of Abraham? *so am I.* Are they ministers of Christ? *I am more.*"

There is one embarrassment in the work I have undertaken which nothing can relieve: the death of my beloved Mrs. Spring must leave a vacuum in these pages which nothing can fill. She was the wife of my youth: it was a joyous union for more than half a century. She was intimate with my entire history; and greatly do I feel the need of her retentive memory, her habits of observation, her judgment of character, her delicacy of taste, her sympathy with my trials, and her jealousy for my usefulness and honor.

Another embarrassment which I deeply feel, is the fact that I am too far advanced in years to have any very strong expectation that my life and health will be prolonged to the completion of that which 1 have undertaken. I am driven to the work; I am running a race with time; it is too hasty an effort.

Could I have had two years for it, instead of the four months it has occupied, it might have been more interesting as well as more instructive. That I shall have courage to finish it, is perhaps more than I may reasonably hope for. With a sweet composure I leave it in the hands of God. I love to think of him; and if there is anything in these reminiscences that dishonors him, I hope they may never pass from under my own eye. In the event of my death before the work is finished, I shall leave the manuscript in the hands of my children, to be disposed of at their discretion.

I love to look back upon the past. Memory lives there, and in treasuring up what we have acquired or observed, it expatiates upon the resources of infinite goodness. I love, too, to look forward to the future. Faith lives there; and in her brightest anticipations sees Him whose presence and love are the joy of earth and time, and also the everlasting joy of heaven and eternity. It is a delightful thought that God is there, God, our own God. There are sombre hues in the past; but there is radiance even on the darkest cloud. "Who is a strong Lord like unto thee, or to thy faithfulness round about thee?" Time is but a dream. "What shadows we are, and what shadows we pursue!" There is *reality* only in the future, and therefore there is gladness—"joy and gladness, thanksgiving and the voice of melody."

CHAPTER II.

MY PARENTS.

OF all the treasures both of faith and of memory, none are more delightful to me than those which relate to my beloved and honored parents. My recollections of their character are not less precious than vivid; and my assured convictions of their present blessedness and their eternal and onward advancement in glory are as full of joy as filial affection can desire.

It was my privilege to have descended from " the seed royal " of heaven and the heirs of covenant blessings. My maternal ancestors, for several generations, were ministers of the gospel, non-conformists, and English Puritans. My paternal ancestry I have not been able to trace beyond the year 1634, when John Spring, with his wife Eliza, embarked at Ipswich, England, for New England, with their four children. They settled in Watertown, Mass., near Boston, where his name is on the earliest list of proprietors in 1636. His descendants were successively John Spring, Henry Spring, John Spring of the third generation, Henry Spring of the fourth, and *John Spring, my grand-*

father, who was settled in Uxbridge, Mass., in that part of it which afterwards became the town of Northbridge. That he was a man of consequence is evident from the fact that when, in the year 1772, the petition for incorporating Northbridge was presented to the Legislature of Massachusetts, it was " headed by Col. John Spring." He was a justice of the peace, a deacon of the church, and a large landholder on the Blackstone river. He was married in Newton to Sarah Read, by whom he had five sons and one daughter. Their two eldest sons were consumed by a fire that destroyed his dwelling-house, during his absence in the year 1740. His surviving children were John, the father of the late Adolphus Spring, Esq., of Northbridge; Mary, who married the Rev. Elias Dudley, of Oxford, Mass.; Ephraim, who remained on his farm at Uxbridge; and Samuel, my father. My grandfather was the owner of a family of slaves. I recollect them well, and that, after my grandfather's death, my father bore his annual proportion for their support in their old age. Their names were Felix and Phelice. They had two children, Rose and Phillis. Felix was a native of Africa, and used to say that he was stolen from home when a child, and carried into bondage. His African name was *Meibi Allah Mahgooma*. My father regarded him as a Christian man; he had great regard for the Sabbath and spent much of his time in reading the Bible. When slavery was abolished in Massachusetts, he was told that he was free, and could go where he chose; but he preferred remaining in the family. He survived his aged master but a few years, and died in Uxbridge, at the house of my uncle Ephraim, near the close of the last century. My grandfather died March 12th, 1794, aged 88 years. My father was accustomed to make him a yearly visit, and always spoke of him with great reverence and love. He was a man of enterprise and wealth, and on his death each of his children inherited a handsome property. More than once, and when from six to ten years of age, I visited him at Uxbridge, and shall not easily forget the enthusiasm, the glee, with which my father returned to the labors and sports of his more youthful days. He had been the most effective and valuable young man on the farm; and though both of his parents were professors of religion, so important were his services at home, that it was with great reluctance his father consented to his wishes to obtain a liberal education. His mother's importunity, added to his own, prevailed, and at rather an advanced period of life, he left the farm, with a view to one of the learned professions.

He began his study of the languages under the tuition of the Rev. Nathan Webb, the minister of Uxbridge, and his own pastor, for whom he cherished great affection and reverence. He entered Nassau Hall in New Jersey in 1766, at the age of twenty-one. Jonathan Edwards the younger was the tutor of his class, and he often adverted to the accuracy, the thoroughness, and the vigor of his instructions. He imbibed a strong attachment to Mr. Edwards while at college, and cultivated it through life. More than once I have heard him say that of all the theologians he had ever known, Mr. Edwards was the most able, and the most withering to an opponent. And I distinctly recollect his making the remark to me, that his superiority in argument consisted in a rigorous demand from his antagonist for a *definition* of his terms.

My father was a great admirer of the president of the college, the Rev. Dr. Witherspoon; and his lectures to the class and his pulpit ministrations were never forgotten. The character of my father's mind was both of a philosophical and practical cast. He was an enthusiast in his pursuit of knowledge, but it was useful knowledge. The age of metaphysical theology had just dawned upon the American Church, and under the instruction of Mr. Edwards he became familiar with various branches of it; while under the conservative, common sense, and scriptural views of Dr. Witherspoon, he placed little value upon speculations that could not be turned to good account. There was a resident graduate in Princeton of whom I have often heard him speak, and to whom he became greatly attached, by the name of Periam, whom he regarded as of very high promise. He was a devoted Christian, a ripe scholar, and died early. I have often desired to have his history. The records of Nassau Hall, I have no doubt, have some notices of this remarkable man. My father could never mention his name without admiration. President Edwards, the immediate predecessor of Dr. Witherspoon, it is well known, was a *Berkeleyan:* my father was interested in Berkeley's philosophy, and but for the influence of Dr. Witherspoon, might have adopted the opinion that the objects of perception are not real existences, and are simply ideas which exist only in the mind.

While at Nassau Hall, he was the class-mate of the late James Madison, the fourth President of the United States. They both graduated in the year 1771. Mr. Madison was younger than my father, and they were room-mates. On a tour for his health through the Middle and Southern States in 1792, he visited Mr. Madison at Montpelier. It was a visit of several days, and in a familiar retrospect of their college-life, my father once interrogated him upon the subject of his personal religion. Mr. Madison merely replied, " Oh, Mr. Spring, Dr. Witherspoon spoiled me for all other preachers." He had a high estimate of Mr. Madison, especially of his integrity and good judgment. He once remarked to a company of gentlemen, who were Mr. Madison's opponents, "You may rely upon this, gentlemen, I know him well; and James Madison will *never do a foolish thing.*" The intercourse between them continued to the time of Mr. Madison's presidency. While he was Secretary of State, and during the administration of Mr. Jefferson, my father requested his influence in favor of the collector of the port of Newburyport, and that he might not be removed from office. Mr. Madison made the following reply :

"WASHINGTON, *November* 13, 1801.

" DEAR SIR :

" I have received your favor of 20th October, and return you many thanks for the friendly sentiments it expresses towards me.

"Having no other knowledge of Mr. Tyng than what I derive from your letter, I can view him in no other light than that of a man of worth and respectability; nor is any circumstance known to me from which I can infer that his removal from office is contemplated by the President. Should his case be taken up with reference to that question, I shall be led by justice to him, as well as by respect for you, to communicate the testimony you bear in his favor, that it may be duly weighed against objections, if any should be urged, to his continuance in office.

"I am sorry to find you sympathizing so much with the anxieties and alarms which are suffered to overcloud the prospects of some parts of the Eastern States. Whatever dislike or opposition may be felt at the removal of particular persons from office, is it possible that the fate of our country or of our Government can depend on an occurrence of no greater magnitude; or can it be right to make use of such a text for all the inflammatory publications which are circulated through the newspapers? It cannot be unsatisfactory to you to learn that other quarters of the Union are more and more every day presenting a very different scene. The reflection must indeed, by degrees, force itself into every mind, that the situation of our country is to be judged of by those great measures which materially affect its happiness and welfare, and not by the question whether this or that man be in or out of office.

"I have, as you desired, presented your respects to the President, who received them with a recollection of your visit to him. I have performed the like task as to Mrs. M., who joins me in very warm congratulations for the recovery of your health, and wishes for its continuance. Since I had the pleasure of seeing you, mine has suffered frequent interruptions, and is even yet less reëstablished than I could wish.

"With great respect and esteem, I remain, dear sir, your friend and humble servant,

"James Madison."

During the war with Great Britain, 1812–1815, and when Mr. Madison was President, my father wrote him a respectful but faithful letter, upon the perils of the country, and especially the state of the public mind in New England. The following is his answer:

"Montpelier, *September* 6, 1812.
"Reverend Sir:

"I have received your favor of August 26. I recollect our collegiate friendship with the same impressions which it gives me pleasure to find you still retain. Nor have I forgotten the pleasant hours that passed between us at a much later day, under my own roof.

"We all feel the weight of the times; and it is to be regretted that all cannot unite in the measures opposed to them. If it were proper for me, it might not be agreeable to you to discuss the subject. But I will not conceal the surprise, the pain I feel at declarations from any portion of the American people, that measures resulting from the national will, constitutionally pronounced, and carrying with them the most solemn sanctions, are not to be pursued into effect without the hazard of civil war. This is surely not the legitimate course. Neither is it the language, on other occasions, heard from the same quarter, nor a course consistent with the duration or efficacy of any Government.

"Permit me to express equal surprise, that this extraordinary opposition to the war declared against Great Britain is most emphatically rested on an alliance or a connection with France, presumed to exist or to be intended, in the face of demonstrations to the contrary, with which the slightest degree of candor ought to be satisfied.

"Without entering into comparisons between different districts of the Union with respect to the sufferings which led to the war, or the objects at stake in it, it is clear that every district felt, more or less, the evils which produced it, and is more or less deeply interested in the success of it. It is equally certain that the way to make it both short and successful would be to convince the enemy that he has to contend with the whole, and not a part, of the nation. Can it be doubted that, if under the pressure added by the war to that previously felt by Great Britain, her government declines an accommodation on terms dictated by justice, and compatible with, or rather conducive to, her interest, it will be owing to calculations drawn from our internal divisions? If she be disposed to such an accommodation, it will be evinced in due time, to the most prejudiced and misinformed, that the earliest and fairest opportunities are not withheld.

"Mrs. M. acknowledges your kind inquiry after her health. Hers and mine are at present both tolerably good. We hope that yours has been entirely reëstablished.

"Accept our friendly respects.

"JAMES MADISON."

My father became hopefully pious while a member of college, and, immediately after he graduated, commenced the study of theology under Dr. Witherspoon. The following letter to his old teacher at Uxbridge may be read with interest even in these days of advanced theological instruction:

"NASSAU HALL, *November* 21, 1771.

"REVEREND SIR:

"The advantages I enjoyed while under your immediate inspection, your willingness and readiness to communicate, the kindness of my never enough to be honored parents, in supporting me through a liberal education, in a singular manner convince me that I owe myself, my services, and my all to the disposal of a righteous God, into whose arms I now commend myself; voluntarily enlisting in the service where his own Son is the leader, resolving by his assistance to fight the good fight of faith, supplicating his will in my being used as an instrument in his hand to overcome and conquer a wretched and sinful world.

"I am now entering upon the study of divinity under Dr. Witherspoon. At present there are eight students; three of whom have the government of college in their hands; two who graduated before me, and two at the same time. The doctor gives us his lectures in divinity on Monday evening ; on Saturday at twelve o'clock we meet again, at which time there is always a discourse delivered by one of us, either practical, theological, or argumentative, when we are favored with the president's accurate way of remarking on all such performances, which not only instructs the young divine, but helps the speaker and makes the writer. Besides attending to the exercises of the divinity school, I have the advantage of the ' Graduate Society,' lately set up, consisting of the tutors and resident graduates, for improvement in the belles-lettres way. This I conceive to be as profitable as anything whatever of the nature ; our officers not looking upon themselves so far exalted but that they perform the stated exercises of the society with the greatest cheerfulness. This is attended with very good effects ; in the first place, because we have the opportunity of hearing their pieces ; and also because we have the advantage of their remarks and observations on our own performances, which is of singular service, since some of them are well skilled in the nice scrutinies and criticisms of the English language. For these purposes we meet and perform regularly every Friday night, between the hours six and nine. By taking a part in these exercises, together with the doctor's lectures to the students on chronology, history, and eloquence, I am apt to think that my time is both advantageously and agreeably spent ; otherwise it must be attributed to my own indolence and want of proper attention, which would be very inexcusable.

"In consequence of the difficulty that attends the study of divinity, and also the importance of gaining a clear insight into the fundamental principles of religion, I am at present determined to spend three or four years in the study; and, in order to divide my time to proper advantage, I think fit to spend the first six or eight months in the manner hinted above, which is not so agreeable to my parents as I could wish. But I trust, upon further consideration, after having heard my reasons for thus doing, they will acquiesce in my tarrying till spring. After leaving this place, which I am persuaded I shall do with great reluctance, as I have spent my time here in the most agreeable manner, I purpose, God willing, to study under Mr. Hopkins, of Newport, Dr. Bellamy or Mr. Hart, of Connecticut; and since my father is satisfied that I should study under either, it is a matter of indifference to me under which, as I am very well persuaded that either of these gentlemen is capable of conveying the hidden truths of the Gospel in the most clear, precise, and intelligible manner.

"The difficulty is great; the work of a minister of the utmost moment, his success uncertain, and myself a feeble, unworthy creature; all which I humbly beg may teach me to go to, and depend on, God for assistance in Christian graces, that I might live agreeable to my profession, and act worthy of my desired calling, and in some measure answerable to the obligations I am under to Him in a special manner for a Christian birth, which I humbly trust I have passed through since a member of Nassau Hall. That this might be the happy case is the earnest request of your respectful and obliged humble servant,

"SAMUEL SPRING.

"To the Rev. NATHAN WEBB."

After my father left Nassau Hall and that youthful school of the prophets under Dr. Witherspoon, he became the student of Dr. Bellamy, of Bethlehem, Conn., Dr. West, of Stockbridge, Mass., and Dr. Hopkins, of Newport, R. I. It was Calvinism of a somewhat different kind from the Calvinism of Nassau Hall which he was now led to adopt. He did not like to be called a Hopkinsian; he called himself "a consistent Calvinist;" he was accustomed to say, "No man can be a consistent Calvinist without adopting the views of Dr. Hopkins." It was never questioned in earlier times that Dr. Hopkins was a Calvinist. The nominal distinction between Calvinism and Hopkinsianism was never recognized in New England until the discussion between Dr. Hopkins and Mr. Mills, of Huntington, on the " doings of the unregenerate." Yet the Calvinism of the Westminster Confession declares that "the works of unregenerate men are sinful, and cannot please God, or make a man meet to receive grace from him." Not till then was the line drawn, and my father called a Hopkinsian. He *was* a Hopkinsian, and understood the system well. The late Chief Justice Parsons, of Massachusetts, a neighbor and friend of my father, and who loved theological discussion, used to say, "Mr. Spring is right; he is a consistent Calvinist; for if I were a Calvinist, I could not stop short of Hopkinsianism." Dr. Hopkins was the correspondent of the celebrated Dr. Ryland, of Bristol in England. He had been requested by Dr. Ryland to designate some person who would consent to continue the correspondence after his—Dr. Hopkins'—death; and he named my father as the ablest, and at the same time as the most safe advocate of his own views. The following letter was the commencement of the correspondence:

"North Street, Bristol, *November* 17, 1803.
" To the Rev. Samuel Spring:
" Dear Sir: Though it may be questionable whether you have ever heard of me, yet I had a respect for you for several years, having become acquainted with your writings, through my very dear friend and correspondent, Dr. John Erskine, of Edinburgh, and Dr. Jonathan Edwards. Through the kind manner in which the former gentleman mentioned me to the latter, I was most pleasingly surprised, about the beginning of May, 1786, by receiving a packet from Dr. Edwards, whose father I had long revered, inviting me to a correspondence, which I continued to enjoy as long as he remained in this world. Having this day been in company with Captain Ryan, who tells me he knows you, lives very near you, I felt inclined to send you a few lines.

" Though I cannot see scriptural evidence for infant baptism, and think immersion is needful to the right administration of that ordinance, yet I feel a sincere affection for all who love Christ in sincerity, and have the highest respect for many who think differently from me in these things. I have, indeed, always lived in the practice of free communion at the Lord's table. The church at Northhampton to which I first belonged has practised mixed communion above three hundred years; and in that at Broadmead, Bristol, of which I am pastor, I have used to break bread to both the Baptist and Pedobaptist church. The evangelical dissenters are very harmonious, and I have a good degree of acquaintance with most of the evangelical Episcopalians. Mr. Sutcliff, of Olney, and Mr. Fuller, of Kettering, and myself, are very nearly of an age, and have long been intimate friends. I suppose no persons in the kingdom have been more industrious in spreading the writings of Edwards and Bellamy. We respect Dr. Hopkins, but cannot quite come up to his standard in all points, though many exclaim against us for our attachment to American divinity. My time is exceedingly occupied, and Dr. Hopkins, I suppose, gets aged and infirm, or I should have been glad to have applied to himself for the solution of certain difficulties which seem to attend his scheme. Indeed, I have exchanged a few letters with him. If you fully agree with Dr. Hopkins, I wish you would undertake to state to me what you would say in defence of man's responsibility and criminality, and the plea that God is the author of sin.

"I have received a friendly letter from the Rev. Samuel Austin, of Massachusetts, to whom I sent a reply some months ago. But I have much less time for correspondence than heretofore. If you would be so good as to favor me with a line now and then, I shall be greatly obliged to you. I earnestly wish you much success in the work of the Lord, and desire a share in your prayers that the Lord would make me faithful unto the death. I request your acceptance of two or three pamphlets, and remain

"Your friend and brother,
" JOHN RYLAND."

Dr. Emmons was a more able man than my father; but his views on several subjects differed from those of Dr. Hopkins. Though my father regarded him as the ablest of the New England divines, he did not approve of some of his published sermons. He endeavored to dissuade Dr. Emmons from publishing his celebrated discourse on God's hardening Pharaoh's heart, telling him it would do more hurt than good.

My father was licensed to preach the Gospel in 1774, devoting three full years to the study of theology. The following year he joined the Continental Army as Chaplain, and accompanied the expedition to Quebec, under Gen. Arnold and Col. Burr. Many are the affecting narratives of the sufferings of that expedition I have listened to from his lips by our home-fireside. He was on the Plains of Abram when Montgomery fell. It was a snowy morning, and in the face of the enemy, Col. Burr made the bold attempt to rescue the body of his fallen leader. One of the daily papers of this city has called in question the correctness of this statement. But my father was no romancer: I have heard him tell the story too often to be mistaken. In confirmation of it, I may allude to events which took place in my own family while I was living in Beekman-street. My father and the Rev. Drs. Beecher and Taylor were our guests. Col. Burr was a relative of my father, his companion in arms, and my father was anxious to see him. I told him that since his murder of Hamilton, Burr had lost caste, and that he had better not call upon him. He yielded to my intimation; but the day before he left, he took me into the front parlor and said, "My son, *I must see Burr.* We went through the woods together; I stood by his side on the Plains of Abram, and when Montgomery fell. I have not seen him since, and *I must see him before I go.* The last time I saw him was after Montgomery had fallen, and *little Burr*, up to his knees in snow, was trying, in face of the enemy, to bring off Montgomery's body. My son, I must see him." We called at his office in Nassau street, but he was out, and did not return the call till toward evening. I will not speak of the particulars of that interview. It was a beautiful, yet a strange interview. Mrs. Spring and the two gentlemen just referred to were present, and listened to many a tale of by-gone days. Burr was no friend of Washington. Said he, "You know, Dr. Spring, that Washington was a coward." Dr. Beecher could scarcely restrain himself. "I wanted," said he, "to knock him down."

The expedition for Quebec embarked at Newburyport for the River Kennebeck. On their departure, my father preached to them from the text, "Except thy presence go with us, carry us not up hence;" and it was this discourse which commended him to the congregation in Newburyport, where, on leaving the army, he became their settled pastor till the day of his death. He was ordained August 6, 1771, and died March 4, 1819.

It is as *a son* that I speak of him, and am sensible that my representations are exposed to the coloring of filial affection. He was a noble man, an intelligent and warm-hearted Christian, and a devoted and faithful Christian minister. His character, in these particulars, is impartially delineated in Sprague's "Annals of the American Pulpit." Ever the advocate of the doctrine of disinterested benevolence, he exemplified it in his life by a higher regard to other interests than his own. He had no fellowship with vanity or meanness, but was distinguished for integrity and honor, and doing to others as he would they should do to him. In questions of doubtful morality, he was in the habit of referring them to the criterion of disinterestedness. "What does disinterestedness say?" was with him the decisive question. He taught this doctrine to his children, and urged upon them the importance of "keeping self in the background." He carried it into the pulpit, and with great power and boldness. With what severity of demonstration and scorching rebuke have I heard him, especially in his extemporaneous discourses, denounce the religion that quarrelled with the divine sovereignty and justice! He would tell his hearers that if their religion took its rise merely from their expectations of the divine favor, it was all delusion. "It is all selfishness," he would say; "it begins in selfishness, and ends in selfishness. Just as though a man, from a supreme regard to himself, could love God supremely, and more than himself." Some of his peculiar views, I have often thought, were the result of his adoring views of the divine character. The great God was his all in all. I have no doubt that the emotional causes of his Hopkinsianism were his all-controlling views of God's direct and personal presence. There was an elevation of moral feeling about him in this respect, which was unusual. God was brought home to the inmost consciousness of his soul. He loved to see God and enjoy God in everything. God's glory, with him, swallowed up everything else. Nature, providence, grace, the cross of Christ, heaven, hell, were resplendent with the manifested and illumined Deity. In his prayers he seemed often lost and swallowed up in God. A lady once said of him, "I love to hear Mr. Spring pray, because he prays as though he loved God." His piety was distinguished for humility, cheerfulness, and decision. He was jealous for himself with godly jealousy, and sat in scrutinizing judgment upon his own motives. Though a severe student, he loved a good joke, and was occasionally full of his fun, especially with his children and his theological students. I have rarely known him depressed, except at the close of his pulpit ministrations on the Lord's day. He would then sigh, "Ah me! who hath believed our report?" He was an enthusiast in sacred music, and then he would walk the room and sing:

> "Weary world! when will it end?
> Destined to the purging fire;
> Fain I would to heaven ascend,
> Thitherward my thoughts aspire.
> Saviour, this is not my place:
> Let me die to see thy face!"

Though they are sixty years since I listened to these words, thus sung, yet I seem to hear them even now, and from the melodious voice of my departed father. He was remarkably scrupulous in the observance of the Lord's day, both personally, in his family, and in the town. He was instrumental in inducing the leading gentlemen of the town to appoint a committee of their own number in order to repress the growing desecration of the day. He would not shave his face on the Lord's day, nor allow my mother to sew a button on her son's vest ; and on one occasion, when his nephew, the late Adolphus Spring, Esq., arrived in haste on a Saturday evening with the message that his father was on his bed of death, he would not mount his horse for the journey of seventy miles, until the Sabbath sun had gone down. His standard of Christian character was high, and applied with searching scrutiny both to himself and others. He had little confidence in religious impulses, and was at a great remove from all those measures the object of which was to produce an excited state of mind. He was a man of strong emotion, but it was emotion that was the result of principle. He was very cautious in receiving persons to sealing ordinances, and more generally put them upon a prolonged probation. Yet his church was not small, and in character and influence one of the most important churches in New England. It was the mother-church of Eastern Massachusetts, then the District of Maine, where family after family removed from his own parish, and where they founded churches which now shine as lights in the world. His diligence as a student, his faithfulness as a pastor, his practical wisdom, and his rare administrative faculties, gave him great influence. He made his mark on the churches, and has left it on the inhabitants of Newburyport. The interest he took in the welfare of the town, and in the public schools, his social qualities, his decision of character, his cheerful temperament, his great hospitality, his public spirit, and his large-heartedness, gave him an honored place among his fellow-citizens of every name.

He lived several years after I entered the ministry, and I shall always be a debtor to his example, his counsels, and his prayers. Four of his sons are still living, and we can all bear testimony to his paternal love and faithfulness. He was attached to the domestic discipline of the Old Testament; and though no father was more kind, we all felt that his word was law. If we have been industrious men, we owe it to the example, the instruction, the discipline of our father. He was a working man in his youth, and a working man in his old age. He knew how to "take hold of things by the right end," and frequently instilled the lesson upon his sons. He was not only watchful of the books we read, the principles we imbibed, the company with which we associated, and the amusements we indulged in, but the *manner* in which we did our work.

His health greatly suffered from his efforts in New England and the Middle States, on a begging tour in behalf of the sufferers by a desolating fire in Newburyport in 1811; but he lived to the advanced age of seventy-three years. His last discourse was delivered on the first Lord's day in January, 1819, from the words: "Behold, now I am old, I know not the day of my death." He died on the 4th of March following. As long as he could sit in his chair, he conducted the religious worship of his family, reading with great delight from Burkitt's Commentary of the New Testament. I did not know of his last sickness until a few hours before his death. It was at noon on the Lord's day that the mournful intelligence reached me. The following morning I left New York, hoping to be in time for his funeral; but a violent snow-storm so obstructed the travelling, that I did not reach Newburyport until the day after his interment. I could not, however, resist the desire to look once more upon that loved and venerated face. I had the grave uncovered—the sexton only with me—and took a last look at the dear form of my departed father, his robe of office inwoven with his shroud. I merely said, "*Yes, it is my father*," and wept.

His views in the near approach of death were such as might be expected from such a man. I made the following record of them at the mournful visit to which I have just referred.

Until within three days of his death, he enjoyed the full use of his reason, and was fully convinced that his end was near. In his last interview with Dr. Dana, pastor of the Presbyterian Church in Federal street, five days before his death,—as Dr. D. sat by his bedside, my father said, "I wish you to pray for me, and for my family, and for my people, that we may all feel aright respecting my poor self. I have a hope in the infinite mercy of God; I have had seasons of discouragement respecting my spiritual state, and I have had seasons in which I hope I have enjoyed the light of God's countenance. As to the truth of the system I have preached, I have no question, but have reason to lament that I have preached with so much coldness. Yet I think I have had some seasons in which I have enjoyed communion with God in my public exercises. I have nothing of my own, not one spark of righteousness to recommend me; I come as a sinner to the Saviour." To this Dr. Dana replied, "God forbid, Sir, that any of us should come in any other way, but in reliance on a crucified Saviour." After a short pause, he said, "I am not adventurous, but I think I can cheerfully venture my immortal soul on the infinite mercy of God in Christ."

To another who inquired, "Do you enjoy the peace of God ?" he said, "I should be miserable without it."

To Dr. Woods, Theological Professor at Andover —on the Monday before he died—he said, "You occupy the most important station there can be in this life. I hope you will be faithful. God be with you, bless you, succeed you, and uphold you."

After considerable weariness he exclaimed, " Oh! let me be gone; do let me be gone! I long to be at home."

Three weeks previous to his death, my brother Samuel asked him " how his life appeared ?" He replied, " Oh! it appears as if it needed grace thrown over the whole of it." "And on what part of your life can you dwell with the most satisfaction ?" He replied, "That I have been permitted to preach the Gospel; that I have been enabled to preach what I believe to be the system of truth; and that I have been the unexpected instrument of establishing the Seminary at Andover, and any agency I had in originating the American Board of Commissioners for Foreign Missions."

He passed away quietly, like a shock of corn in his season, fully ripe. As a deserved tribute to his worth, the Church at Newburyport caused the following inscription to be placed on the stone that marks his last resting-place:

"In memory of Rev. Samuel Spring, D.D., born at Uxbridge, Mass., Feb. 27, 1746; graduated at Princeton College 1771; licensed to preach 1774; ordained as pastor of Second Congregational Church and Society in Newburyport, August 6, 1777; deceased March 4, 1819, aged 73. A man of an original and vigorous mind, distinguished for a deep sense of human depravity, and especially of his own unworthiness, and for his exalted views of the character and perfections of God the Redeemer; of great integrity, firmness, benevolence and urbanity; an able, faithful, and assiduous pastor, an example to the flock over which he was placed; a kind husband, a tender father, and a sincere friend. He was a 'Visitor' of the Theological Seminary at Andover from its commencement; President of the Mass. Missionary Society; Vice-President of A. B. C. F. M., and bore important offices in most benevolent Societies around him; he lived eminently useful, beloved, revered, and died universally lamented."

The following letter, addressed to me soon after my

father's death, it is due to his memory here to insert:

"FRANKLIN, *April* 28, 1819.

"To Rev. GARDINER SPRING:

"DEAR NEPHEW: I received yours of 29th March, with both pleasure and pain. It was painful to have my afflictive feelings called up afresh respecting the late decease of your dear father and my dear brother. There was no other man in the world with whom I had been so long and intimately united in sentiment and affection. I share largely, and I had almost said equally, in this bereaving stroke of Providence. But since the will of the Lord is done, it is my duty as well as yours to mourn with submission. I did not know till you informed me, that your father was so much tried on account of Mr. Murdock's appointment at Andover. I had heard of his appointment, but not of his acceptance of it. I greatly regret the event, for, as you intimate, I have always thought, and often said, that Orthodoxy would languish and die there as soon as your dear father deceased. I have feared, and do still more and more fear, that that richly endowed Seminary will ere long become the fountain of theological errors, and disseminate them through all New England, if not through America. I have for some time been fully convinced, that neither the teachers, nor the taught, strictly adhere to that excellent creed upon which the institution was professedly founded. They are fast verging towards the absurdities of old Calvinism, and the tide of popularity is setting so strongly in their favor, that I can do nothing more than save my single self from being carried down the stream and overwhelmed. This I intend to do, and hope I shall be able to do. You are at present in a safe harbor; but I fear your cotemporaries in Massachusetts will soon imbibe that *neutralizing* spirit which will both disable and indispose them to combat the abounding errors of the day. I rejoice that your pious father *kept the faith* to his dying hour. There is but one true system of Divinity, and the more clearly and intelligibly that is unfolded and supported, the more it will detect, refute, and bear down every false system. The peculiarities of Orthodoxy afford a minister the best *defensive* and *offensive* weapons. It is the wisdom as well as duty of a preacher to employ these weapons as freely and forcibly as possible. * * *

"Please to write to me as often as you can, and with the utmost freedom; for in me you shall find a faithful friend as well as an affectionate uncle.

"Nath. Emmons."

CHAPTER III.

MY MOTHER.

The year 1766 was memorable in the town of Hadley, on the Connecticut river, for the destruction of a private dwelling-house in the centre of the town. It was with no small difficulty that the large family which occupied it escaped the flames. It was a cold night in midwinter, and the owner of the house, then in the vigor of manhood, was almost frantic with anxiety for the safety of a *beloved daughter*, then but six years of age. She had escaped at the first alarm without being noticed, and was running in her night-dress, and with naked feet, when a kind lady took her in her arms and carried her to her own bed. In the midst of his deep agony for his beloved child, the father was told that his daughter was safe, when he turned to the blazing mass and exclaimed, "*Now burn!*"

That little child, so kindly cared for by a watchful Providence, was *my beloved mother*. She was the daughter of the Rev. Samuel Hopkins, D.D.—a wife meet for such a husband as my father; in piety, in personal accomplishments, and activity, fitted to be his helper, his adviser, his comforter in his arduous work.

Her venerated father, notwithstanding his name, was a Calvinist of the school of Baxter and Doddridge. His father was the Rev. Samuel Hopkins, of West Springfield; his mother was the eldest daughter of the Rev. Timothy Edwards, of East Windsor, in Connecticut, and the sister of Jonathan Edwards. He graduated at Yale College in 1749, and held the office of tutor in the college for three years. He made a public profession of religion in 1752, and was received into the church of which his father was pastor. He was ordained over the church in Hadley in the month of February, 1755, and remained its beloved and faithful pastor for fifty-six years, and to the day of his death. He was married to Mrs. Sarah Williams, the widow of his immediate predecessor, by whom he had eight children, of whom my mother was one. The Rev. Dr. Lyman, of Hatfield, his intimate friend and neighbor, in a discourse delivered at his funeral, says of him, " I have seldom known his equal for the constancy and fidelity of his friendships, and for so much innocent pleasantry, mingled with so much solid sentiment and profitable instruction. He was an able and sound divine, and well able to vindicate the faith once delivered to the saints. His manner as a preacher was grave and solemn, but not the most animated and interesting: what was deficient in manner was compensated by important truth. He was a man of remarkable prudence and judgment, and shone with peculiar lustre in ecclesiastical councils, and in the associated bodies of his brethren in the ministry."

He lived to the advanced age of eighty-one years, and died on the 8th of March, 1811. I have seen nothing of my grandfather's publications, except his half-century discourse to the people of Hadley, from the words, "Yet have I set my king upon my holy hill of Zion," in which he presents ample illustrations of the mediatorial prerogative of King Jesus, and a condensed and valuable historical view of the town and church, and towards the close of which he says, "Neither preacher nor hearers can escape the wrath to come, but by flying to the Atonement of Christ, and to divine mercy through His blood for forgiveness."

My maternal grandmother, Sarah Porter, was a descendant, in the first generation, from John Porter and Rose his wife, who came from England, and were among the first settlers in Windsor, Conn. He died in April, 1648, and his widow died in about twenty years after. They had five sons and six daughters, most of them born in England. Samuel Porter, their third son, born in England in about 1659, married Hannah Stanley, daughter of Thomas Stanley, of Hartford and afterwards of Hadley. They settled at Hadley, where he died on the 6th of September, 1689, and she died on the 18th of December, 1708. They had eight children born at Hadley. The Hon. Eleazar Porter, their fourth son, was born 25th of February, 1698, at Hadley. He married Sarah Pitkin, daughter of the Hon. William Pitkin and Elizabeth Stanley, of Hartford. Mr. Pitkin was chief justice in the Connecticut colony in 1713, and died 8th of April, 1723. The Hon. Eleazar Porter and Sarah Pitkin, his wife, settled at Hadley, where he was a very distinguished and influential man. He died November 6, 1757, and his widow died June 6, 1784, in the eighty-second year of her age. They had twelve children, born at Hadley, most of whom died unmarried. *Sarah Porter*, their second daughter, was born April 28, 1726, and married the Rev. Chester Williams, of Hadley, who died October 13, 1752. She then married, in 1756, the Rev. Samuel Hopkins, the minister of Hadley, and had by him two sons and six daughters. Their third child, my own mother, was *Hannah Hopkins*.

She was born August 10, 1760, and was married to my father November 4, 1779. They had eleven children, eight sons and three daughters, the first of whom, a son, survived his birth but twelve short hours. The names of the others, in the order of time, are Margaret Stoddard, Gardiner, Hannah, Walton, Samuel, Lewis, Mary, Pinkney, Charles, and John Hopkins. Margaret became the wife of the Hon. Bezaleel Taft, jr., of Uxbridge, and died July 25, 1816. Gardiner is still living, and is the pastor of the Brick Church in New York. Hannah died May 16, 1795. Walton died May 18, 1809. Samuel is still living, and was till recently the pastor of the church in East Hartford, Conn. Lewis was lost at sea in 1814. Mary died August 13, 1796. Pinkney died at New York, September 9, 1820. Gardiner, Samuel, Charles, and John Hopkins, all old men, are the only survivors of the eleven.

Our dear mother, both in her pensive and cheerful moods, was wont to indulge herself in the use of her pen. On one of my last visits to her, she playfully told me what she thought of us all; and then, changing her tone, said, with touching tenderness, "Take *that*, my son, and read it at your leisure." May I not be allowed to record it here? I give it in her own words:

"The Rev. Samuel Spring, D.D., and Mrs. Hannah Spring, the parents of this circle, look round upon them with mingled joy and grief. It was their privilege early to devote their children to God in the bonds of the covenant; they have endeavored to impress their minds with the *infinite importance of religion.*

"In their covenant God in Christ is their only hope for themselves and their children. Thankfully and anxiously do they look round on their surviving offspring; nor do they repine at the hand that has hidden the greatest half of their number in the silent tomb; firmly believing that eternity will open a scene respecting them *all*, in which all holy beings will rejoice. Oh! may they be so happy as finally to present themselves before God, and say, 'Here, Lord, are we, and the children which thou hast given us.' Amen!

1. "Ah, beauteous babe!
    Just didst thou sip the cup of life,
Then from it turned. Just twelve short hours filled up
Thy mortal span. Transplanted, as we hope,
From this to heavenly ground."

2. "Child of our hopes, and comfort of our declining years,
And must thou die? Yes; high heaven
Has so decreed. 'Be still, and know that I am God.'"

3. "*Still lives* to bless the world; our hope, our joy!
O keep him, Holy God, and let him as
A signet be on thy right hand, and with
His years increase his love for souls."

4. "O child of promise! shall we much deplore
Thine early exit from this world of woes?
We hope thou wast prepared for realms of bliss;
Soon we shall follow thee."

5. "The manly, noble, persevering mind,
And beauteous form, just entering
On the busy scenes of life, must find
An early grave. And what *can* soothe
Parental anguish here? God reigns;
And no injustice can be done."

6. "O child of many hopes and many fears,
Endowed by God with talents clear and bright,
Still must we hope that they will be
Improved for noble purposes."

7. "O can we ever cease to mourn
The enterprising mind, the energetic
And the vigorous man, the heart
Replete with every social virtue;
The noble and the generous friend!
If e'er there was a call for deep submission,
Sure we have it here."

8. "A rosebud of the brightest hue!
Lent by God a few short months,
For reasons far more wise than we can scan,

Called from this active scene ; soon
Did she follow her departed sister
Where side by side their monuments
May now be seen."

9. " Sweet child of sensibility ! let not
The fondest hopes of parents, cherished
In thy infant days, be blasted
In thy manhood ! Let talents given
Be nourished and improved, to bless
Thy parents, and to bless the world."

10. " However fair the promise of thy youth,
And hope looks forward with propitious eye ;
Yet sure the heart must tremble
For thy future destiny, while
Destitute of grace."

11. " Last, but not least beloved, of sons,
Much may we hope from thee,
If God direct thy mind. Let not
The wishful eye be turned on thee in vain ;
Be thou the prop of our declining years."

Thus spake the heart of *a true and loving Christian mother*. The death of my brother Lewis, lost at sea, was a most afflicting providence to her, and she says of it, " If ever there was a call for deep submission, we have it here." He was bold and enterprising, and had embarked as supercargo on a vessel from Cape Cod on a perilous voyage, during the last war with Great Britain. Some persons now living may remember the fearful snow-storm in January, 1814, in which the United States schooner *Sylph* was wrecked, if I mistake not, off the Jersey shore. My brother Lewis sailed the day before; and it is the opinion of mariners that, from the violence of the gale, not being able to bring his sharp and heavily-laden craft—she had a full cargo of salt—into the wind, she was put before it, and ran under, and that in less than forty-eight hours after he left Barnstable, the vessel and all hands were lost in or near the Gulf Stream. Neither vessel nor crew have been heard of since. The agitated family waited for tidings month after month, but no tidings came. My mother's emotions, in view of this mournful event, will be most truthfully presented by the following letters, addressed to me in New York:

"Newburyport, *May*, 1815.

"My Dear Son:

"We received yours of the 28th ult. this morning. You ask if I am waiting for a letter from you before I write? By no means, my son; I have not felt myself at all neglected by *you;* but other reasons have prevented my writing of late.

"Since our distressing apprehensions respecting your dear brother Lewis, we thought it not best to write, or burden your mind with the same anxious suspense in which we were held. But after waiting many weeks, and from every source of information, your father wrote.

"To describe to you, my son, the state of my mind for these two weeks past, respecting our dear Lewis, would be impossible. Indeed, I need not. You are a *father*. You can look forward and conceive your sons grown to manhood, and become companions for you, promising to be the support of your declining years. Enterprising, promising in the view of all around you as it respects *this world;* to you tender, respectful, dutiful, affectionate, to have such an one taken without comfortable evidence of his preparation for a better world! O, my son, *I must not dwell here*—I must look up to the throne of God; I must look to the great Arbiter of all events, who governs the universe in infinite rectitude. I must, I do believe that He hath done all things well. I hope *I feel it*, and that, though my heart now bleeds with anguish for my son, yet the time will come when—if my heart is right with God—I shall rejoice at this very event. O, how unspeakable the consolation that *the Lord reigneth!*

"You will perhaps say, 'Mamma, you write as if you had no hope respecting Lewis.' I confess, my son, I have very little; I can scarcely say I have a hope. It is now more than fifteen weeks since he sailed from Barnstable, Cape Cod, for Georgetown, S. C.—a voyage which might have been performed in six, eight, or ten days at most in good weather. We have heard from Bermuda, from Halifax, from Cuba, from many of the West India islands, where it is most probable he would have been carried in if captured. I know it is *possible* he may be taken and carried to England, but I think it not *probable*. He sailed Saturday, January 14. On the Monday night and Tuesday following occurred one of the most tremendous storms ever known on our coast. Have we much room to hope?

"You say you are 'amazed at his temerity in

sailing with a cargo of salt in the month of January.'
He expected to have sailed at an earlier date; but
the vessel he bought was not sold according to the
first advertisement, and the postponement of the sale
deferred his voyage. I said to him, when he was
planning it, 'Lewis, had you not better be contented
to stay at home this winter? It is dangerous going
abroad. I dread your encountering our coast at this
season of the year; you must suffer a great deal, if
you escape the enemy; perhaps something may turn
up for you to do by spring.' He answered me,
'Mamma, I am now past my twenty-first year; I
have no one to depend on me at present; I have
nothing to depend on but my own exertions; I am in
the prime and vigor of life; now is my time to make
something to begin the world with. If it were safe
to go into any kind of business at home, I would not
sail; but you know it is not. I have something that
I can venture abroad with, and I am ashamed to be
seen in the streets in idleness. As to the danger of
our coast in the winter, I expect to strike right out into
the broad ocean, and not keep on our coast. I know
I shall be exposed to the enemy, but I think I can escape by outsailing them; if not, and I am taken and
lose all, I know the English so well that I know I can
get into business with them, and I shall not return till
the war is over.' Thus he reasoned, and had you
been here, you would have felt differently from what
you now do. I think I gave him the best advice I
was capable of, and it is a satisfaction to me that I
wrote to him and sent him on his Bible after he left
home. While conversing with him on serious subjects

a little before he went away, he observed to me, 'Mamma, I believe all you say is true, and I wish I felt about these things as you do, but I am sensible I do not.' I have written just as things were spoken, that you may judge of the state of his mind as well as I.

"I very much rejoice in the goodness of God towards you and your people. O may the Spirit still continue to descend like gentle dew upon you. I have hardly left myself room to assure you that I am still

"Your affectionate mother,
"Hannah Spring."

"Newburyport, *September* 3, 1815.

"My Dear Son:

"As the privilege of conversing with you is denied me, I take this method of communicating to you some of my feelings and exercises, in reference to the loss of your dear brother Lewis. I am persuaded that when you turn your thoughts towards your father's house, and think of the sore dispensation that attends us, you are sometimes ready to exclaim, 'O that I had wings like a dove, that I might fly to my friends, and spend one hour at least in conversing with my dear parents and brothers! I flatter myself that you are sometimes ready to ask, how does my dear *mother* bear this trial? I answer, I hope I am not altogether stupid under the rod; though I sometimes feel very insensible. I realize the truth of the old adage, 'What the eye does not view, the heart does not rue.'

We did not witness the *agonizing struggle*, the *dying strife*. If we had, perhaps our hearts would be more deeply affected. But, oh! there was an eye that *did* see; a hand that *could* save; a God who ordered all these events according to His own infinite wisdom. And shall we reply against our God, or call in question the wisdom or perfection of His government, because our worldly hopes and expectations are cut off, and our dear children hidden from our eyes? Have I been so long in the school of Christ, and not learned the lesson of submission to my Heavenly Father? If so, I have poorly profited by His example who, in full view of a most bitter death, said, 'Father, not my will, but thine be done.' But can the feelings of the *mother* be extinguished? Can the heart cease to yearn over the son? No; God does not require it; and should I cease to feel as a mother, I fear I should cease to improve the trial as a Christian.

"God has dealt gently with me under this trial. I will relate to you what I wish no eye to see but your own. About a fortnight after he sailed, when we had no uncommon concern about him—not then knowing how terrible the storm had been on our coast—he was showed me in a dream in a drowned state. Every feature had the appearance of a person who had lain in the water about ten days, which I have now reason to think was really the case at that time. You will perhaps think it weakness in me to mention the circumstance, but I then feared, and I now think, that Providence designed to prepare my mind by this appearance for the certainty of this dreadful event. In this view I mention it.

"When in the course of providence we became very doubtful of his safety, my principal distress was for his precious soul. O could I be sure, or even have comfortable evidence of his eternal welfare, the loss would be nothing. But while endeavoring to call up every favorable circumstance respecting him, and to find something to rest a hope upon, I was forcibly assailed by this Scripture, '*Except ye believe that I am he, ye shall die in your sins.*' I saw clearly that unless he was brought to accept an offered Saviour, he must have gone to the bar of God with all his sins about him. I was silent before a righteous God. I knew a Saviour was provided and had been offered him all his life long, and if he had gone out of the world rejecting him, God's justice would be glorified. In this state I remained a number of days, when those words passed through my mind as though audibly spoken, '*And in the fourth watch of the night, Jesus came to them walking on the water.*' I know that Jesus was able to appear for him in his last moments, and to save him from sinking in endless destruction. I cannot be without *hope* that this was the case; yet I know that my consolation must be drawn from a different source. *The Lord reigneth.* If you think me guilty of great weakness in mentioning these things, I only say, suspend your judgment till you have passed through a similar trial.

"On looking over this, I am almost disposed to withhold it. I find I have not communicated my feelings as I wish; you will have a very inadequate idea of them, but conclude to send it.

"When I reflect on the dealings of God with our

house, I am ready to say, Why has he dealt thus with us? Why is our beauty and our strength cut off? My Saviour answers me, 'Every branch that is in me that beareth not fruit he taketh away; and every branch that beareth fruit he purgeth it that it may bring forth more fruit.' You, my son, will not cease to pray for us that this may be the fruit of our affliction. My ardent prayer to God has been that he would sanctify my children. I *hope* he is answering my prayer, but it is by terrible things in righteousness. God's ways are not as our ways.

"God bless you and yours, prays your affectionate
"Mother."

I will not trouble the reader with my answer to my mother's letter. Oh, Lewis! Lewis! We all loved him. In form and feature he was the noblest of the family. His name vibrates on my heart even now at the distance of half a century. He had fine business talents, and was a worldly man. But who can tell that my mother's day-dream was not realized? She was wonderfully peaceful after it, and we all rejoiced to see her thus comforted. Jesus came walking on the sea.

She was a devotedly pious woman, and was well instructed in the truths of the Gospel. She once told me that she had read Henry's Commentary *through* before she was fifteen years of age. How early she became pious I do not know; but it was in early youth. She made a public profession of her faith at the age of eighteen, a year before her marriage. Her intelligence, her tenderness, her prayers, her weeping solicitude for the immortal welfare of her children, her Saturday evening instructions from the Bible, more to them than all the Sunday-schools in the world, made impressions on their minds which nothing can efface. If they did wrong and denied it, those lips of hers would quiver, and that little foot of hers would shake the floor with emphasis, and her rebuke would cover us with shame; but if we were frank and "owned up," she was all forgiving gentleness. She had a piercing eye, and though a woman of small stature, she was a woman of great courage. Many a time, by the fireside, she would recite to us the deeds of her father during the Indian wars, and stimulate us to noble daring. I have ever admired woman's valor, and often thought that a courageous mother would not be likely to have a coward son. She taught us that this world is not all sunshine and flowers; she often premonished us of coming evils, and bade us prepare for them, and, trusting in God, manfully to breast ourselves for the battle of human life. She would laugh at us when we complained of the winter's cold, and tell us to go and warm ourselves by shovelling away the snow. My father was generous to a fault; he cared nothing for money, and in his last sickness it was a grief of heart to him that he had been so lavish that my mother would be left comparatively poor. My mother was economical, rigid in her economy; and but for her, my father's ample inheritance, for years dwindling away, would have been exhausted.

Two illustrations of her solicitude for the spiritual welfare of her children may here be noted, one furnished from memory by Dr. Hawes, of Hartford, and the other forwarded for record by my brother Samuel.

During an illness of my father, his pulpit was supplied for a season by the senior class at Andover Seminary. On one occasion Mr. Hawes preached, and after the services of the day, the family were gathered round the tea-table. Mr. Hawes had preached in the afternoon a sermon to the young, and my mother was very anxious that the solemn impression made by it on her own mind might reach the conscience and heart of my brothers Charles and J. Hopkins, who heard it, and who were then at the table. She had been, as was her wont after coming from church, to her closet, and no one can doubt what was the burden of her prayer on that Sabbath afternoon. She came to the table with her heart full. She said nothing; but all noticed that the tears were trickling down her cheeks as she poured out tea. The young men were not slow to divine the cause, and her sympathy soon communicated itself to them. They could not eat, and soon left the table in tears. It is not known whether the impression then made was lasting; but they have both long been exemplary and useful members of Christian churches, and, I doubt not, attribute their conversion, under God, to the undiscouraged efforts and prayers of faithful and believing parents, and especially their godly mother.

The other event may be more briefly related. Soon after my brother Samuel began to venture to hope that he had found a Saviour, he was one day conversing with our mother, and giving her some account of his religious exercises. She listened with interest, and closed the conversation with this remark: "*Every Christian grace, but one, has its counterfeit.* You may love; but it may be a selfish love. You may have faith; but it may be only the faith that trembles. You may have hope and joy; but they may be spurious. But there is one grace you cannot counterfeit." "And what is that, Mamma?" "The grace of *perseverance*, my son."

She was a sweet mother. Oh! we loved her, and we love to dwell on her memory. I feel, while writing these few pages, as though she was near me and communing with me. I told my family at breakfast, this morning, that I was going to-day to enjoy her company. Yes; she was a loving mother, a loving wife, a loving child of God. She was our earthly refuge. The church loved her, as much as they did their pastor. With his increasing years and infirmities, my father loved her more and more, and confided more in her judgment to the last. The whole town, with all their denominational differences, loved and respected Mrs. Dr. Spring. She was at the head of their charitable institutions, alike honored by the rich and sought after by the poor. She was fifteen years younger than my father, and survived him but a few short months. He died on the 4th of March, she on the 3d of the following June.

I find the following thoughts in my Diary in relation to the death of my parents :—" Feb'y 24, 1820. The past year, both my parents have gone to their rest. Ever since I left my father's roof, at the age of fifteen, it has been my practice and privilege to write to them on my birth-day. Little did I think, a year ago, that I was writing my last birth-day letter. I feel to-day that one of the most pleasant and useful habits of my life is broken up. I do not weep for my beloved parents; I have no doubt they are in a better world; I only mourn that I shall see their faces no more; no more be encouraged by their counsels; no more benefitted by their prayers. 'They were lovely in their lives, and in their death they were not divided.' Since their death I have felt myself very much like an *orphan*. I could not reach that house of mourning in time for my father's funeral, but had the satisfaction of passing the week after his death with my sorrowing mother. It was a blessed week to her, to the family and to me. On the morning on which I left, I saw that my poor mother was much depressed. As I bade her farewell, I simply said at parting, Dear mother, let *not* your heart be troubled! I could say no more. It was the last sentence I ever uttered to my mother. We wept and parted—I for my field of labor, she for her rapid maturity for heaven. Sorrow had accomplished its mission; her sorrow was soon to be turned into joy. In the following June I was called to visit her, but on my way from Boston to Newburyport, I learned that by a fatal hemorrhage of the lungs her spirit had fled. On my arrival I found it so. I entered the chamber where she was dressed for the grave. DEAR MOTHER! I said as I kissed the clay-cold corse! I could not utter another word. We followed her to her last resting-place, and carefully deposited her by the side of her husband and our father."

The most affecting thought to me on the death of my parents was, *that I had lost their prayers.* From how many exposures and sins had their prayers protected me! How often had their prayers relieved and refreshed me in seasons of sadness and discouragement! How many blessings, and how rich, had their prayers procured for their unworthy son! I stood alone now. God was my only helper.

The following inscription is on the stone which marks her grave:

"In memory of Mrs. Hannah Spring, wife and relict of Dr. Spring, and daughter of Rev. Samuel Hopkins, D.D., of Hadley, Mass.; born August 10, 1760; died June 11, 1819, aged 59 years.

"A wife worthy of her affectionate husband; a woman of eminent holiness of life, beloved and respected by all; peculiarly active in promoting the interest of all benevolence; a help meet for a minister of the Gospel, abounding in prayer, in faith, and good works; an excellent mother, and peculiarly endeared to all her friends and acquaintance. Truly they were lovely and pleasant in their lives, and in their death were not far divided.

"In testimony of the grateful estimation with which the memory of their pastor and his consort is cherished, this monument is erected by a bereaved and affectionate church and congregation. 'The righteous shall be had in everlasting remembrance.'"

Many a time have I blessed God for such parents; and I will praise him for them while I live. I mourn that I ever grieved them, and praise him for all the comfort they derived from my subsequent history, and for their frequently expressed and adoring views of God's goodness to their children.

My mother was a most faithful correspondent.

Her letters to me after I left home for Yale College, and after I became a minister of the Gospel, have been treasured up, and more than once read with tears. The following letter discloses so much of that anxious, loving, believing heart, that, humbling as it is to myself, I may not suppress it. It was given me by her own hands. Have I not reason to bless God for such a mother?

"*August* 10, 1810.
"My Dear Son:
"I am this day fifty years old; and this week, I have reason to think, you have been separated to the work of the Gospel ministry, consecrated an ambassador of the King of Glory to guilty man. I would bless God that I have lived to see this event: far greater is my joy than to have seen you crowned an earthly monarch. And now, my son, as I am not only by bodily infirmities, but by age, called to look into the grave, I desire to set my house in order, that I may be ready to depart at the sovereign call of heaven. For the honor of a faithful, prayer-hearing God, and for your encouragement *in prayer*, I now record some things *respecting you.*

"You have often heard of my extreme sickness at your birth. Perhaps by that my mind was the better prepared to receive you as the peculiar gift of God. I think I have more evidence of acting faith in devoting you to God in baptism, than in the case of any one of my other children. Your own memory will be the best witness for me, as to the pains I took, in your education, to impress your mind early with a sense of divine things. I am not conscious of doing more for you in this respect than for my other children; but when in your early years you discovered a propensity to vice, how great was my distress for you! I know that you often witnessed my *tears*, but to the anguish of my heart you were a stranger. And when in the face of all instructions, entreaties, warnings, reproofs, and corrections, such as rent the heart of a mother with anguish inexpressible, you still persisted in that course, what could be my resort but the throne of grace? You well remember the day of fasting and prayer set apart by your father and myself on your account. My heart was that day overborne with sorrow. I thought it would be comparatively easy to follow you to the grave, to what I then suffered. But my heavenly Father was pleased to show me, before the day was out, that my help and hope were only *in Him;* and to Him did my heart turn as to its only refuge, insomuch that when the day was ended, I felt as though *my* work was but just begun. It is impossible for me to describe to you, unless you know experimentally what it is to 'wrestle with God,' the ardor of my soul before God on your account. At first I seemed to be content to plead for restraining grace; but I did not long rest there. The covenant promises of God respecting the righteous *and their seed*, were very sweet to my soul. I knew that God would be inquired of by the house of Israel to do this for them. It was God's constituted way to bestow the blessing. Therefore I had confidence to plead with him; my work seemed plain before me, and I had no disposition to relax in it at all, until God should appear for you. I told no one my feelings, not even your father;

the work was between God and my own soul; I firmly believed that God would in his own time answer my prayer. That you may the better judge of my feelings, I relate one circumstance. In the course of a few months after those impressions on my mind, I was taken sick. I was at first attacked violently, and thought that perhaps God was about to remove me from the world. *You* were *then* the nearest on my heart of any object in the world. My work as to you was not done, and to whom should I commit it, if I were removed? I determined to wait for more decided appearances in my disorder, and if I found myself failing, to commit this work to your father, enjoining it on him as my dying request, never to cease wrestling with God for you till you should be gathered into his sheep-fold. But God, in mercy to you, and to my other children, I hope, restored me, and with renewed vigor I returned to my closet. When the first serious impressions were made on your mind, that I was acquainted with, I felt a new and fresh engagedness in my work, and sometimes at least the midnight hour has witnessed my prayers and tears for you. You will not now wonder that I was anxious to know your particular state of mind when you were absent from me. Sometimes, indeed, I was ready to limit the Almighty, and say, 'Oh! let the salvation of God come *this night* to my child!' But God taught me more commonly to lie at his feet, and humbly to implore the blessing in his own time and way. In his own time he has, I trust, brought you forth to the light, and you behold his righteousness; yes, the complete righteousness of Jesus, your advocate on high.

"When I am sleeping in the dust, look over this sheet, and give glory to God, who has wrought such wonders for you. Look upwards, and be animated to double your diligence in the work of the Lord; remember that short is the space between us, and as we are both infinitely indebted to free, rich, sovereign grace, will it not be unspeakable pleasure to celebrate that grace forever and ever?

"And when you leave this mortal stage, may your children be left on earth, a seed to serve the God of their fathers, that, through us, his praise may be handed down to latest generations.

"To Mr. Gardiner Spring, the child of my prayers, tears, and vows, this paper is dedicated when I am no more."

As already intimated, I was in the habit of writing to one or both my parents on the return of my own birth-day. My mother carefully preserved these letters, and at my last visit put them into my hands. I leave them to my children, but will take leave to insert some of them at the close of the present chapter.

"NEW HAVEN, *February* 24, 1809.

"I send you this to tell you, my dear parents, that I have not forgotten my birth-day. *You* have not forgotten it. Neither have we forgotten each other, and I will add, we have not, I trust, wholly forgotten the God who has borne us up under the pressure of many trials; who has preserved us for so many years, and who gives us this day some feeble tokens of his regenerating mercy. The whole course of my life has been marked with sin, while it has clearly borne the traces of infinite love; but *this precious birth-day* is crowned with rich testimonials of *special grace*. I never saw such a birth-day as this. I never before saw that birth-day on which I could say, even with the fear with which I now say it, that I *hoped* I was a child of God. I confess the multitude of my daily sins shakes my confidence, and the increasing weight of my guilt almost bears down my hope. But amid this darkness of fearful apprehension, there is a pale glimmering of rising joy. Yes, my parents, the boundless mercy of God through Christ has, I hope, reached your poor son. Oh! the riches of infinite grace!

"Twenty-four years ago I was born in sin. For the space of these long years I have lived in sin. For most of this period I have been despising the blood of Jesus, rejecting the cup of salvation, and greedily drinking the bitter draughts of sin and woe. Sin has been the 'sweet morsel' under my tongue. And yet God has had mercy on me a sinner; through the exhaustless, sovereign grace of God, this troubled conscience, this guilty heart, has felt that peace which the 'world cannot give,' and, blessed be God, which 'it cannot take away.'

"What infinite reason have I to be thankful that *I have been born!* And, my parents, what joy have you in the thought that you have given being to a soul that will never die; what joy have you, in that you have trained up an immortal mind for an eternal existence at 'the right hand of God in the heavens.'

This is enough to repay you for all your care; this is enough to call you often to your knees in earnest and humble prayer to God for his gracious blessings upon me, and upon your other children. There is an inexpressible pleasure *in being*. Now time appears precious; 'tis the door to eternity. But what a sullen blank are these past years! Ah! what are my *days*, my *moments now!* Full of sin; stained with the guilt of resisting the influence of my blessed Comforter, and sending him grieved away; perplexed with unbelief; harassed by the sin and temptation of a wicked heart.

"In this letter, I feel as though I were writing to my parents, and unfolding my heart to the confidence of Christians; I put no constraint upon my words or my feelings. I may talk plainly *with you*.

"I have told you that I trust in God's mercy. But I am full of doubt, and ignorance, and error. I am indeed a great sinner. But, oh! there is joy—joy to you, joy to me: they were sinners whom Jesus died to save! The humble Jesus of Nazareth—the babe of Bethlehem, the Judge of the world—died, and died *for us*. And who are we? Oh, what mercy! Ah, here we rest; 'tis enough; we lean on the arm of an omnipotent God. Here we have strength for weakness, holiness for sin, life for death. Here all our deficiencies are supplied. Are we vile? Christ is holy. Are we weak? He is our strength. Are we ignorant, and walking in darkness? He will lead us by the still waters; he *will never leave us nor forsake us*. Are we doubting, and, while walking on the sea of sin and danger, do we fearfully tremble like Peter?

He rebukes our unbelief, and bids us trust in him. His promises, His precious promises, bear up our spirits; His *covenanted mercy* bids the trembling eye of faith look away beyond the everlasting hills to the bright mansions of glory. When, in times like the present, we fear for the welfare of his children, He assures us that 'the gates of hell shall never prevail against' them. When we look around us and mourn for the depravity of our friends and the world, He comforts our hearts, and tells us that 'though Israel be not gathered, yet shall he be glorious in the eyes of the Lord.' Christ is indeed precious. *He is all.*

"Dear father, dear mother, I would on this day write something to give joy to your aged hearts. I would dwell upon a theme dear I know to you, dear I hope to me. It is the blessed Jesus; 'tis his cross; 'tis his Gospel; 'tis his intercession; 'tis his great salvation. Oh! let us love and adore him; glory in his cross; seek an interest in his prevailing intercession; feel the peace and joy of his Gospel; receive his great salvation; be thankful for it, and tell it to others. Oh! my parents, is this list of infinite blessings, before which the swelled catalogue of fame, pleasure, wealth, and all that this frail world can give, dwindles down into a despicable scroll,—is this Jesus, this cross, this Gospel, this salvation, *ours?* Could we be doubled, or manifold in our existence, how cheerfully should we give all that we are to our blessed GOD! I well know, that if this salvation were not a *great* salvation, it would not be ours. If it did not proceed from a *great* God; if it were not founded on a *great* covenant; if it did not save *great* sinners from *great* punishment, it would be none of ours. But it is exactly suited to the exigency of our case. From all that is threatening in divine vengeance; from all that is terrible in fear; from all that is wretched in sin; from the curse of the law; from the sting of death, and from the power of the grave, this salvation saves. ' *Thanks be unto God for his unspeakable gift.*'

"You see I must close. Before I do it, I will once more thank you for all your parental love; for your warnings, your instructions, and your prayers. I thank God for them also. I hope they have been blessed for the good of my soul. Pray for me still. I need your prayers every day I live. Remember, every prayer you put up to God for me is heard; every prayer strengthens me in my duty, and encourages me to go on my way rejoicing. I did hope that God would call me to a profession remote from the temptations of the world. He may yet. I do not wholly give up the object. But now I am in all the bustle, the noise, the wickedness, and, what is worse, the temptations of *a most ensnaring profession*. May divine grace guard me! O that I could live free from sin! One holy hour would be worth all my days and years of transgression.

"I often think of you, dear parents, and almost as often fear that I shall see you but little more on this side the grave. I have been very little with you since I was fifteen years of age. I shall not be with you much more. How should I weep at the thought if I could not look beyond this vale of tears! You were always dear, dear to me; *now* doubly so—*you are my parents in the Lord.* We shall soon leave this world; it is of little consequence how soon; God will direct. We shall tarry here while our Master has anything for us to do; we wish to stay no longer. He who hears the ravens when they cry, will take care of what we leave behind.

"You, papa and mamma, may soon drop. Forget not me and mine; and when you go to your Father and my Father, to your God and my God, remember to mantle us with your blessing. Unless I am under a miserable delusion, *I shall see you in heaven.* I hope we 'know in whom we have believed.' Oh, may we live for eternity. May we feel the spirit of the Gospel, and let our light shine. Give my love to all. Recommend Christ to my brothers. Dear papa, be faithful to *the souls* of men. Preach Christ and him crucified; dwell much upon the doctrines of the cross.

"With much affection I am, my dear parents,
"Your dear son,
"GARDINER SPRING."

"NEW YORK, *February* 24, 1815.

"BELOVED PARENTS:

"I know you are looking out for a line from your son. I should be strangely forgetful of my privilege should I disappoint you. You have called to mind more than once that this day completes my thirtieth year. The son of your prayers, your tears, and your vows, I know has not this day been forgotten. I have set apart the day as a day of fasting and prayer, and I know not how to fill my sheet to better advantage, than to open to you the thoughts which have passed through my mind. Shall I write without restraint? Yes, I may. Parents will impute no unworthy motives to this retired hour; they will indulge a child.

"After some devotional exercises, a part of the morning was set apart to the examination of my own state and character. Perhaps I shall use too much freedom on this subject even to you. I have never abandoned my hope in Christ, nor let go my hold of his sure covenant, since I made a public profession of religion. Notwithstanding all my sinfulness, and all my awful defection from duty, and in defiance of some efforts to give up the hope of an interest in the blood of sprinkling, still I cherish it. I have very little of that deep and abiding sense of my own vileness which I find in many others, though my sins often appear very great. I have no such sweet views of the Lord Jesus, nor of the character of God, as many others enjoy; though Christ does appear precious, and the character of God without a stain. My hopes are usually bright. God has his own ends in view in surrounding my path with so much light; but I am often astonished when I contemplate the fact. Strange as it is to myself, and more strange as it would be to others, did they read my heart, I am generally free from perplexity and darkness as to my own good estate. I feel safe in the hands of God. I think I can say that I think more of my duty than I do of my allotment in a future world. I cannot tell how it would be if I expected to be lost; but this I know, that without any reference to future happiness or misery, I have vastly more anxiety about my increasing conformity to God, and increasing usefulness in the ministry, than I have about my own acceptance. I have tried to doubt, and to fear, and to tremble; but after all, I hope I am quiet as to this great concern. If I could be as holy as I wish, I think I should be happy. I trust I habitually feel that it is my highest privilege, and my sweetest portion, to do the will of God. Sometimes these thoughts encourage me; and sometimes they distress me. I fear I am presumptuous. I hope—I hope strongly, even in my coldest and most sinful seasons.

"I have been reviewing my mercies. If I should count them, they are more in number than the sand. In the review of my life and of the past year, I find reason for incessant praise. While reading over the precious record of your struggles and tears for your poor son, my dear mother, and of God's dealings with you in relation to him, you will not wonder that I have been led to-day to think of the privilege of being born in a gospel land, the child of believing parents, and early consecrated to God in baptism. Long, too, have I been the child of Providence. In many instances, in the early part of my manhood, an ever-present God has delivered me in the midst of severe temptation, and restrained me from those outbreaking sins which would forever have tarnished my character, and diminished my usefulness. I knew not how to value the blessings *then*. I trust, also, I have been plucked as a 'brand from the burning,' and am to the present hour a monument of saving grace. I have been brought into the ministry of reconciliation, where, ill-deserving as I am, I may exhaust my strength, and wear out my days, in the sweetest of all employments. And I have been blessed in my labors. The past year has been a year of distinguished mercy. Though it has been a year of sin, and of greater sin than any other year of my life, still it has been a year of greater mercy than any year of my life. Though it has been a year of severe conflict both within and without—a year of unusual temptation, and not without seasons of unaccountable stupidity; yet it has been a year in which I have enjoyed more and sweeter fellowship with the Father and his Son Jesus Christ; more and sweeter engagedness in the work of the ministry; more and stronger and sweeter hungerings and thirstings after righteousness; and I think I may say, more faithfulness to the souls of men, as well as more of the common blessings of divine providence, than I have enjoyed during any preceding year of my life. I cannot tell you how much reason I have for thankfulness as I review the year. Hitherto hath the Lord helped me. The God of Jacob has been my help. The Lord liveth; and blessed be my Rock, and let the God of my salvation be exalted!

"From my mercies I have passed to my sins. Here I am distressed—not because my sins affect me, but because they do not affect me. I *need* the contrition of a broken heart. I see sin enough to make a heart of adamant bleed at every pore; but so stupid am I, O God, that I am as *a beast* before thee. Pray for me, my dear parents, that I may have a broken and contrite spirit.

"A portion of the day I have devoted to prayer for my parents—for my brothers and sister—for my family—for my people. But my thoughts have been chiefly turned towards my own soul. It is a dull seacon with me. My soul cleaveth to the dust. It is a time of need with me, my dear parents. Pray that I may find grace to help. I want the religion of Brainerd. I long to be increasingly useful in the ministry. I would engage an interest in your supplications that the God of all grace would strengthen me with all might in the inner man; that he would endue me with that vehement desire for the advancement of his glory that shall constrain me unreservedly to devote my heart, my time, my talents, my interests, my thoughts, my studies, my devotions, my life, my all, to the great work in which I am permitted to engage. My momentary fervor seems all to die away in a few good resolutions, without ever breaking forth into living engagedness, and vigorous, patient exertion. Oh! that my *meat* may be to do the will of Him that sent me, and to finish His work.

"Accept my love. Make it to my dear brothers. Beg them not to make Mammon their God. Beg them, from me, to be reconciled to God through atoning blood. I long to see them rejoicing in the truth. Shall there be none of my father's house to sustain the conflicts, to be supported by the hopes, and enjoy the rest which remaineth for the people of God, besides their eldest brother? Oh, my dear parents, be not discouraged! Their hearts are in the hands of the Lord. He *can* turn them as the rivers of water are turned.

"All are well, and send love. The return of peace, I fear, is dissipating the little seriousness among our people.

"Your affectionate and dutiful son,
"Gardiner Spring."

"New York, *February* 24, 1817.
"My Respected and Beloved Parents :

"This day reminds your son of a debt he can never pay. A child must always be in arrears to its parents. Thirty-two years ago you watched my beating pulse, and guarded my helpless frame, with all the solicitude with which I now watch and guard the little infant that sleeps beside me. None but a parent knows how to feel the obligations of a child. Thanks to God, and thanks to you, my parents, that I have had a being in this world of hope. The solicitude which watched my infancy has long since passed away. But there are some anxious thoughts remaining. Yes, and to these kind affections I address this birthday salutation.

"Parental solicitude is ready first of all to inquire, What progress has this son made in grace? It has been a part of the business of this day to make and answer this inquiry. It has been a day of seclusion from the world, and converse with God and my own soul. The sad, the reproachful result, I must not withhold. When I ask myself, at the close of the day, what advance I have made in the divine life this year, my answer is, *very little.* I feel condemned, as I review the year. As I compare it with the two preceding years, I am convinced that my growth in grace is less this year than it has been for several years that are past. I have grown in knowledge; I have grown in influence; I hope I have grown in usefulness; but I have grown less in grace than in either. Oh, I could not have believed that I should ever have been constrained to feel the truth of this bitter confession. I have seen the seasons when I thought I could not rest without pressing forward; when it was a trial to have heavenly things at a distance a single day; but, alas! I am now too contented to live away from God. I have been ready to ask myself to-day whether the pursuit of any object, be it ever so good, and be it designed to advance the Redeemer's glory ever so much, that interferes with personal progress in the divine life, is justifiable. I see the evil, my parents; I see the canker that has been preying at the root of the plant of righteousness. I have been dreaming of being a *great man*. And I see I must dismiss the delusion, or ruin my soul. I must begin to live anew. God has not left me; and I hope I have not altogether left him. But I see no evidence of having *gone forward*. I cannot tell you the feelings of my heart at meditating upon this feature in our Saviour's character, '*He made himself of no reputation.*' I see that I have not been willing to do this. God has kept me from public departures from duty; but, oh! my secret departures from duty stare me in the face. I have not, indeed, been induced to leave my closet; my closet is sweetly precious; but it is not even there as it was in months that are past. I have been ready to say to-day, I am afraid my parents have not prayed for me so much as they used to do. Is it so, my dear parents? Oh! I need your prayers now! Sometimes my heart melts, and my eyes flow, when I sit down and ask myself how much more useful I might be to the church of God, if I were as pious as Edwards or Brainerd. I do yet long to be holy.

"My mercies this year have been very great. I have seven children, and mother and children all comfortably well. I have had health—not a Sabbath during the year have I been taken from active duty. My labors have been, and still are, blessed. The cause of truth is advancing. Among the signal mercies of the year, I number the hopeful conversion of that dear deceased sister, that beloved brother, and a poor adopted servant-girl in my own family. Poor Kate has found a Saviour. I number also the protracted lives of my parents, and my own spared life and soul. Mercies everywhere surround me.

"I received your two letters by Mr. Lord and Mr. Tappan. All things are much as they were. Yesterday was the most solemn Sabbath among my people since the revival. We hope God is about to visit us again. Newark is again highly favored. There are not less than five hundred persons *very solemn.* We know not what is to take place here. Enemies bitter, unyielding, powerful, beset me on every side. The devil has come down in great wrath, and we hope his time is short. The Lord, we trust, is about to lift up a standard against him. There have been of late some attempts to injure the character of your son, but the Lord has kept me from the 'strife of tongues.' The principalities and the powers of New York mean to kill me, if they can. I have David's refuge, 'Hold thou me up, and I shall be safe.' But Mr. Lord has told you our difficulties. Blessed be God, all is peace in our own congregation. Mr. Skinner is fast in Philadelphia, and Mr. Whelpley does not go to Boston. The wrath of the Philadelphia Synod is praising the Lord. We shall have a battle in the spring, and lay a heavy hand upon that report. I shall not hesitate to take my life in my hand, if Providence allows me to go to the Assembly.

"I must close with much love and thankfulness, my dear parents, for the favors of infancy, youth, and manhood. I am your son still. I can write to you but few more times on the 24th of February, perhaps no more. It is not very probable that all of us will see another year. God give us grace to fill up what remains with arduous and successful duty, is the prayer of

"Your dutiful and affectionate son,

"GARDINER SPRING."

"NEW YORK, *February* 24, 1818.

"MY DEAR MOTHER:

"You are already in waiting, I suppose, for a line from your son. The 24th of February, I know, will never be forgotten by you; I hope it may always be remembered by me. I have great reason to be thankful that I have lived another year, and that I am allowed to write, and you to receive, one more birth-day letter. Years roll so rapidly away, that I am in habitual expectation that some birth-day, not far distant, will find that you have no son to remember you, or I no parents to be remembered.

"For many years I have found it good to set apart the anniversary of my birth as a day of fasting and prayer. It is a season which is calculated to instruct, humble, and encourage me. I must confess I know not what to think of myself, when I look back upon the year that has just gone by, and I know not what to think of the sentiments and affections with which I have been endeavoring to review it. I began the day, fearful that I should mock God in its duties, and put myself farther from him, rather than be brought nearer to him. But, notwithstanding a very obdurate heart, God has enabled me 'to come near, even to his seat, and fill my mouth with arguments.'

"I find I have lived thirty-three years. Amid the rapid current of time, there are very few objects we observe with less care and distinctness than ourselves. To one standing on the shore, the tide appears to pass by with inconceivable swiftness; but to one who is himself gliding down the current, the stream is unruffled, and all around him is a dead calm. It is only when I look back—when I discover here and there a distant land-mark, that I realize I am going forward. Yes, I am rapidly going forward. For the sake of taking a retrospect of the dispensations of divine providence towards me, the past year, I have, as it were, endeavored to-day to make a pause in my being. But I find I cannot stay the progress of time. Even now I am going forward. But though still advancing, I can see a great distance behind; and what comforts me most is, that I can see everything so full of God. The retrospect of the past year brings with it recollections that confer distinguished honor on the divine goodness. Surely, I have had to do with a God of forbearing mercy. The return of this anniversary is enough to convince me that it is of the Lord's mercies that I am not consumed. Amidst all the sins of the year, I and mine are still in the land of the living. I can survey many signal and peculiar mercies. One I have recorded, never, I hope, to be forgotten; I mean the almost miraculous preservation of our daughter, Mary Norris, after her dangerous fall. The footsteps of mercy I see everywhere through the year.

"A review of the past year is singularly calculated to give me an impressive view of my own character, as well as the divine goodness. My wicked heart has poorly stood the test of the mercies and trials which have visited me. In reviewing the history of the year, every page appears blotted by sin. I have been endeavoring to look at my sinfulness, but I find my heart strangely unaffected with it. I desire to go to God with this bitter complaint against my own soul, that I do not bewail my iniquities. I see enough in the past year to break a heart of adamant; but mine, oh, how hard! But while I say this, my dear mother, I close this day with hope—hope of God's presence—hope of more and greater faithfulness in duty—hope of increase of grace, and perseverance therein to the end. I have endeavored to remember not only my own soul, but those of my parents, my children, my wife, my brothers, my people. I have had the comfort of the thought that I have met you at the throne of grace to-day. God grant the object of our united prayers.

"When have you written to me? You are greatly in my debt on the score of letter-writing; in everything else no one more in yours than

"Your affectionate and dutiful son,
"G. Spring."

CHAPTER IV.

MY EARLY LIFE UP TO MY ENTERING THE MINISTRY.

THE town of Newburyport, in the State of Massachusetts, is situated three miles from the ocean, on the west bank of the Merrimack river, and skirted on the west and north by a rich and fertile back country. The township was an extensive one, comprising what was once Newbury Old town, Newbury Byfield, Newbury New town, and the plains. In the year 1764, that part of the township which bordered on the Merrimack was erected into a separate and distinct town, as the port of Newbury, or Newburyport. It was a bleak, cold climate, but not unfitted to the spirit of English Puritans.

In descending from the high elevation of my parentage to speak of their eldest son, I may well cover my face with shame. I was born in the town of Newburyport on the 24th of February, 1785. I recollect nothing of my infancy, very little of my childhood, and nothing so early as my proneness to evil. As far back as I can remember anything, I can remember that I was a selfish, wilful boy, and very impatient of restraint. As I grew to riper years, my sinful tendencies were expressed, sometimes in bold, and sometimes in deceitful forms. And I have remarked with pain and deep humiliation, that the sins I struggled against in manhood, and even now struggle against in old age, were the dominant and cherished sins of my youth. The poison rankles there still. I clearly see, as I look back upon the past, that the natural tendencies of my mind were all on the wrong side of the question. I was "by nature a child of wrath."

I was not without serious impressions in my childhood, especially under the instructions and expostulations of my beloved mother. The Spirit of God strove with me; my conscience was tender, and in seasons of depression I had occasional resort to secret prayer. I distinctly remember the time when, and the place where, my honored father requested me to read the twentieth chapter of Exodus, as far as the twenty-first verse, and then to read the eighteenth chapter of the Gospel by St. John; thus early impressing upon my mind the two great facts, that "the wages of sin is death; but the gift of God is eternal life, through Jesus Christ our Lord." These instructions, together with the death of my sister Hannah, who died at the early age of seven years, deeply affected me, though I was but ten years old. But these impressions were not permanent. I soon returned to the blindness and infatuation of my nature, and cast off fear and restrained prayer. I had no outwardly vicious habits, but was impatient of control, and thought it a hard and severe discipline that I was not allowed to enjoy the ordinary amusements of boys of my age, and only wished that I was old enough and strong enough to flee out of my father's hands. I have often wondered at the patience of God towards me in my younger years, and adored the mercy that kept me out of hell. Yet I was tenderly attached to my parents, and this attachment was a powerful restraint upon my conduct; so that when I left home, the thought of my parents and my love for them absorbed my youthful heart, and kept me from wickedness.

I left home, for a short period, when I was about twelve years of age. My parents had devoted me to God, with the earnest desire that I might become a minister of the Gospel; and with this view I was sent to the Berwick Academy, in the State of Maine, to pursue my classical studies under the instruction of one of the most accomplished preceptors in New England. But I had no heart for study; I had no heart for anything but *home*. I left Berwick Academy, and shall never forget my father's tenderness in consenting that I should pursue my studies in my native town. I began my Latin grammar under the care of the late Eliphalet Gillet, D.D., then a young man studying divinity with my father, and teacher of the town classical school. He was a man of great loveliness of character, a ripe scholar from Dartmouth, and took a deep interest in my progress. He was subsequently settled in the town of Hallowell, on the Kennebec river, and was one of the ablest and most useful ministers of the State. The closing years of his life he spent in the service of the Domestic Missionary Society of Maine, as its watchful and efficient secretary; and many a feeble church in that State, and many a waste place in Zion, has had occasion to bless God for his faithful care of their interests. His name is fragrant in Maine.

I remained in the Newburyport grammar-school until the June before I entered college. My classmates were Carey, Andrews, Morse, Swett, and Gerrish, all, except myself, preparing for Cambridge. They were young men of good families and high culture : it was a noble class, and none of us dishonored our training. Colonel Swett, of Boston, and myself, are the only members of it now living. Our preceptor was an Irishman, whose name was Michael Walsh, a Protestant and a Christian man, to whom I was a troublesome pupil. Well do I recollect, when in after years, and on a visit to my parents, I called on him in his old age, how he wept, and said, "O Gardiner! a minister of the blessed Jesus! I shall come to-morrow and hear you preach!"

The last three months before I entered college were employed in the family, and under the instruction of the Rev. Dr. Crane, of Northbridge, in Worcester county, Mass. Here, also, I was associated with noble class-mates, Frost, Taft, Reed, Metcalf, and Barstow. Of Reed and Barstow I know nothing. Frost became a useful physician ; Taft a member of the Massachusetts Senate and Governor's Council ; and Metcalf is now the Hon. Judge Metcalf, of Boston. Dr. Crane was as full of his fun as of Latin and Greek, and we greatly enjoyed them both. He was a thorough instructor in the classics. Besides those already mentioned, Dr. Calvin Park, Rev. Cyrus

Kingsbury, of the Choctaw Mission, Rev. Dr. Preston, of Savannah, Dr. Brown, of Boston, and Professor Fisher, of Yale, who was lost in the Albion in 1822, were his pupils.

In the year 1799, at the age of fifteen, I entered Yale College. It was a sad mistake to have entered at so early an age. I was a severe student, and as ambitious as Julius Cæsar. Though a mere boy, and the youngest of my class, I was placed by the side of such young men as Seth Norton, William Robinson, Abel McEwen, John C. Calhoun, and Bennet Tyler. I struggled on, but my eyes failed me, and my health was impaired. At the close of the first year, and not a little in opposition to my own wishes, my father determined that I should leave College, and employ the year at home. God so ordered it that this summer of 1801 was a memorable summer in regard to my spiritual interests. It was the last series of Sabbaths in which I sat under my father's preaching. The most impressive discourse which I then heard from his lips, was from the words, " God so loved the world, that he gave his only begotten Son, that whosoever believeth on him should not perish, but have everlasting life." I recollect that discourse now, after the interval of more than half a century; nor shall I ever forget the glowing views it presented of the *wonderful love of God*. An evening discourse from that venerable man, the Rev. Jotham Sewal, delivered in my father's pulpit, also made a still deeper impression on my mind. It was from the words, "Ho! every one that thirsteth, come ye to the waters." I wept much during the service, saw that I was lost without an interest in Christ, and was led to more frequent and earnest prayer. During this summer, I took a short voyage to the eastern part of the State of Maine, in company with the late John Pearson, Esq., where we walked eight miles on the Sabbath to find a place of worship. The autumn and winter following were devoted to study, under the direction of the late Dr. Adams, a distinguished scholar, then the Principal of the Leicester Academy, and subsequently the Professor of Mathematics in Dartmouth College. Here I was room-mate with the late Eleazer Foster, Esq., of New Haven, who was a man of excellent spirit, and the assistant of Dr. Adams. My studies were directed to Algebra, Geometry, and Conic Sections; while, in consequence of the sickness of Dr. Adams for some weeks, I heard the upper classes in Latin and Greek, and, though with a self-righteous spirit, conducted the devotions of the Academy.

With restored health and courage, I reëntered Yale College, but in the class below that in which I first entered. During the whole of my course, Dr. Dwight was the President of the College, and, as the Professor of Divinity, occupied the College pulpit. I was greatly instructed by the preaching of this remarkable man. The series of his discourses constituting his system of theology, was delivered in the morning, the whole of which it was my privilege to hear; his afternoon discourses were more practical and pungent.

In the summer of 1803 there was a remarkable outpouring of the Spirit upon the whole College, and my own mind was deeply affected. I had been in the habit of secret prayer from the time I *first* entered College, but had never ventured to cherish the hope that I had passed from death unto life. But I now felt that the great question for eternity must be decided. Occasional letters from my parents, especially from my mother, increased my anxiety to such a degree, that it seemed to me, if I continued to grieve the Spirit of God, that I should be left to perish. One Saturday afternoon, while my room-mate was absent, I resolved to devote to prayer, and not leave the throne of grace until I found mercy. There, in the south entry of the old College, back side, middle room, third story, I wrestled with God as I had never wrestled before. Nor do I, at this distance of time, recollect anything about that season, except the intensity of my desires, and one passage of Scripture which I urged with great earnestness: "For my thoughts are not your thoughts, neither are your ways my ways, saith the Lord. For as the heavens are higher than the earth, so are my ways higher than your ways, and my thoughts than your thoughts." It was exceedingly pleasant to me to repeat these words, and remind God of what he had thus revealed of his abounding mercy. I rose from my knees, not with any hope that I had found mercy, but less burdened and more tranquil. I had a deeper sense of sin, but an indefinite sense of relief. The predominant sentiment of my soul was the ABOUNDING MERCY OF GOD. Deep as was my sense of sin, and desert of the divine displeasure, the boundless mercy of God in Christ swallowed up every other thought. It was towards evening, and just as the sun was going down, when I left my chamber in order to call at the post-office for letters from home. As I stepped upon the College campus, it seemed to me that everything was new—it was so inexpressibly beautiful. My steps were elastic; my heart was buoyant, though solemn. Everything around me was changed, though it did not occur to me that I saw with new eyes. Everything was joyous; nor was there a pensive emotion in my bosom. The green upon the trees, the mild beams of the setting sun, the whole scenery, was perfectly beautiful. It seemed to me that the world God had made was a most beautiful world; I never looked upon it in the light in which I then beheld it. The next day was the Sabbath; and before it closed, I began to hope that God had brought me out of darkness into his marvellous light.

This was in the month of June, and my peace of mind and my enjoyment in the private and social duties of religion, not only continued, but increased, until the fourth of the July following. And now, marvellous to be told, amid the arrangements and speeches, the songs and glee, of that memorable day, my religious hopes and impressions *all vanished*, as "a morning cloud, and as the early dew." I could not account for it; but thus I remained for several weeks, and in the sad conclusion that a deceived heart had turned me aside, and that my imagination, my sympathies, and natural affections, lay at the bottom of all my religious experience. But while I gave up my hopes, strange to say, I was not unhappy. Though I did not abandon my closet, nor forsake the society of my religious class-mates, I returned to my studies with my wonted zeal and ambition, and lived from week to week as though all my calculations were bounded by the present world. Thus I passed through the remaining period of my College life; sometimes catching a glimpse of better things, but for the most part influenced by mad ambition, the pride of talent, and the dogged determination to excel. There was an outpouring of the Spirit upon the College the following summer, and the most I recollect about it now is, that I had no sympathy with opposers, but rather rejoiced to see so many of the students pressing into the Kingdom of God, while my own heart told me that I had no lot nor part in this matter. My class graduated in the year 1805, and in my valedictory address to them I was foolish and wicked enough to adopt the vainglorious maxim, "Aut Cæsar, aut nullus." My father was present, and when he took leave of me, it was to commend me to the care of a kind Providence, and to throw me upon my own resources. I told him that I had no fears, and that while I should never forget his bounty, I was well satisfied to depend on my own exertions. I was twenty years of age, and launched forth upon the turbulent sea of life with a proud and self-reliant spirit that buoyed me above the billows.

I had made up my mind for the legal profession, and immediately entered the office of that eminent jurist, the late Judge Dagget, of New Haven. He was for the most part absent from the office in his attendance upon the State Courts; but gave me the use of his library, and directed me in all my elementary course of reading. I was a severe student, and profited above many, mine own equals, in the knowledge of the law. After reading Coke upon Littleton, and

Blackstone's Commentaries, I pursued my studies by *subjects*, and wrote largely upon every subject, consulting with care all the treatises and reports which were in the Library.

When my father left me, I had four dollars in my pocket, and I began to cast about for means to defray my necessary expenses. With this view, I wrote to Moses Brown, Esq., of Newburyport, a man of great 'wealth, and who was subsequently one of the founders of the Andover Seminary, and frankly told him my arrangements and my condition, and requested him to loan me two hundred and fifty dollars, at the same time giving him to understand that if my health failed, or my prospects were in any way obscured, I had no means of returning the loan. With his characteristic liberality, he at once sent me a check for the money, and *on my own terms*. I had at the same time an invitation to take charge of the Academy in Wethersfield, Conn., but this I declined from a determination to pursue my legal studies. I had also another resource: I was fond of music, and accepted the place of Precentor in the Church then occupied by Rev. Moses Stuart, my tutor in College, and this, with the charge of a large singing-school, kept me from want.

During the autumn of the same year, I was unexpectedly requested to go to the Island of Bermuda as a classical and mathematical teacher. The offer was a tempting one, and I accepted it, and remained in that Island fifteen months, at the same time pursuing my legal studies under the advice of the late Chief Justice Esten, then in the heyday of his professional career, and whose courtesy laid me under lasting obligations.

While at Bermuda I addressed the following letter to my father:

"BERMUDA, *July* 4, 1807.

"DEAR PAPA:

"In a letter which you wrote me from Salem, which I received *via* New York, you ask this question: 'Tell me if you intend at some future day to be a V. D. M.?'

I *have* felt as though a race of political and legal glory would be the great object of my heart. From my youth up, however, I have generally been disposed to engage in a more noble cause. No employment can be more honorable, none more useful, none more productive of personal and domestic happiness, and none more *alluring* to the man of genius and piety, than that of a teacher in holy things. I am very strongly biassed in favor of the office of a clergyman. The grandeur and beauty of the subjects would gratify my pride; the opportunity of engaging in literary and scientific pursuits, would be pleasing to my taste; theological discussion would interest me, and, above all, the hope that I could do *something* for the cause which I have so long rejected, *something* for that God who is daily showering his blessings upon me and my family, *something* for the Saviour who bled for me, and whom I have so ungratefully despised—this hope, even faint as it is, would yield me no ordinary satisfaction. I think, *were I a true Christian*, and could *earnestly* engage in an employment like this—could I devote the few talents which God has given me, to the advancement of his glory—I would not change my situation for the glories of that man who is nursed in the palace of luxury and splendor, or rolled on the wheels of affluence and fame. Diadems and thrones would be nothing to me.

"There are moments in which I loathe all earthly pleasure. It is like a dream, that is half forgotten. These are the moments when divine grace is *striving* with my soul. I have had in former religious impressions a deep conviction of the vanity of the world. Vanity is enstamped on all. All that can gratify the sense, or give pleasure to the fancy; all that pride, with her long train of gratifications, can present; or ambition, with her flattering glories, can enjoy; all these are but a bubble inflated by expectation, which, for a while, rises in the air and glitters in the sun, but at a moment vanishes. The things which are the most alluring are often the most destructive; and those which are the most flattering in their promises are the most fruitless in enjoyment. Everything here changes, decays, comes to an end. All floats on the surface of that river which with a swift current is running towards a boundless ocean.

These sentiments, you will say, it is easy to express, but more difficult to feel, and perhaps still more to practice. My life is a proof of the remark. Although the office of a clergyman, and the faithful performance of the duties which belong to it, would even to *me* be a source of more gratification than any which would arise from other employments; yet with me there are great difficulties in the way of the profession. If the inspired apostle could say, Who is sufficient for these things? with how much more propriety can *you*, can any clergyman, and with how much greater force can I, ask the same question, Who *is* sufficient for *these things?* Many worthy men— many clergymen—have endeavored to persuade me to enter the ministerial profession. Whether it has been from the persuasion that I am prepared for the office, or from the interest they take in my welfare, I know not. If from the former, they are in a great error. '*Credat Judeas Apella; non ego.*'

"The ministerial character should concentrate many peculiar qualifications. Talents, education, health, prudence, sound doctrine, and divine grace, are indispensable requisites in the character of him who stands at the altar. Were I convinced *truly* that I had all these qualifications, I would not for a moment halt between two opinions, but would eagerly embrace an object no less pleasing to myself than gratifying to my parents. But, alas! my father, my virtues are too much of the negative kind. As to talents, I am like most other men; as to education, better than many; as to health, I have nothing to boast of; as to prudence, I am neither one thing nor another—I am greatly influenced by the impulse of the moment, and act frequently from wrong motives; as to sound doctrine, I am no heretic, but like the rest of our family, I need instruction.

"Now I come to the main point: Am I a renewed man? I will tell you in a few words what is my state as to spiritual matters. I believe I have many feelings which are apparently right, and more which are undeniably wrong. You shall judge of me by the *best* and by the *worst* of my symptoms. When I look back upon my youth, I find that I have some views and feelings which I had not in former years. The world appears more vain; the character of God appears more lovely; my own more odious; holiness appears more lovely and sin more detestable. I feel a burden on my heart which I cannot remove; my sins often press very heavily upon me, and I am ready to sink under them. I could not complain against God, should he damn me eternally; I deserve it, and he will finally appear glorious in the destruction of sinners. I feel as though I loved God's people, and his cause has my warmest wishes for its welfare. I hope there are none so bad as myself, and if I go to hell, I would fain go alone, and see God's children numerous and happy. I sincerely pray for the prosperity of Zion. Peace be within her walls, and prosperity within her palaces. I should wish to go to heaven, because I should be pleased with its employment. Were all my sins mortified, and I rendered perfectly holy, I think I should be happy. Nothing is so miserable as to be under the reigning power of sin. Could I join with the hundred and forty-four thousand who stand before the Lamb and praise God forever and ever, I think the joy would be unutterable. If I am ever saved, it will be through the abounding grace of God in Christ. Sometimes I can say, Lord, I believe; help thou mine unbelief.

"But, Papa, notwithstanding all this, I roll sin as a sweet morsel under my tongue. Wickedness abounds in me. I am attached to the world. I am avaricious;

and in the present state of my family, make *money* my god. I strain honesty as *far as I can* to gain a *little.* I am *altogether* dissatisfied with myself. I am an *almost* Christian. I am not sufficient for *these things.* It will not do for me to be a clergyman. I am not taught myself, and I cannot teach others. I serve God and Mammon. I am vibrating between heaven and hell, and unless God's infinite mercy preserves me, I shall fall to the abyss of unutterable woe, forever to be an enemy to God, to all goodness. Oh! wretched man that I am!

"I have no time to deliberate. I must be in *some* business. To prevent my falling into want, I take to the law. I am afraid I shall go very near heaven, and never get there.

"You ask, with emphasis, 'Are you, my son, *determined* to pursue the law? If so, write me, and if not, write me.' What I have written I have written. If I were not so inconsistent, I could answer you more directly. But I sin one moment and pray the next. I know not what more to say. I engage in law with great reluctance. Often I feel as if every step I took, I was upon unholy, upon forbidden ground.

"Your affectionate and dutiful son,

"GARDINER SPRING."

There were not wanting considerations of personal interest and affection, which it was no easy matter to resist, in determining to leave New Haven. At the weekly singing-school, I had become acquainted with Miss Susan Barney; and before I was aware of the attachment, my heart was led captive by one who had captivated more hearts than mine. She knew my character in College; she knew my poverty; she had confidence in me; and though I urged her to an absolute engagement before I left for Bermuda, she gave me no other encouragement, than that I might correspond with her, and if I returned *unscathed*, she would then be happy to see me.

I opened my school at Bermuda very soon after my arrival. But I was utterly disappointed, and became well-nigh a discouraged and dispirited man. The sparsely scattered inhabitants were high-church in their principles; they were no ardent friends of the United States; their minister, a Mr. Thompson, was a dissipated, drunken fellow, and the Lord's day was no rest to me. But for an incidental visit one Lord's day to a neighboring parish, where I found a devout Presbyterian church, under the ministrations of the Rev. Mr. Matson, I should at once have quitted the island in disgust.

The families that patronized me were among the aristocracy of the island; and though they treated me with great courtesy and kindness, made me feel that, though the instructor of their children, I was but a Yankee school-master. They marked my depression and my proud spirit, and were not less dissatisfied with me than I with them. Before the close of my first quarter, they paid me a full quarter's salary, and plainly told me that if I could not be contented to remain, they would release me from my engagement.

The Sabbath I spent in the neighboring parish, to which I just alluded, was a day not to be forgotten. I was in the midst of a God-fearing people, and heard an evangelical sermon. I wept much, and the people saw it. The singing was miserable; I endeavored to unite with it; and at the close, the minister and the elders came around me, to inquire the name of the musical stranger. I was alone, and again I wept. They took me by the hand, introduced me to their families, and after becoming acquainted with my history and my object at the island, engaged to establish a school at a place called the Salt Kettle, and to give me permanent and profitable employment. I found many lovely Christian families there, where, stranger as I was, I was treated as a son and a brother. Before opening my school at the Salt Kettle, however, I returned to New Haven, with the hope of inducing Miss Barney to go back with me to the island.

Susan was embarrassed by my return; but, in opposition to her father's wishes, and in compliance with those of her devoted and pious mother, she consented to my urgent request. We were married on the evening of the Lord's day, May 25, 1806, by her pastor, the Rev. Moses Stuart; and after a flying visit to my parents at Newburyport, returned to New Haven to make our arrangements to embark for Bermuda. My parents did not approve of my sudden and hasty marriage, though they were then and ever after greatly pleased with their new daughter. My father especially was gratified with my choice, and when he questioned the wisdom of the procedure, I simply replied, "My father, you threw me upon my own resources," and pointing to my bride, added, "you see now what they are." The evening before we left our parents at Newburyport, we were seated by an open window, in the month of June, and my father, himself a great lover of music, requested us to sing one of the songs of Zion. We did so; they were the words beginning with

"Pardon, and grace, and boundless love
Streaming along a Saviour's blood."

It was a sweet hour to us all. My father wept, and said, "I don't wonder that Gardiner and Susan have concluded to mingle their voices." He then turned to the Bible, and requested me to read the forty-fifth chapter of Jeremiah. When we came to the fifth verse, and I was reading the words, "Seekest thou great things for thyself? seek them not," my father said, "Stop! that is enough." This was his parting counsel. "Seekest thou great things for thyself? seek them not."

We left the much-loved home of my childhood amid the prayers and blessings of my parents, and returned to New Haven by the Boston and Hartford turnpike. In passing through an almost uninhabited country, called Douglas Woods, and which lies between Uxbridge and Pomfret, there was a total eclipse of the sun. It was dark at noon-day. The stars were visible, the domestic fowls were crowing, the birds were hastening to their homes in the leafy forest, and the young cattle were lowing, as it were, their evening hymn of praise. The whole scene was fitted to inspire solemn and affecting thoughts. We looked up at the sun, we looked beyond and above it, and we looked at each other. Forty-eight years after this, and while attending the General Assembly at Buffalo, I received the following letter from Mrs. Spring, pleasantly referring to this scene:

"NEW YORK, *May* 23, 1854.
" MY DEAR HUSBAND:

" I received your dear letter yesterday, and it made me glad the whole day. It was so delightful to see a little sprig of love bloom out, after forty-eight years of the stern realities of life, that it makes me young again.

" We had a full church on the Sabbath; and Dr. Ferris gave us an excellent sermon; but it was not my husband. There is no movement in the affairs of the church, though I have heard it intimated that, to make up for past deficiencies, they think of raising your salary to five thousand dollars. I am glad it will be during your absence, and without any request or suggestion from yourself.

" There is to be a grand excursion on the opening of the railroad from Chicago to the Mississippi, and our long-tried friend, Mr. Knapp, has procured tickets for us for the whole route, from New York to St. Paul's and back, free of expense. He called last evening with the invitation and tickets, and says he cannot believe it possible that we can refuse so grand an offer. If you would be satisfied with so long a journey, and return by the way of Canada, for such is Mr. and Mrs. Knapp's arrangement, and then go with me to some quiet place in the country, I should like it. Your friends here think you ought to go.

Write to Mr. Knapp, for he is very earnest, and very kind. If you go, we will meet you at Buffalo.

"I am going out on Friday to Susy's, to see the eclipse; you will have a better view of it at Buffalo. When you look at it, will you remember *Douglas Woods* and 1806, when two children stood there, looking up into the darkened sky, and then into each other's eyes? My heart swells when I think of all God's goodness to us since that time up to this very hour. Shall we not render love and praise? Adieu, my dear husband. Do not forget us in your prayers.

"Yours till death,
"SUSAN SPRING."

On our arrival at New Haven, all our arrangements were made for our departure for the Island of Bermuda. Having obtained our passports, we embarked on board the brig Harmony, Capt. Stevens, with a deck-load of live stock for the West India market. Our passage was long and tedious, and we did not reach Bermuda until some time in July. It is a marvellous entrance from the north side of the island to the port of St. George's, to which we were bound, lined on either side by submerged rocks of immense size, visible to the eye from the deck, and leaving scarcely channel-way enough for the brig to pass through. At one moment you seem to be dashing against the sunken rocks, and then, at the cry, "*helm a port*," or "*helm starboard*," you would suddenly turn a right or left angle out into a new channel-way. We reached St. George's at dinner-time, where porgie, gruper, and the delicious angel-fish, furnished us with a welcome dinner on dry land. In the afternoon, after visiting the barracks and the parade-ground, we took a boat for the interior of the island, where our friends at the Salt Kettle and Heron Bay had provided permanent lodgings for us, on a healthful point of land, washed on three sides by the ocean, and nearly facing the town of Hamilton. It was called Lowe's Point, after our hostess, Mrs. Lowe, or Aunt Lowe, as we soon were wont to call her. God was very kind to us in this provision for our comfort and usefulness. Mrs. Lowe lived alone, and was attended only by two female slaves. She treated us as though we were her children, thought it a privilege to attend our family worship, and loved us to the last. I never look back upon this first year of our wedded life without associating it with Aunt Lowe. Here, in our lonely chamber, consecrated to God and one another, on the 1st of April, 1807, our first child came into the world. We called him *Samuel ;* we lent him to the Lord, and prayed that he would honor the honored name of his paternal grandfather. I can scarcely realize that fifty-eight years have passed away since that well-remembered day. The Bermudians are all called *Porgies.* Our Samuel was called the little Porgie, and was claimed as a native-born subject of George the Third. Mrs. Spring's chamber was amidst beds of geranium, and her rapid recovery was amid the gratulations of the young and the old, and a wilderness of roses showered upon her pillow and the little Porgie's cradle. Here I had a very flourishing school, and remained somewhat more than a year. It was a delightful year. Everybody loved and respected us, and we loved and respected all about us, except the poor slaves, who were liars and thieves. One of them, however, we loved. She was a middle-aged black woman, who was Samuel's nurse; and when we left the island for home, with tears she entreated us to buy her; and when we refused, it seemed as if her heart would break. Poor Kate!

The occasion of our leaving the island was solely the apprehension of a war between Great Britain and the United States, in which event all the citizens of the United States who had remained on the island more than a year, would be regarded as prisoners of war, or be constrained to take the oath of allegiance to Great Britain, neither of which we could consent to.

God had prospered us. We left the island with fifteen hundred dollars, enough, as we hoped, to support our little family until I could be admitted to the bar. Our small capital, except an allowance for daily expenses, together with three hundred dollars which Mrs. Spring had put into the hands of a relative, was mostly swept away by the failure of the parties to whom it was entrusted. Living in a residence together with another family, the expenses of housekeeping were not large; our health was good, and I returned to the study of the law, in the office of the late Nathan Smith, of the United States Senate, with diligence and zeal. Mr. Smith was a true friend, not only as an instructor, but by introducing me to the incipient practice of the profession before those inferior courts of justice, where students at law were allowed to appear. I gladly availed myself of these privileges, sometimes arguing cases in connection with my instructor, and on one occasion, not a little to his surprise and amusement, attaching myself to the opposite counsel. I was admitted to the bar on the 15th of December, 1808, and forthwith opened my office in the business part of the city of New Haven, over the store of Bulkley & Austin.

My religious impressions had not entirely disappeared. From the second evening after our marriage, we had maintained morning and evening worship in the family, both at home and abroad, in Bermuda and New Haven. We were regular attendants on the ministry of the Rev. Moses Stuart, under whose faithful ministrations my convictions of sin were renewed, and my hopes of acceptance with God were revived and invigorated. It was at a Sabbath evening prayer-meeting, in a large hall opposite the college, that I was more encouraged and animated than I had ever been before. Dr. Dwight was in the chair. As the exercises closed, and the crowded worshippers rose to sing the Doxology, I felt that I could "praise God from whom all blessings flow!" Praise! praise! It was delightful to praise Him! On the 24th of April following, I united with the visible church under Mr. Stuart's pastorate, and began to be an active Christian. Under the direction of the late Jeremiah Evarts, an older member of the bar, and also a member of the same church, and a man whose name is as ointment poured forth, a Sabbath evening service was instituted in two of the rural districts of the city, with which it was my privilege to be associated. I had more of the confidence of my Christian friends than I deserved, and in cases of dangerous illness in the neighborhood of our residence was, greatly to my surprise, called upon to pray with the sick and dying. My daily employment called me to my office, where, with rigid punctuality and exemplary diligence, I was enabled to discharge my duty to the few clients who employed me, and in great patience to wait for more. I had no cause for discouragement, and my success was quite equal to my hopes. But, while I did not relax my diligence, my enthusiasm in my profession was greatly abated, and my relish for the law sensibly declined. I began to think of another profession, and to long for our weekly meetings in the suburbs of the city. So far as I can now recall the facts, the first individual to whom I ventured to suggest my views, was Mr. Evarts. He did not *discourage* me; but, with all characteristic kindness and wisdom, counselled me not to be hasty in deciding so grave a question. Among the many testimonials to the excellent character of this remarkable man, I may add the letters of President Day and Mr. Bates, in the Appendix.

At the following commencement of Yale College, I was to take my degree of A.M., and to deliver an oration. My theme was the "Christian Patriot:" nor were my views as yet decided with regard to the change in my professional career. Early on the morning after the commencement, the Rev. Dr. John M. Mason preached his great sermon on the text, "To the poor the Gospel is preached." As I led the choir, I sat immediately opposite the preacher. And never did I hear such a sermon. I could not refrain from weeping. Hundreds wept. Dr. Dwight wept; Dr. Backus wept like a child; senators wept. When I left the church, I could think of nothing but the *Gospel*. I crossed the green exclaiming, "the Gospel! the Gospel!" I entered the little parlor where my lovely wife was nursing her babe, and exclaimed, "the Gospel! the Gospel!" I thought, I prayed, I resolved, if the providence of God should prepare the way, to become a preacher of the Gospel. I said nothing but to Mr. Evarts. My purpose was formed.

But how to carry it into effect? I was ignorant, and had no resources except a mind disciplined to hard study; but I had a strong confidence that God would carry me through. My family depended on my exertions, and I resolved at all events not to leave them to suffer. In this exigency I wrote to my honored father, telling him of my state of mind, and acquainting him with my pecuniary condition. He was a man of great disinterestedness and a man of expedients. He wrote me, that I could not prepare myself for the pulpit in less than a year's time, and I was reluctant to throw upon my self-sacrificing parents the burden of my growing family, or upon my family the burden of absolute dependence. But the God of providence relieved me from this embarrassment. Mrs. Mary Norris, of Salem, a lady of great wealth, hearing of my plans, generously offered to take us all (for we then had two children, Samuel and Edward), into her family, and make provision for all our wants until I was settled in the ministry. She was a widow, mostly alone, and gratified with our society, and often said she should be the gainer by the proposed arrangement. "Hitherto the Lord helped" me.

But the embarrassments did not all vanish. I had not whispered the matter to my dear wife. She was not a professed Christian, though she rejoiced that I had become so, and seemed to enjoy our religious privileges at home. A little circumstance, of deep interest to my own feelings at the time, I may here record. One morning she came unexpectedly into my chamber, and found me on my knees. She made no apology: she uttered not a word. Instead of retiring, she threw herself beside me, put her arm upon my shoulder, and remained kneeling until the close of the prayer. I never shall forget it. It was but the beginning of the end. Yet was she a worldly woman, and sought the honors of the world for her husband. I knew not what to do. I could not broach the subject without a contest with emotions which I desired only to gratify. Abraham said nothing to Sarah when he was called to offer up Isaac. I then began a course of conduct which I have ever since pursued, and that was, in all cases where my own duty was plain, and my resolution formed, quietly to carry my resolution into effect, and meet the storm afterwards. I did so in the present instance, though there was no other storm than a plentiful shower of tears. I said nothing to my wife; nothing to any one except Mr. Evarts. I sent my wife on a visit to my only sister, the wife of the Hon. Bezaleel Taft, at Uxbridge, the native place of my father, where I engaged in a few weeks to meet her, and make a further visit to Newburyport. She had no suspicion of my views, and left me with the confident expectation that she would return to New Haven.

In the meantime, after she left me, I was busily employed in arranging my affairs for my removal to Andover. I announced my purpose to the church at the next prayer-meeting, and received a fresh impulse from their prayers and benedictions. Mr. Evarts took my office and my business, and closed up my unsettled accounts with his accustomed accuracy, and my ledger now records them. Mr. Smith, my old teacher, laughed at me; Judge Daggett was silent. Judge Rossiter said to me, " Mr. Spring, the pulpit is your place; you were formed for the pulpit rather than the bar." My business in New Haven was closed; my debts paid; my household furniture, small as it was, was carefully stowed away; my law-library, worth about four hundred dollars, was disposed of, and I was on my way to Uxbridge, Newburyport, Salem, and Andover.

When I reached Uxbridge, and was once more in the bosom of my little family, I felt that the trial had come. I could not at once disclose my plans to my wife, and was saved that painful interview by the suspicions of Mr. Taft, who told her that he believed I was going to be a clergyman! She laughed at him; but she saw a change in my deportment, and began to suspect it herself. I told her all. She went to her chamber and wept, and for a long time. But she came down, subdued indeed, but placid as a lamb, and simply said, " It is all over now; I am ready." Oh, how kindly has God watched over me! It seems as though the promise was fulfilled, " Return unto thy country and to thy kindred, and I will deal well with thee." Some day or two before we left Uxbridge, Mr. Taft said to me, " Brother Spring, I have a case before Justice Adams this morning; you are still a lawyer, and I want you to go and argue it with me." The thought struck me pleasantly, and I resolved to go; but, instead of assisting him, without his knowledge I engaged myself to what I thought the weaker party; and my last effort at the bar was in battling with my sister's husband, and in the place of my father's nativity.

We reached Newburyport in safety, and received a most cordial welcome from our parents. In due time we accepted the hospitalities of Mrs. Norris, and I hastened to the class at Andover, where I pursued my studies for eight months only, and, without my father's knowledge, or the knowledge of the professors, was, by the influence of the late Dr. Worcester, of Salem, licensed to preach the Gospel.

While at Andover I supplied the vacant pulpit at Marblehead, three miles only from Salem, where my family was, for eight successive Sabbaths, where God was graciously pleased to give me some seals of my early ministry, and to anoint me afresh for my work. I was the guest of a truly Christian woman, Mrs. Reed, the mother of the Hon. William Reed, of the United States Senate. Mrs. Reed's only daughter, afterwards the lamented wife of Mr. Ropes, of Boston, dated her conversion from the period of my residence in their family. I met this lovely woman for the last time at Northampton, at the annual meeting of the American Board. At her request, Mrs. Spring rode with Mr. Ropes, and she took a seat in my chaise from Northampton to Enfield, where, with Dr.

Morse, Dr. Beecher, and others, we had an amusing night of it, sleeping and not sleeping, the ladies in one room in a field-bed, and the gentlemen in another.

Before I left Andover I received a call from the South Parish, but it was not unanimous, and though I greatly desired the position on account of its literary advantages, I could not accept it. I also received a call from the Park-street Church, in Boston; but it was not unanimous, and I declined it. In May, 1810, I left Andover with a view of visiting the General Assembly of the Presbyterian Church, then holding its sessions in Philadelphia. On my way I spent a Sabbath at New Haven, preached to my old friends, was received by them with great cordiality, and offered a call from the church of which I was a member, lately vacated by the removal of Mr. Stuart to Andover, but which I discouraged them from prosecuting. I passed through New York, and, in the absence of the Rev. Dr. Romeyn, occupied the pulpit in Cedar-street, at an evening lecture, where, I have been since informed, a number of persons belonging to the Brick Church, learning something of me from Professor Stuart, mingled with the audience. The result was, that on my return from Philadelphia, after preaching for a single Sabbath, I received a unanimous call to become their pastor.

I accepted the call, and after a very lame examination, and not without a prolonged discussion in the Presbytery, and some doubts as to my orthodoxy, was received under their care. My trial sermon was a frank avowal of my sentiments, and a bold and unequivocal statement of the views I THEN entertained upon the subject of human ability. It was this that embarrassed the Presbytery; and but for the strenuous efforts of the late Dr. Miller, who told the Presbytery that if they condemned *Mr. Spring* for those views, they must condemn *him*, so far as I could learn, they would have refused to ordain me. I was not present at their discussion, but was told that the ground of their decision was, that Mr. Spring appeared to be a very pliable man, and that a better acquaintance with Presbyterianism, and his brethren in the ministry, would lead to a modification of his views more in accordance with their own. The Rev. Ezra S. Ely, who had just become a member of Presbytery, and who for a few months had been my room-mate in College, took leave to say that " the Presbytery did not know that young man; that the views he expressed to-day were the views he would express to-morrow, and to the end of the chapter." After receiving me, the Presbytery appointed two of their number to have a kind and fraternal interview with me on the subject, one of whom was a most lovely man, the late Dr. Milledollar. About a week after my ordination, he invited me to take a drive in his carriage, when the whole subject was discussed, and the result was, that in his judgment, "the best way of curing a man of such views was to dip his head in cold water;" and there the matter ended. Our subsequent intercourse and an occasional exchange of pulpits were unembarrassed, and of the most fraternal character. I visited this beloved man of God in his last sickness, ripe for heaven, and proved with him the preciousness of " the communion of saints."

CHAPTER V.

MY ORDINATION AND MY MINISTRY.

I WAS ordained as a minister of the Gospel, and installed pastor of the Brick Church, on the 8th of August, 1810, by the Presbytery of New York. The service was on a week-day morning, and the house filled to overflowing. Few are now among the living who were witnesses of that solemn scene. A little boy was there, who stood upon a distant seat, supported by a devoted mother, who well remembers the kneeling minister, as the venerable Dr. Rogers and his co-presbyters laid their hands upon his youthful head. He is still among us, and for years has held the office of Ruling Elder in the church, alike honored at the bar and in the house of God. By solemn oath I was pledged to my work, and set about it in earnest, though with fear and trembling. I neglected everything for the work of the ministry. I had a strong desire to visit the Courts, and listen to the arguments of the eminent jurists of the city; but I had no time for this indulgence. I had none for light reading, none for evening parties, and very little for social visiting, or even extensive reading. Everything was abandoned for my pulpit ministrations. I had warm friends in the Presbytery, in New England, in New Jersey, and in the eastern section of Long Island. And more than all, I had good courage. Three of the eight sermons I had prepared before I left Andover I had preached in New York already, and the remaining number was kept good for several years. Under God it was this laborious and unintermitted effort that saved me from shipwreck. Through His marvellous loving-kindness, and amid many proofs of His sustaining hand, I have remained the pastor of the Brick Church to the present time; and it is wonderful to look back upon the varied work and scenes of so prolonged a ministry.

Not every man, either among ministers or their hearers, is aware of the incessant and severe labor that is called for in the successful prosecution of the ministerial office. He must be thoroughly " a working man." It is work, work, work, from the beginning of the year to the end of it. There is nothing of which I have been constrained to be more economical and even covetous than *time*. I have ever been an early riser, and even in mid-winter, used to walk from Beekman-street round the "Forks of the Bowery," now Union-square, before I broke my fast. I usually went into my study at nine o'clock, and after my removal to Bond-street, more generally at eight, though my study was opposite the City Hall, and more than a mile from my residence.

> " Oh, there is a charm
> That morning has, that gives the brow of age
> A smack of youth, and makes the life of youth
> Breathe perfume exquisite."

Nor have I ever been the advocate of night-studies or night-parties. These last would long ago have been the death of me. In whatever else I have been wanting, my habits have been habits of industry. When I have, from time to time, looked over my desk, my drawers, and my trunks, I have been surprised to see the amount of labor which I have been enabled to perform. Nothing could have sustained me but a fulfilment of the promise: "As thy days, so shall thy strength be." I have been greatly favored of God during my whole ministry. More especially would I record it with thankfulness, that I have *loved the work* of writing sermons and preaching the Gospel. I can conceive of no service so delightful to my own heart. Investigation of the truth and import of God's word—the proof, illustration, defence, and application of that truth to the minds of my hearers, have ever interested me. I think I have been favored in this state of mind. *Truth* has been my object, the truth as God has revealed it in his word. I never, consciously, had any reluctance to abandon a wrong view because I had long cherished it, nor to adopt different views because they countervailed my former opinions. I have often thought that if men of different theological sentiments, but of fair and ingenuous minds, would prosecute their inquiries under the impression that they are equally interested in ascertaining the truth, and that nothing is gained but much is lost by their adherence to error, there would be very little religious controversy.

The *great end and object* of the ministry, though very imperfectly, I have endeavored constantly to keep before my mind. I have generally found that laborious ministers gain their object. If it is to write *elegant* sermons, they write them, and gain their object. If it is to write *learned* sermons, they write them, and gain their object. If it is to *enrich their discourses* with the pithy and concentrated sentences of other days and great men, they do it, and gain their object. If it is to be *popular*, they are popular, and there the matter ends. They look no farther. They gain their object, and have never thought of anything beyond it. It was not the conversion of sinners they were aiming at, and therefore they never attained it. I know a most worthy minister who preached more than a year to the same people, and his preaching was sound in doctrine, logical, and able; but during that whole period I have yet to learn that a single sinner was alarmed, convinced, or converted to God. And the reason is, that was not *his object*. He did not study for it, nor pray for it, nor preach for it. He gained his object most effectually, but it was not the conversion of men.

I have adverted to this kind of preaching, because, as it seems to me, this is the snare of the modern pulpit. I have listened to not a few sermons within the past ten years, in which there was no want of instruction; they were full of solid and weighty truths; great pains were taken, in the use of metaphor and illustration, to indicate the preacher's progress in science, and to show that he stood abreast with the improvements of the age; but in which the great end of preaching was lost sight of—the turning of the wicked from the error of their ways—the salvation of the immortal soul. The preachers had power, but their minds were not directed to this great object. With all their intellectual effort, there was a want of amplification and earnestness in addressing the different classes of their audience, and crowding the conscience of the impenitent. Why is it that there is so little adaptation in so much of the preaching of the present day to produce the conversion of men? Too many ministers preach now as though they thought all their hearers were Christians, overlooking the multitudes who are dead in trespasses and sins, and pressing on in the broad way that leads to destruction! When the ascended Saviour met Saul of Tarsus on his way to Damascus, he said to his prostrate persecutor, "Rise and stand upon thy feet; for I have appeared unto thee *for this purpose*—to open the eyes of those to whom I send thee, and to *turn them from darkness to light, and from the power of Satan unto God.*" This is the great object of the ministry, and the minister who so regards it will gain his object. Paul gained it. He " was not disobedient to the heavenly vision, but showed first unto them of Damascus, and at Jerusalem, and throughout all the coast of Judea, and then to the Gentiles, that they should *repent and turn to God, and do works meet for repentance.*" And he gained his object by turning many to righteousness.

Dr. Doddridge says of himself: "I had nothing in the world I have desired so much, in the prosecution of my ministry, as the glory of God and the conversion of souls." His Theological Seminary was, in every view, a model school. Intellectual culture did not satisfy him: "It is my heart's desire and prayer to God," says he, "that no one may go out from me without a heart tenderly concerned for the salvation of perishing souls. What are all our studies and pursuits to this!" One of the rules for the guidance of his conduct, while himself a student, and not twenty years of age, was: "In all my studies let me remember that the souls of men are immortal, and that Christ died to redeem them."

I have generally aimed to preach on *important subjects*. The more important they were, the better were they suited to my taste and my wishes. I have labored to distinguish between the precious and the vile; to insist largely and earnestly on the difference between the friends of God and his enemies, and " say to the righteous it shall be well with him, and say to the wicked it shall be ill with him." I began my work rather with the view of being instrumental in the conversion of sinners, than of comforting the people of God. I have found, too, that the discourses prepared for unrepenting men more generally interested, and, indeed, comforted the people of God. I early found that I could more easily prepare a good sermon from an awakening and alarming subject, than from one that is more comforting. The fact is, I knew more of the terrors of the Law than the preciousness of the Gospel. My own obligations to holiness, the strength and the evil of sin, my absolute dependence upon sovereign grace, my infinite and everlasting desert of God's displeasure, were subjects with which I was familiar. I knew much about them from my own experience. Of other and less distressing thoughts, though they have not been hidden from me, and have sometimes made my bosom warm and my tongue glow, I knew less, and felt less deeply. I could never understand why the great body of ministers preach with less embarrassment on fearful themes, than on those which are more attractive, unless it be that an alarmed conscience has more to do with our preaching than a loving heart; nor how this can be, except that the heart is by nature desperately wicked. The difficulty of *preaching well* on the more attractive and winning themes, has sometimes alarmed me, and made me fear lest after having " preached to others, I myself should be a cast-away."

I have preached many, very many, very poor sermons, but very rarely one that was hastily written. I have found that my mind was uniformly most active at the close of my Sabbath services; and for a series of years I rarely retired to my pillow of a Lord's-day evening without having selected my subject for the following Lord's day. I found great advantage in doing this, in that my mind was not embarrassed by conflicting subjects, or no subject at all; in that I had a subject to think of, to pray over, and sometimes to dream about; and in that one subject naturally led to another. More generally, and almost uniformly, I began my sermon on the morning of every Tuesday; so that if I finished it by Friday noon, I had one day to spare for general reading. If my subject required more than a week's study, I gave to it two weeks, sometimes three, sometimes four, and in one instance six weeks, and was greatly the gainer by so doing. One sermon thus elaborated and prayed over, is worth to the *settled pastor* and to his people, more than a score of hasty discourses. In order to carry this arrangement into effect, I obtained help from my brethren, or fell back upon the old store, or preached with no other preparation than a few outlines of thought treasured up in memory and delivered without notes. I say " delivered without notes," because I found by experience, that when my mind was divided between my notes and my invention, I was more embarrassed than when my invention was left unshackled. I have reason to believe that some of my best and most profitable discourses, saving a few outlines of thought, were truly extemporaneous, and so literally extemporaneous that from beginning to end I did not know beforehand what would be my next sentence. I say " literally extemporaneous." In one view only is this true, and in another it must be borne in mind, that they are the result of some mental discipline, and express the thoughts laid up by previous study and the use of the pen. If he has self-possession and the use of language, attained by reading, writing, and study, and any interest in the object of his vocation, any man can preach extemporaneously, and preach well. Heneage Finch, Earl of Nottingham, and Lord Chancellor of England, adopted as a maxim, that " a lawyer ought to read all the morning, and talk all the afternoon." With some modification, this maxim is not less important to the Pulpit than the Bar.

In writing for the pulpit, I have been careful to leave space enough in my manuscripts to interline new thoughts as they occurred from my general reading, and, what is of quite as much importance, to cultivate the habit of striking out old ones that were needless.

I have sometimes begun a sermon without any fixed method in my own mind; but have almost uniformly found it lost labor. For the most part, my divisions and arrangements have been thoroughly premeditated; and so thoroughly that, under the impression that the practical application was the most important, I have in many instances written the application first, and the body of my discourse last. I have rarely been embarrassed for want of subjects. The wonderful facility with which one subject leads to another—the state of the congregation—an interview with some individual or family—a watchful observance of the leadings of divine providence—intercourse with ministerial brethren—some unexpected suggestion during the night-watches—a solitary ride on the saddle—my "index rerum,"—and the inexhaustible treasures of the Bible, furnished me with subjects which I have not yet overtaken.

My reading has been uniformly with a view to enrich my mind for my pulpit ministrations. To this end I have not slighted the works of the great Errorists; and have felt strong for the truth of God the more I have possessed myself of their sophistical reasoning. I have never felt it an easier task to defend the great doctrines of grace than when I have risen from a careful study of Dr. John Taylor, Dr. Whitby, John Locke, Adam Clarke, Dr. Priestley, the Unitarian divines of New England, and Dr. Nathanael W. Taylor. No man, no set of men, no confession of faith, has biassed my mind in these investigations. I respected the form of doctrine which has exerted so powerful an influence on the Church; but I still felt at liberty, nay, I felt the obligation, of testing it by *the Law and the Testimony.* And not a little to my joy did I find that it honored the test. As beautiful symbols, from my heart I adopted the Westminster and Heidelberg Confessions; as safe expositors of the mind and will of God, I have found none more profitable than Matthew Henry, Thomas Scott, and Charles Hodge. Nor may I overlook " Doddridge's Family Expositor," in my judgment a beautiful work, more to my edification than Olshausen, or Rosenmuller. Bishop Warburton, the author of " The Divine Legation of Moses," was a warm friend of Dr. Doddridge, and his intimate correspondent. When he read the second volume of the Family Expositor, he wrote to Doddridge: " The greatest thing I can say of it is, that it is equal to the first; and the truest thing I can say of both, that they surpass anything of the kind." The late Rev. William Jay remarks: " Doddridge's Expositor I have diligently and regularly consulted. It is the work of an accomplished, laborious, and devout student of the New Testament. His practical reflections are the gems of the work. I consult Guise and Orton with frequency and benefit, but not with the pleasure and advantage generally that I examine Doddridge. I love Doddridge because he is so affectionate and devout."

I have been instructed by the exegetical publications of my venerated pastor and teacher, Rev. Moses Stuart; but he is too rash and fanciful to be a safe guide to young ministers. My models for the services of the pulpit have been Samuel Davis—of whom William Jay says, " I must confess, no discourses ever appeared to me so adapted to awaken the conscience and impress the heart,"—Nathanael Emmons, Edward D. Griffin, Asahel Nettleton, Edward Payson, John Howe, and Thomas Chalmers. I do not hesitate to include the name of Emmons in this enumeration, because, while in my judgment he has some errors, he has more truth than any writer whose works have fallen under my notice. The young minister who refuses to read Emmons because his name has been proscribed by the Princeton Reviewers, will remain ignorant of truth which, as a preacher of the Gospel, he ought to know. Those preachers to whom I have referred, seem to me to have the great object of preaching in view. They humble the creature and exalt the Creator. Their great aim is to leave the sinner without excuse for not being reconciled to God, and to urge the saint to aim at high spiritual advancement and usefulness.

When Dr. Beecher was on his dying-bed, a ministerial brother said to him, "Dr. Beecher, you know a great deal; tell us what is the greatest of all things." He replied, "It is not theology; it is not controversy; it is to save souls." This is the great secret of good preaching. His biographer remarks that "the one idea of Dr. Beecher's life was the promotion of revivals of religion." Well do I recollect his influence on my own mind, during a few days when he was my guest in Beekman-street. So long as an honest and earnest effort for the salvation of men is honored in the Church of God, will the memory of Lyman Beecher be a rich treasure to the American churches. Oh, how differently would some truly evangelical ministers preach, if the conversion of men were the great and uppermost thoughts in their preparations for the pulpit! I repeat the thought, that not a few excellent ministers of the present day preach the Gospel as though there were no impenitent men in their audience. They ought to know mankind better than this. They preach sound doctrine, but they have not learned the art of bringing it home to the conscience. I look around me upon a generation of ministers more learned than myself; yet I am not moved by their preaching. It lacks the urgency of Paul, Baxter, Edwards, Nettleton, Payson, and Skinner. They are wanting in heavy attacks upon the corrupt citadel of the human heart, and therefore fail of producing that impression of inexcusableness which is the great element of genuine conviction. A better age is coming, and one of the first indications of its approach will be, that the pulpit has recovered the use of its senses.

On the subject of preaching with notes or without them, it is difficult to express any satisfactory views. A minister's mind needs the careful and laborious culture of the pen; where this is attained and persevered in, the more he preaches without notes, the better. If he has the spirit of devotedness to his work, intellectual resources, self-possession, a free command of his mother-tongue, intense interest in his subject, and confidence in God, he will preach far better with nothing before him but God's Bible and the God of the Sanctuary. If a man can lose sight of himself in preaching, and rise above the fear and applause of his hearers; if he can be so thoroughly master of his subject that in his illustrations his memory shall not embarrass his invention, he will preach better without notes than with them. The danger with extemporaneous preachers is, that they are not students; the defect and danger of written discourses, that the preacher has not the confidence to look his audience in the face, unless he is endorsed and sustained by his manuscript. My own discourses on the Lord's day have been for the most part written out, and with care, because I am conscious that I lack those prerequisites for a purely extemporaneous preacher. My weekly lectures have never been written; I have rarely carried anything in the form of paper into the pulpit, in these services. They have cost me no labor except a solitary walk, or a ride on the saddle; yet they have been among my best discourses. They have been *studied* discourses, not of the day, but of years of study long since past, gathered up and concentrated for the hour. A fanatical and ranting preacher once appointed a religious service in the town of Bethlehem, where Dr. Bellamy was the settled pastor. Dr. Bellamy went to hear him; but in the presence of this distinguished man, the interloper refused to open his lips. After much disappointment, Dr. Bellamy was urged to conduct the service, and he did so, and preached without notes and with great power. " Mr. Bellamy," said the stranger, " did you never *study* that sarmont ?" "YES," vociferated Dr. Bellamy, " *twenty years ago.*"

I may venture here to advert to a singular and foolish incident in my own history. In returning to New York, from an annual visit to my parents at

Newburyport, I passed the Sabbath at the town of Ashford in Connecticut. It was the habit of New England to observe their Sabbath "from evening to evening." I had not much the appearance of a clergyman, and as I dismounted, inquired if I could have accommodations for myself and horse for the Lord's day. After supper, the landlord said to me, "Pray, sir, are you not a clergyman?" "I am a clergyman." "Because if you are a minister, I think our parson would be glad to have you preach for him. He'll be over to rights to see you." Soon the settled pastor came, and was introduced to me. He is one of the best of men, the Rev. Mr. Judson, though we were then perfect strangers. "I understand, sir, that you are a minister of the Gospel, and propose to pass the Sabbath with us." "That is my character, and such is my purpose." "I should be happy to ask you to preach for me, if I knew who and what you are." "As to *what* I am, I am no Methodist, no Baptist, no Unitarian; as to *who* I am, you will allow me to say, you will remain ignorant; I came here a stranger, and such mean to remain." "But will you not favor me with your name?" "Excuse me, I have reasons for desiring to remain unknown." Mr. Judson was embarrassed, but eventually requested me to occupy the pulpit, which I consented to do on condition that he would not ask my name. He gave his assent, and I preached for him. My sole object in wishing to remain unknown, was to ascertain whether I could not preach without notes, with unembarrassed freedom, before an unknown audience. And the experiment was full of encouragement. I preached in the morning from the text, "The law was our schoolmaster, to bring us unto Christ;" in the afternoon, from the words, "Unto you, therefore, which believe, he is precious." I never preached better, nor to a more attentive and affected audience. I left the town at the going down of the sun, unknown by a single individual. Mr. Judson, though I took tea with him, did not ask for my name. Some years after, he was present at an evening service in the Old Brick Church, and taking me by the hand, said, "Do you remember the Sabbath at Ashford? It was a memorable day *to us*. That day God made bare his arm; it was the beginning of a work of grace among my people."

I am more and more disposed to favor extemporaneous preaching. I regard it as the most successful way of wielding the sword of the Spirit; we cut and thrust then, this way and that way, and every way. The most powerful appeals I ever heard from the pulpit, and the most powerful I ever made, were extemporaneous. Through dimness of vision by cataracts, I preached several months without notes, and I believe it is the universal judgment of my people that I never preached better.

CHAPTER VI.

THE EMBARRASSMENTS AND ENCOURAGEMENTS OF MY EARLY MINISTRY.

The first of these was my own conscious incompetency for the work. My theological attainments were very limited. I am surprised at myself in consenting to take charge of so large and so important a congregation. My course of study at Andover had been limited to the short period of a single year. Next to my weekly preparations for the pulpit, therefore, I resolved to supply my deficiencies by a thorough investigation of the great doctrines of the Gospel. I had a tolerable supply of the best authors; while I was abundantly furnished from the library of my predecessor, the Rev. Dr. Rodgers, the library of Dr. Miller, and the more ample library of Dr. Romeyn. In addition to these resources, I corresponded with my seniors in the ministry, with the view of satisfying my own mind in relation to several topics by which I was embarrassed. Some of these communications are valuable. The two following are from the late Professor Stuart, of Andover.

"ANDOVER, *March* 1, 1813.

"MY DEAR BROTHER:

"No version of the Old Testament was made, except that of the Septuagint, before the first Christian era. The Pentateuch was translated about three hundred and eighty years A. C.; the other books gradually, and by different hands. The Targums, *i. e.*, Chaldee translations, may some of them precede the Christian era, but this is uncertain; 'et hoc sub judice est.' Many eminent critics place them much later; as Origen and Jerome appear to know nothing of them.

"Of the New Testament, the Syriac version was probably made in the second century; but the proof is not direct. Latin translations were certainly made —many of them; but all, except fragments, are lost. All the other versions are so late, as to afford no evidence of the kind which you desire. Moreover, the Apocrypha was included in some of them.

"On the whole, the argument is not worth anything, except from the Septuagint. The testimony of Josephus and of Philo for the Old Testament, and of Melito, Origen, and other fathers for the New Testament, is abundantly sufficient. Lardner gives the latter. The other is fully exhibited in the introductions to the Old Testament; I presume in Horne's, although I have not read his work.

"The *genuineness* of the scriptural books rests on the same kind of evidence as the genuineness of Virgil and Homer. The *authenticity* is a very different question.

"Mrs. S. desires to be very affectionately remembered to you and yours, with

"Your friend and brother,
"M. STUART."

"ANDOVER, *October* 7, 1813.
"MY DEAR BROTHER:

"I am quite mortified at the fate of your letter to me, dated some time last spring. As it contained matters which seemed to require some attention, I have concluded it to be my duty to write, in answer to some of the questions which you put.

"In respect to the EXEGESIS of Canticles, I have had, and still have, my doubts; viz., doubts which of the methods of interpretation adopted by commentators (Christian and Jewish), is most correct. I may, perhaps, be permitted by Dr. Romeyn to have some doubt here, without peril of the חֶרֶם חֲרָמִים which he so readily deals out; inasmuch as there have never yet been any two commentators, Christian or Jewish, patristical or modern, Asiatic, African, European, or American, that have been agreed about it. The seven times seven senses of the Rabbins, have been literally given to this *offendiculum criticorum*. Now, who shall decide where *doctors* disagree? For my humble self, if I doubt whether the forty-nine senses can all be applied to the book; or whether any one of the forty-nine can be applied agreeable to the laws of sane interpretation, and must be a heretic on this account, I say with Vitringa, '*Ego sum in hac hæresi.*'

"But in regard to the point of *canonical* rank (which is the point stated in your letter), I would that you might put Brother Romeyn to the test of stating his *evidence*. More than eight years since, I went thoroughly over the ground of the Old Testament canon, and satisfied myself of the fact that the Canticles were undoubtedly comprised in the Canons of Scripture used by our Saviour and his apostles. The result I embodied in a public lecture. *That lecture I have regularly read every three years since to the whole Seminary.* To questions often asked me by doubters about this book, on account of its speciality of composition and diction, I have always replied, that the fact could be clearly established that it belonged to the canon in the time of our Saviour; and that all hope of getting rid of the difficulties of it by ejecting it from the body of the sacred writings, were in vain. We must look these difficulties in the face; and if we cannot solve them, leave them (where we must leave a multitude of passages in the Scripture) to a future day, and better knowledge than ours, to solve. All hope of changing the Hebrew Canon is even more groundless than in respect to that of the New Testament. The Saviour and his apostles have given it a definiteness which admits of neither addition nor diminution.

"Such are the sentiments that I have always, *in public and in private*, maintained ever since I had any definite knowledge of the subject. I challenge any person to produce any evidence of the contrary. Dr. Romeyn will do me the justice, at least, to believe my testimony on the subject of my own opinion.

"I certainly do not think it worth the trouble of writing this to save myself from the imputation of heresy, among those who make all divinity heretical that is not *triangular*. This method of theologizing, however, is not confined to those who inhabit the region of triangles. 'What said Father Paoli to his brother Jesuit, who was less dexterous in combating for the mother-church than himself?—What did Scarpi say at the meeting of the order?—He said he doubted whether the infallibility of the Church could be predicated of the Pope alone, or whether it resided in an ecumenical council.—Most abominable! and what did you tell him?—I told him that the Pope was the successor of St. Peter.—Well, and what said he?—He said that he did not read in the New Testament of Peter's having appointed any successor, and challenged me to produce the passage.—Challenged you to produce the passage!—Yes; and I was not able to recollect it.—Able to recollect it! why did you not tell him that the Fathers believed as we do?—I did.—And what said he?—Why, that the Fathers were not the Pope, and so were not infallible. —Why didn't you tell him that he would endanger the faith of the whole Church by such *innovations?*— I did try to argue with him about them.—*Argue* with him! you stupid blockhead (fatuus Diaboli)—*argue with him! Why did you not call him* HERETIC, and tell him that he was going to perdition? I more than half believe you must yourself, at bottom, be like him in your sentiments, because you manage in such a way. These heretics are to be confounded by blows, not by arguments (fustibus non argumentis confutandos).'

"Thus believes Brother Romeyn, as truly as Father

Paoli, and for as good a reason. If you think strange of this, you have only to recollect that two pennyweights of brains are a sufficient apparatus for the purpose of guiding a march through the whole round of hard names and abusive insinuations, while it needs several pounds to manage an argument, and confute a *heretic*. But, peace! The self-complacency of those who are St. Peter's successors—*Non invideo, miror magis.*

"To be serious—the love of truth, and implicit confidence in what the BIBLE declares, is my motto. Other *orthodoxy* I prize or neglect, just in proportion as it agrees with this. 'It is, moreover, to me a small matter now, to be judged of men's judgment.' He who sees the heart, knows whether I love His word, and count everything discrepant from it, supported as it may be by ten thousand thousand voices, as the dust of the balance. THY WORD IS TRUTH. Blessed Saviour, who uttered this, make thy disciples to know its full import! Even so!

"Sincerely and affectionately yours,
"M. STUART."

Among the embarrassments of my early ministry, was the practice of my predecessors on the subject of *infant baptism*. Dr. Rodgers, Dr. McKnight, and Dr. Miller had been in the habit of baptizing *all the children* of the congregation, without regard to the Christian character and profession of either of the parents. I felt constrained to adopt a different course, and to baptize only those children, one of whose parents was a professed Christian. I felt bound to this course by the obvious principles of the Abrahamic covenant, the example of the apostles, and the spirit of the Gospel. I could not understand how any conscientious parent could consistently consecrate his child to God in baptism, who could not consecrate himself; nor how such a parent could presume to pray for his child, when he himself is a prayerless man; nor how he could instruct his child in the knowledge of God, and, by precept and example, persuade his child to become a Christian, when he himself is a stranger to God and his Christ. The confession of the Presbyterian Church affirms that " not only those that do actually profess faith in and obedience unto Christ, but also the infants of one or both believing parents, are to be baptized." The same principle is repeated in the 166th question of the Larger Catechism. I have known some persons who were grossly immoral, who desired to present their children to God in baptism; and who does not see the manifest inconsistency of this? Can such persons consistently bind themselves by a solemn engagement to train up their children in the nurture and admonition of the Lord? Do they mean to do it? and, if not, ought they to be allowed to make any such engagement? And are not the ministers who countenance them in so doing, chargeable with the same inconsistency? And where the parents are not immoral, but are professedly irreligious and prayerless, is there not the same inconsistency? When they offer their children to God, they profess to believe the Gospel; and if the profession of faith is a profession of obedience, is it not a hypocritical profession? You tell me that no sincere professor perfectly obeys *all* the commands of Christ, and that the parent thus offering his child is like all other professors. Even though he neglects the Lord's Supper, it is but a single violation of Christ's command. But what if he honestly tells you he *does not intend* to obey this command: wherein does he differ from the man who *avows his purpose* not to obey some one command that arrays itself against his besetting sin? Yet such is the unvarnished truth in relation to those who offer their children in baptism, and at the same time avowedly violate the precept, "This do in remembrance of me." Oh, how is the religion of Christ exposed to the contempt of the world, when they see Christless and irreligious men thus making light of its claims! Is it not religious mockery? Is any professedly impenitent man thus entitled to the blessings of God's covenant for his child? Is there no distinction between the church and the world? If it be said that the children of believers baptized in infancy are the children of God's covenant, and are members of the visible church, and as such are entitled to baptism for their children; I grant that they are members of the church, and that, when of suitable age, they should be required to acknowledge that relation; but they should do it truly and uprightly, and not merely for the sake of obtaining baptism for their children. It is true, they are members of the church by the covenant of God with their parents, and on the faith of their parents, but not personally, until they become so on the profession of their own faith, and do that for themselves which their parents did for them in their infancy.

It was no easy matter for me to introduce what is called the "strict practice" on the subject of baptism. I preached five sermons on the general subject of baptism, and, in dependence on God, relied for my success on the force of truth. Nor have I, with one exception, during a ministry of fifty-six years among the same people, ever varied from the strict practice; and that was in the case of a sick and dying grandchild, whose father was a man of prayer, but not a communicant, and I myself professed to stand *in loco parentis.* I now look upon the whole transaction as wrong. Nor have I, except in a single instance, *positively refused* to baptize every child that I was requested to baptize; and that was the child of a distinguished foreigner, who was connected with one of the families of the congregation, and who, after much expostulation on his part, turned from me with the remark, "I perceive, sir, that you baptize only the children of the aristocracy." I have been enabled always so to present the subject, as to throw the responsibility of the refusal on the parents themselves. A member of the congregation once came to me, with the request that I would baptize his child. He was not a religious man. I endeavored to show him the solemnity and the privilege of the transaction. I requested him to look at the subject deliberately, and ask himself if he was prepared to give up himself and his child to God. I prayed with him, and requested him to see me again. He went away, and being requested by his wife to have another interview with me, replied, "No; you will not catch me there again."

I had been justified in the course I pursued by the

views and conduct of the late Dr. Romeyn, who was established in the Presbyterian church in Cedar street, about a year before I came to the city. He was the first man who introduced the strict practice in the Presbyterian churches in New York. He took a firm and noble stand on the subject in the General Assembly of 1812. Dr. Richards, Dr. Miller, and Dr. Romeyn were the committee appointed to "draft a plan for disciplining baptized children;" but Dr. Romeyn was the author of that able report, exhibiting the views of our own Confession of Faith, of the best churches at the period of the Reformation, in different parts of Europe, and also of the first churches in New England, and in which he shows that no parent can use baptism as the seal of God's covenant, who does not *profess his faith in Christ and obedience to Him.*

There was another subject, also, on which I had no small difficulty, and that was the subject of fashionable amusements. But in this matter "Old Adam was too hard for young Melancthon." It is a foregone conclusion that our young people will dance. I regret it in Christian families, but I cannot prevent it. Our mercurial youth live for folly and fun. "The heart of fools is in the house of mirth." I have observed one thing, however; that when the Spirit of God is poured out upon us, there are no balls and assemblies; there is more prayer and praise than dancing. It is a grief of heart to the ministers of Christ that Christian families are so extensively the patrons of fashionable amusements. The giddy companions of the world, the sons and daughters of pleasure, give little proof of a Christian training.

But there were more serious embarrassments than these; they were threatening indications of dissatisfaction from some of my respected ministerial brethren, both in the Presbytery and in the city. The Rev. Ezra Stiles Ely had published his celebrated work entitled "The Contrast," the object of which is to show the points of difference between the views of Hopkinsian and Calvinistic theology. It was addressed to prejudice and ignorance, and was aimed at the youthful pastor of the Brick Church. I did not answer it, because I had more important work to perform; because I did not adopt the *peculiarities* of Hopkinsianism; and because I believed that after free and candid discussion by other parties, the religious public would gradually come to the conclusion that its object was mischief. It is a very imperfect contrast, because it takes no notice of the great doctrines which Hopkinsians receive in common with Calvinists; because it is a perversion of their real views; because it imputes to them doctrines they do not believe; and because it is throughout so utterly destitute of candor and honesty. I had no other way of quieting the alarm excited by "The Contrast," than by preaching "the truth as it is in Jesus," and more plainly and pungently. This I was enabled to do. I endeavored to exhibit the fundamental doctrines of grace as the great means of bringing the benighted and lost out of darkness into God's marvellous light. I dwelt largely upon the divine attributes; upon the spirituality and obligations of the divine law; upon the unmixed and total depravity of man; upon the all-sufficiency of the great atonement, the fulness there is in Christ, and the unembarrassed offer of pardon and life to all "that have ears to hear;" upon the great wickedness of unbelief; upon the absolute dependence of saint and sinner upon the power of the Holy Spirit; upon the divine sovereignty and electing love; upon the perfect righteousness of Christ as the only ground of the believer's acceptance with God; upon the self-denying nature of that holiness without which no man can see the Lord; upon the immediate duty of repentance toward God and faith in our Lord Jesus Christ; upon a punctual attendance upon all the appointed means of grace and salvation; and upon the solemnities of the world of everlasting retribution. For a series of years I had two principal objects in all my preaching. One was to exalt God and humble the sinner at His footstool; the other was so to exhibit God's truth as to leave the unrepenting and incorrigible without excuse. I endeavored to make them see that they had no cause for outward complaint or inward murmuring against God; that in rejecting the Gospel, they are condemned by their own consciences, by every page of God's word, and would finally stand condemned at the bar of God, and would have no reason to complain when they are sent to hell. It is true, this was not popular preaching. It stirred up no small opposition. But this was no proof to me that it was not God's truth, nor that it ought not to be preached, nor that it was not well timed. It was true; it was timely; and it was doing its work.

My confidence was in God. I was not discouraged. There were praying men, and *praying women*, not a few, who held up my hands. The God of Israel was inquired of to work for us, and he did work wonders. Opposition did not hinder nor retard the work, but rather promoted it, showing beautifully how the wrath of man can be made to praise the Lord. These great truths were not preached *eloquently;* they were presented earnestly and urged home. It was not rashness to urge them; the event showed that it was sound wisdom and prudence. Their practical tendency was Christian. God's Spirit came down, and in a succession of outpourings "took forth the precious from the vile," enlightened, sanctified, and confirmed his own children, took out from the world a people for his praise, and, as the older Christians died off, raised up a generation to serve him, and enlarged, and beautified, and perpetuated the church, and gave it a name among the more useful and honored churches in the land.

The conflict related mainly to the doctrine of original sin, human ability, and the extent of the Atonement. Some of the members of the Presbytery stood in doubt of me, and the late Dr. Romeyn, of the Church in Cedar-street, with true Christian courtesy and love, proposed to me, in writing, the following inquiries, to which I gave him the annexed replies:

The doctrinal points about which we want specific information are the following, to wit:

1. Did God, in his decree of election, first determine to save a certain number of our fallen race, and then, for executing this his purpose of mercy, constitute Christ as their Redeemer, to deliver them from death, and restore them to eternal life?

Ans. God did, from all eternity, determine to make a manifestation of his pardoning mercy to the intelligent universe, in the offer of it to all the human race, and in the actual exercise of it towards the elect. In the execution of this purpose, he constituted Christ as the Redeemer; who should, in his mediatorial character, make the exercise of mercy *practicable* to all, and by covenant engagement with the Father, *certain* only to the election of grace.

2. Was Adam the federal head, or representative of all his posterity, in the covenant of works, so that all mankind, descending from him by ordinary generation, sinned in him, and fell with him in the first transgression?

Ans. Adam *was* the federal head and representative of all mankind in the covenant of works. By *his obedience* all his posterity *would have* come into the world in a state of holiness and life; but by *his disobedience* they *are* brought into the world in a *state of* sin and condemnation.

3. Is the *guilt* of this first transgression imputed to, or laid to the account in law, of all mankind descending from him by ordinary generation?

Ans. The *guilt of this first transgression* is not *transferred* to his posterity, so that, if they had continued perfectly holy from the beginning to the end of their lives, they would have been damned for his sin; but it is *imputed*, so that they are, by reason of their connection with him as their federal head and representative, ORIGINALLY in a state of *sin and righteous condemnation*.

4. Does the disability to do good extend to the

whole moral constitution of the soul, the understanding as well as the will and affections, so that we need the illumination of our understanding, as well as the subjugation of our will?

ANS. The whole moral constitution of the soul needs *spiritual* illumination before it can be the subject of any holy affection. The understanding is darkened by reason of the blindness of the heart, and must be enlightened by the Spirit of God.

5. Is the Lord Jesus Christ in the covenant of grace the head of the elect, and their representative, so that they are viewed by God as his seed?

ANS. He is.

6. In assuming our nature and being made under the law, did he design the redemption of his people, his seed, and none else?

ANS. In assuming our nature, and being made under the law, Christ made an atonement for the sins of the *whole world;* but designed the redemption or final deliverance from sin and hell of his people or seed, and none else.

7. Are his sufferings and obedience, or, in other words, is his righteousness, imputed to those who believe, *i. e.*, laid to their account in law, so that they are acquitted forever from all the condemnation of the law, and adjudged to eternal life?

ANS. His righteousness is thus imputed.

8. Is faith in Jesus Christ the only mean or instrument of a sinner's being united to Christ, so as to be viewed in him as a member of his body?

ANS. It is, except in case of those who die in infancy. I have no proof from the Bible that all infants are to be damned; still, they can be saved only by the free grace of God, reigning through the righteousness of Christ. They are originally sinners, and deserve the curse.

9. Is union with the Lord Jesus real and inseparable, but spiritual and mystical, and not merely a union of sentiment and affection?

Ans. They are distinct persons; but their union is real, mystical, and inseparable.

10. Can there be, in fact, any evangelical repentance, or repentance unto life, without an apprehension of God's mercy in Christ?

Ans. *Repentance unto life* is exercised in view of God's *whole character* AS IT IS; merciful as well as just. Still there may be repentance unto life, without any such apprehension of the divine mercy as implies the persuasion, or the expectation, that it is to be exercised *towards* ME *in particular*. We have the warrant to believe that all who repent and believe WILL *find mercy;* but no individual sinner has the warrant to believe that he HAS *found mercy*, until he has some evidence that he has repented of sin, and believed on the Lord Jesus Christ.

11. Must sinners be discouraged from using the means of grace?

Ans. *No, by no means.* Still, they ought to be told to use them rightly. We would never tell them to sow tares, and then assure them that God has given them the promise of anything better than tares for a harvest. They ought to be strongly encouraged to use them.

12. Are Christians required to love God so disin-

terestedly as neither to desire nor seek any benefits from him?

Ans. No; that would not be disinterested love.

13. Ought God to be called the author of sin?

Ans. No.

Additional questions relating to certain doctrinal points:

1. Arising out of the answer to question first. Did the Lord Jesus Christ, by his perfect obedience, and sacrifice of himself, which he, through the eternal Spirit, offered up unto God, purchase reconciliation, and an everlasting inheritance in the kingdom of heaven, for any but those whom the Father hath given unto him from eternity?

Ans. No.

2. Arising out of the answer to question sixth. When it is said, "Christ made an atonement for the sins of the whole world," is anything more meant, than either the all-sufficiency of the merits of his sacrifice of himself, or the fact that he is the mercy-seat, or *propitiatory*, from whence God, in the Gospel, can treat with all mankind in a way of mercy?

Ans. Both, and nothing more.

3. Arising out of the answer to question tenth. Can there be repentance unto life without a persuasion that God CAN, and actually does, exercise mercy towards such of our fallen race as are penitent?

Ans. The fact of God's having proclaimed himself a *forgiving God*, does not constitute the obligation to repentance; but without this, we have no reason to believe there would have been a penitent.

On the subjects of atonement and human ability, I have long been convinced that where the terms are clearly defined and understood, the discussion is mere logomachy—a war of words. On the subject of atonement, Dr. Romeyn, and the brethren in whose name he addressed me, were satisfied, and the controversy was abandoned. On the subject of human ability, he had already committed himself, as I have shown in a note contained in " The distinguishing traits of Christian character," and in favor of the distinction between natural and moral ability and inability. Less is said about the importance of that distinction at the present day, and perhaps wisely : the most zealous advocates and the most zealous opposers of the distinction both agree that " no man *can* come to Jesus Christ unless the Father draw him ; " and that both saints and sinners are alike absolutely dependent for holiness on the power of the Holy Spirit. I have never changed my views on this subject; but I have modified my statements, and, as I think, more in accordance with the Word of God. The distinction is valuable ; and though I do not now say the sinner can repent *if he will*, because the assertion implies that an unholy volition produces holiness, yet I still maintain that his duty stands abreast with his intellectual powers, and his faculty of moral discernment. If he is capable of sin, he is capable of holiness ; else is he under no obligation to repent and believe the Gospel. This truth, though not always expressed, *underlies* all faithful preaching. Those pulpits which teach that it is impossible for unrenewed men to repent and believe the Gospel, rarely urge this duty upon the impenitent, and never with the earnestness with which it is urged in the Word of God. No man is required to perform *impossibilities*, nor is there any impossibility in the case, except that which arises from unmingled wickedness, and which leaves the sinner without excuse. Men who have the faculties of moral agents, who are capable of knowing what is right and what is wrong, if they are not saved, perish because they " will not come to Christ that they might have life." They have perception, reason, and conscience; to plead their blindness and wickedness as an excuse for not coming to him is only to " take advantage of their own wrong." There the solemn declaration stands : " To him that knoweth to do good, and doeth it not, to him it *is sin*." God makes no allowance for a wicked inability. We must take heed how we silence the voice of conscience. Many a good sermon has been neutralized by a single untimely sentence. There is a sense in which men *can* come to Christ, and there is a sense in which they *cannot* come. Saints and sinners are alike dependent on Omnipotent grace, and alike under obligation to be and do all that God requires. I am unable to see why the Scriptures, reason, and common sense, do not justify and demand this representation ; and why there is not perfect consistency in saying that, in view of their perception, their reason, and their conscience, impenitent men *can*, and, in view of their unconquerable depravity, they *cannot*, repent, and believe the Gospel.

For several years after my ordination, the interest excited throughout the churches in these discussions was unabated. Nor have I any doubt that the discussion did good. It led both Calvinists and Hopkinsians to be more cautious in their statements, and to have more confidence in each other. It led the people *to think*, and this is what they needed; and it issued, as we shall hereafter see, in a glorious work of grace in some of our churches.

I survived these embarrassments; but it was only through the divine favor. Lord Mansfield, whose superior is not to be found among the chief justices of England, has the following remarks on the subject of human applause: "I will do my duty unmoved. The lies of calumny carry no terror to me. I wish popularity; but it is that popularity which follows, not that which is run after. It is that popularity which, sooner or later, never fails to do justice to the pursuit of noble ends, by noble means." A minister of the Gospel, as well as a judge on the bench, occupies too exalted a position to be influenced by any other than the approbation of God and good men. He can afford to suffer from the arrows of falsehood and malice, if it is in the pursuit of truth and duty.

I have alluded to my correspondence with ministers in various parts of the land during my theological inquiries. The following communication I insert as a specimen:

"LITCHFIELD, *June*, 1817.

"MY DEAR BROTHER:

"I learned immediately, by a letter from Cornelius, the decision of the General Assembly on the synodical letter. Let the name of the Lord be praised; for it is His doings. It is a great event, and in its consequences an everlasting victory to truth. It unfolds, perhaps, his meaning in defeating your magazine, and teaches *you* and *me* never to move, when God, in His providence, shuts the door, confident that He has provided some other way. If a magazine be desirable, still the necessity cannot be, I should think, so urgent, and I am confident that Mr. ———— must not be the man. Whatever may be his talents at writing, his temper is not good, and will ruin the cause which makes him its organ. *Non tali auxilio tempus eget.* Besides, I do believe more good will be done by your meeting them single-handed. In the first place, you will write better, circumstanced as you are (if the spirit of the prophet be subject to the prophet), than any other person can write. Most of the great and good things which have been given to the church of God, have been extorted from unwilling men by the force of circumstances. I believe that God intends that you shall add to the stock of useful things, by bringing you into such circumstances, and that, if you take counsel, you will do better than any other man. Whatever I can do, will be done cheerfully. There will also be loss by attempting too much, and, moreover, the gain of sympathy by your standing alone.

"I am ever affectionately yours,
"LYMAN BEECHER."

The following letter from my ministerial friend and townsman, the Rev. Dr. Tyng, of St. George's Church in this city, was very kindly addressed to me, on the opening of our new church-edifice, on the corner of Fifth avenue and Thirty-seventh street.

"St. George's Rectory, *November* 2, 1858.
"Reverend and Dear Sir:
"My old and venerated friend: My mind has been awakened to grateful feelings, by the fact of your entrance into your new Brick Church. I recall my first knowledge of you in 1814, when you preached for some successive evenings in your father's church in our native town; on two of which I was permitted to hear you, from the two texts, 'Are not Abana and Pharpar,' &c., and 'It is hard for thee to kick against the pricks,' &c. I often think, from the impressions then produced upon my mind, that preaching was really a different thing then from now. My whole soul seemed to respond under those two sermons, all the attending circumstances of which are as fresh before my mind this moment as when they occurred. I remember your volume of Essays that I was then induced to read, in consequence of those sermons, and the power and delight which attended their truths to my mind. And now forty-four years have passed, and we are both old; and you still, in your old age, beloved and delighted in, as well as reverenced, by thousands.

"I recall my removal to New York, by which I became your neighbor, and the kindness with which you welcomed me here. And when our minds at St. George's were forced to an early removal, I feared that my venerated friend would hardly live to accomplish his renewed position, without which, it seemed to me, the Brick Church must be dissolved. And now, I have been laboring in my new church just ten years, and you have been spared to perfect your work, and been allowed to perfect it in its own characteristic style

—the Brick Church still. For myself, though so much your junior, I feel the pressure of age coming on, and acknowledge its many infirmities. You have passed threescore years and ten, and yet are, like Moses, of enduring ability to go in and out before the people of God. Many years, in your new work, of course, you cannot have. But it is enough for all your friends, that God has permitted you to inaugurate it in your own person, and to see with your own eyes the certainty of its result. It cannot but be one of the strongest and most prospering churches in our city. And I must be permitted to say, that you have no friend who more truly enjoys this prospect, and feels a livelier interest in your renown and happiness in your closing years, than I. Soon our common work will be completed, and we shall join in giving praise in a higher sphere, to Him who hath loved us, and washed us from our sins in His own blood, and made us kings and priests unto God, even the Father. May you be cheered in your upward path with much affection from your many friends, and with abounding divine consolations, from the best of all friends, our glorious Emmanuel.

"And among the many congratulations you will receive, over this very triumphant opening, be pleased to accept and welcome mine, as the expression of a long and most affectionate friend. The Lord be pleased to prosper the whole work for His own glory.

"Your faithful friend and brother,
"In our glorious Lord,
"STEPHEN H. TYNG."
"Reverend GARDINER SPRING, D.D."

CHAPTER VII.

PRINCIPLE AND EXERCISE.

THE terms *principle* and *exercise* are not familiar to the present age. The great controversy on this subject was at its height while I was pursuing my theological course. The leading advocates of the Exercise theory were Dr. Emmons, my father, and Dr. Woods, though Dr. Woods has since modified his views. The principal advocates of the Taste theory were Dr. Burton, Judge Niles, of Vermont, Dr. Griffin, and the old Calvinists. The advocates of the Exercise theory maintained that *all sin and all holiness consist in positive exercises of the mind;* that the law of God neither requires nor forbids anything else; and that, anterior to these, there is no moral character. The advocates of the Taste theory maintain that *anterior to all positive exercises, there is a moral nature, a principle of sin, in the unregenerate,* and *a principle of grace in the regenerate, a moral taste or tendency of mind*, a "heart of flesh," or "heart of stone," which is the foundation of all moral acts.

In this controversy, Dr. Burton, a man of distinguished ability, found a very able coadjutor in Nathanael Niles. He was a graduate of Nassau Hall in 1776, and Judge of the Supreme Court in the State of Vermont. Few persons wrote more on metaphysical and ethical questions, or more ably. I have now on my table a manuscript volume loaned me by his son, Dr. Nathanael Niles, of this city, and written between 1789 and 1805, which covers a wide field of moral and philosophical investigation.

Judge Niles studied divinity with Dr. Bellamy. He became a Congregational clergyman, but was never a settled minister. On his first interview with Dr. Bellamy, the Doctor told him, that if he wished to become a thorough theologian, he must dismiss all his previous notions, and come to the study with a mind not preoccupied. At a subsequent interview, in a conversation upon the character of God, he remarked, " Dr. Bellamy, I don't believe *there is* any God." " What ! " said the Doctor, " come to study theology, and don't believe there is any God ! " " Why," said he, " I used to think there was ; but you told me to dismiss all my previous belief ; and now I don't believe there is any." Judge Niles was an original thinker, a powerful debater, an ardent patriot, and fond of political life. He was three times a member of the Legislature of Vermont, the Speaker in the House of Representatives, a member of Congress, a strong Republican, and six times elector of President. The celebrated song called " The American Hero," the song of the Revolution, and beginning with the words,

" Why should vain mortals tremble at the sight of
Death and destruction on the field of battle ? "

was written by him. Dr. Nathanael Niles, his son by a second marriage, was the Secretary of Legation at Paris, and *Chargé des Affaires* at Sardinia.

Among other topics of interest, Judge Niles discusses the questions, " Is action necessary to morality ? What is that in the mind which is itself blamable ? Is divine sovereignty consistent with blame ? What is the relation of the understanding to praise and blame-worthiness ? And of choosing between indifferent things, or those which are equally eligible." After an elaborate dialogue between Evangelist and Moralist on the subject of Taste and Exercise, he relates the following

"FABLE OF THE MORALIST AND THE RATTLESNAKE.

" The Moralist, walking in his meadow, saw a rattlesnake lying at his length on the grass. He stopped short and cast his eyes here and there, in quest of some weapon with which he might safely kill the snake. The snake at the same moment saw him, drew himself into a coil, and raising his head from the middle of it, he fixed his eyes on him, and waving his tail from side to side, seemed to say, ' Keep your distance.' The Moralist, loth to lose sight of the snake, lest he should slide beyond his reach, alternately watched him, and looked for a weapon. At length, the snake, surprised at his manner, inquired why he looked so many ways almost at the same time ?

" ' I am,' said the Moralist, ' looking after a stick.'

" ' For what ? ' said the snake.

"'For the purpose,' said the Moralist, 'of destroying *thee*, venomous reptile.'

"*Snake.* But why would you destroy me?

"*Moralist.* Because it is fit thou shouldest die.

"*Snake.* Pray, how have I merited death?

"*Moralist.* By thy poisonous and malignant nature.

"*Snake.* If I mistake not, thou hast lived in this vicinity several years, for frequently, when lying concealed beneath the brake, I have seen thee passing and repassing. Now I ask, hast thou ever known me injure man or beast?

"*Moralist.* While I have lived here, which has indeed been several years, a number of people have been wounded, and some of them mortally, by the venomous bite of thy cursed species, and I know not but by thee.

"*Snake.* I grant it has been so; but I well remember, the report in every one of these cases was, that the offending individual was killed immediately after the offence was given; was it not so?

"*Moralist.* Such, indeed, was the report; and, upon recollection, I believe it was just.

"*Snake.* The consequence is, that I hurt none of them. Why, then, hast thou doomed me to death? Shall not every one tried at the bar of so good a man as thou art, be judged according to his deeds? And what have I done, to deserve death?

"*Moralist.* I know not that you have *done* anything to deserve it, but *you are* what deserves it. You are a rattlesnake, and all rattlesnakes ought to be killed.

"*Snake.* Is it possible that a man of so much discernment, candor, and goodness of heart as you possess, can decide so hastily upon such irrational grounds? According to your own acknowledgment, you can charge me with no one act, or series of acts, on account of which I am justly liable to death; and yet even you, who are so scrupulously tenacious of justice, have pronounced upon me this heavy sentence. My life is my all. You can take no more. If men are deprived of their natural life, their more important existence still remains unimpaired. To treat a man as you treat me, you must destroy him forever.

"*Moralist.* Your reasonings are as vain as they are futile and fallacious. That you are of a mortally poisonous nature, you will not deny; and this nature of yours is full of future acts which only wait for an opportunity to show themselves. Your nature is active as well as poisonous; and it is both to such a degree, and so unequivocally, that whosoever sees your nature, sees you poisoning every man who shall be so unfortunate as to fall within your reach. You and your nature are alike. You carry in your bowels a brood of young snakes, which, perhaps, have never yet seen the light, and your nature is full of snakish actions. Both those broods now exist, though they are not at present immediately visible. Your nature is little, if indeed anything, else than a collection and concentration of such acts in embryo.

"*Snake.* You say, then, that I deserve to die, not for what I have done already, but for what you suppose I shall do hereafter?

"*Moralist.* It is even so.

"*Snake.* But does this decision agree with your general rule of right ? Do you treat your own species in this manner ?

"*Moralist.* It is only from an apprehension of what one will do, or to deter others from the like conduct, that men punish one another. Punishment makes no atonement or compensation for what one has already done. Suppose you should bite and kill a man, and that you should be killed in your turn: what pleasure could your death afford to the bereaved family, except by gratifying their spirit of revenge, which ought never to be gratified, or else by gratifying their benevolent wishes, that you may do no more mischief? And what dispositions but these could be gratified in any other being on such an occasion? This shows that while no benevolent being will inflict evil except for the sake of doing good, every such being will in his proper department inflict it, when it is necessary to the procurement of some great good which will more than counterbalance the evil inflicted. This is the general principle on which men will always kill rattlesnakes, while they cautiously spare the butterfly. While, therefore, it is sufficiently evident that you have this nature, and that you will act it out when you shall find opportunity, the evidence against you is complete, and you certainly deserve to die.

"*Snake.* But how are you assured that such is my nature?

"*Moralist.* I know it from your resemblance to those which uniformly, when opportunity offers, perpetrate this kind of deadly mischief.

"*Snake.* But every like is not the same. Does it follow that I have all the qualities of the rattlesnake because I look like one?

"*Moralist.* Should the toad or the fly which you are about to devour, oppose you with such a question, would not your conduct show how unworthy of an answer you think it? Be satisfied with this, that with the same measure you mete, it shall be measured to you again.

"*Snake.* But even on the hypothesis that such is my nature, how are you assured that, if suffered to live, I shall act in the manner you assert?

"*Moralist.* How am I certain that a heavy body thrown into the air will fall to the ground? I am certain of it from the heavy nature of the body. How are you certain that flies, worms, and toads will nourish you? Because you have experienced that all things produce effects agreeable to their respective natures.

"*Snake.* You say, then, that because others have offended, I must be punished, although I have never done anything to deserve punishment.

"*Moralist.* No; you are to be punished for being what you are, and because, being what you are, you would do mischief, unless prevented by a deprivation of your power to do it.

"*Snake.* You are very unreasonable to judge of my propensities by the shape of my body, or to deem me noxious because some of my kind are so, especially when it is considered that but a small portion of them have actually injured any one. But even on the supposition that we are all poisonous, I ask, on what occasions does this fact appear? Do we act on the defensive only, or do we offend? Your kind seek us out in our dens to destroy us. But has any one of mine ever been known to pursue you? We often find you sleeping beneath the cool shade, and, sliding from under the brake, play harmlessly around you, until your awaking menaces our lives. Only suffer us to indulge ourselves, and we should never hurt you. Every circumstance of our biting proves no more than that we are disposed to defend ourselves. We were never known to pursue a retiring enemy.

"*Moralist.* I grant you speak the truth. I believe you would not exert your poisonous powers, if we would clear the way for your desires for their several objects. But those desires thwart the happiness of man, which is certainly of more value than yours can be. If we would give you the path and effectually keep ourselves beyond your reach, you would not hurt us. But must we, whose nature is so much more dignified than yours, give way to your perverse inclinations, which are so unfriendly to society?

"*Snake.* They are not unfriendly to society among my kind. Witness our lying in the most friendly embrace and in great numbers, through the long winter. And we should be as friendly to man, were we not instructed by our nature that he is our enemy. But you say that the happiness of man is of more worth than that of snakes. I remember to have heard you, the other day, in conversation with a person, whom you called Evangelist, when you urged to him that there was no other standard of happiness than as it referred to him whose happiness it is. My happiness is worth more to me than that of all other beings besides, just as you reckon yours of more value to you than that of the whole universe besides.

"*Moralist.* It is in vain to talk, since there is not a principle in my nature capable of being touched by your reasonings, unless you could by some deep sophistry wholly pervert my reason, or by some deeper magic make me believe that your nature is innocent. The sum of the matter is this: You are most evidently a poisonous, noxious reptile; I have found a stick, and you must die.

"*Snake.* Let me beseech you to consider, that, be my nature what it may, it is not a thing of my own making, nor was I at all consulted about it. It was given me at the will of another, and altogether without my desire. I heard you say that to punish in such a case would be a cruelty you would not exercise towards a dog. And is there, indeed, such cruelty in your good nature?

"*Moralist.* What I said the other day, has nothing to do in the present case. Mankind are not snakes, nor have they the poison of snakes. It is of little concern with me whence your nature proceeded. Though it was the work of God's own hand, it is not the less noxious.

"The man raised the stick. The snake began to speak: 'Remember,' said he, 'you have a nature.' The stick fell, and put an end to the dialogue. 'Proud reptile!' said the man, 'to reason concerning thyself as though thou hadst held the rank of human nature.'"

Whether the particular acts of the will are the fruits and effects of something else in man; whether or not there is an antecedent taste or disposition which gives to the will all its preferences, and to the outward conduct all its moral character; whether or not the moral character of men is determined by being what they are, or doing what they do; these are questions on which the Moralist and the Rattlesnake had different and opposite views. " Who shall decide when doctors disagree ? " The following sportive letter from my old friend, Dr. Perrine, may well follow the fable of the Moralist and the Rattlesnake :

"AUBURN, *Nov.* 12, 1834.
" MY GOOD OLD FRIEND, G. SPRING :

" Are you still in a world of confusion, turmoil, and strife? Alas! we have our pilgrimage in troublous times; but soon, my dear brother, our conflicts will cease, and our journey will come to an end. Happy the man who shall finish his course with joy, when so many things occur in this world to disturb and agitate his mind. But after all, there is, occasionally, a kind of amusement in our very vexations. I have just been looking over, for the first time, the three numbers of the Literary and Theological Review, published in your city, and truly I feel vexed and amused. While reading, I frequently thought of the severe and pointed manner in which you condemned many of us at the 'West,' who have been accustomed to think and to speculate with you on theological subjects, as having departed from the faith, and as holding 'new and dangerous doctrines.' Now, it seems that you, and others, have got up the Literary and Theological Review to correct our errors at the 'West,' and I must say, you do it 'with a witness.' This wonderful luminary does, indeed, pour upon us a flood of light from the East. All we have got against it is, that it so affects our eyes as to make us see objects upside down. There are two articles that present things about in the position in which we have been accustomed to view them, and we think them orthodox, viz., one in No. I., 'Christian Sanctification;' the other in No. III., 'The Song of Angels.' On the other articles, touching theology and its philosophy, allow me to make a few remarks while I feel a little playful, and glad in finding that the confounding light of the sun of orthodoxy, rising in the East, has not actually, and completely, put out all our eyes at the West.

"It seems to us errorists at the 'West,' that you theologians and mental philosophers at the East make strange work with your 'Disposition, heart, inclination, susceptibility, tendency, propensity, organ, pre-adaptation, congenerous and similar, previous aptitude, moral requisite, bias, moral habit,' &c., &c. These words and phrases, and many like them—for you have ransacked Webster's Dictionary for expressions of the kind,—we say, these words and phrases you appear, to us, to use in the same sense, and to express the same *state*, or the same *something* of the *mind*, or of the soul, or of the *something* that belongs to man. It also appears to us that you give to this disposition, heart, inclination, &c., &c., a moral character; or, if you prefer it, you make this disposition, &c., &c., to constitute the moral character of man. This appears queer to us 'Western errorists,' and makes us think that you, down East, must be ahead of us in mental philosophy and theology, sure enough. By this improvement in philosophy and theology, you have made discoveries which confound us. The discoveries which the good man at Salem, or somewhere down East there, made a few years ago, of what Paul heard, 'which it is not lawful for a man to utter,' can't be compared to yours. You admit that Adam sinned, because, I suppose, he did sin; you also admit that he fell, at a certain time, after he was created, and began to act, because, no doubt, he did fall, at a certain time, after he was created, and began to act. This is such philosophy as we errorists adopt at the 'West.' But now for your discoveries with respect to the manner in which Adam fell. Adam, say you, had, from the first, different dispositions; for awhile he followed his good disposition: in process of time, God ceased to sustain his good disposition; Adam then followed his bad disposition, and fell! From the *first* he had a *bad* disposition, and disposition gives character to man. Alas, poor Adam! he was down before he fell!! Truly, you are keen fellows, down East there, I tell you. It will not be safe for us Western boys to grapple with you,—you will *have* us down, before we fall!!! But hold a little, before you have us on the hip: say, how do you folks, down East, know that Adam had a bad disposition from the first? 'Oh,' say you, 'because dispositions are *only* known by their exercises.' There you have it! Well, had he a bad *habit*, too, from the first? Another question, as you seem to know a thing or two: after Adam was fairly down, and had fallen, too, did he continue to have different dispositions? 'No,' you say, 'we judge of dispositions *only* from exercises: unregenerate man has no good exercises, therefore he can have no good dispositions; besides, if unregenerate man had a good disposition before he was regenerated, he would be holy before he was renewed.' This is queer; you have a way, down East there, of knowing things, and not knowing them, but directly different things from the same notices, just as it suits you. Adam had no bad exercises, and he had bad dispositions. Adam had bad dispositions, and had no bad character. Unrenewed man has no good exercises, and he can have no good dispositions; and he can have no good dispositions, for then he would have a good character. Well, you must have your way! It now seems that you make regeneration to consist in man's receiving a good disposition. May I be so bold as to ask, how do you see what is in the inside of a man, or how do you know that he receives a new disposition with regeneration? 'Oh,' you say, 'we see and know what is in the inside of a man by looking at what is alongside, or on the outside, of him. After man is renewed, he has good feelings, emotions, and exercises, and we know that there must be a previous disposition of mind to the exercise of good emotions.' And again, 'disposition is the cause of a man's pursuing one particular course rather than another, for President Edwards says so.' You have keen eyes in seeing what is in man, and in the writings of President Edwards. If disposition is a *cause* of an emotion, and pursuing a certain course, can there be a disposition without *these effects* —remember Adam—may not these *effects*, then, exist without a *disposition as their cause?* President Edwards is speaking of a state of mind *generally* existing out of which volitions arise. In his Treatise on the Will we must look for his philosophy on this subject. There he tells us what may unite in forming this *state of mind*, and that the strongest motive, philosophically considered, is the cause why man chooses one thing and not another. His son shows us that he (President Edwards) does not exclude the influences of the Spirit in the good emotion or volition of man. Don't abuse President Edwards, we warn you, and drag him in to help you make holiness consist in a previous aptitude to certain exercises. Adhere to your own 'new' and superior light. What farther have you to say in support of regeneration consisting in disposition? 'Why,' say you, 'there must be a correct classification between mental acts and their sources. Affections cannot be referred to the will, but the heart; affections must have a source as well as volitions.' Oh, philosophy! oh, Burton! Have you anything further? Oh, yes: 'Men are susceptible of being regenerated by the Holy Spirit; therefore, when they are regenerated by the Holy Spirit, they *may* have a new disposition given them;' *i. e.*, a thing cannot be done in two ways; if it *may* be done in one way, it *must* be done in that way. You reason like unicorns down East there. We think you might do us more good by presenting us with what is in the precious old Book. Oh, Brother Spring, in what company do we find you! Our souls bleed.—My paper is too small. Oh, forgive my playfulness and folly! Do come out from among the * * * , we entreat you; we love you; we can't lose you; they don't love you as we do. Will you write a word to your old friend,

"M. L. R. PERRINE.

"Love to Mrs. S. I have no more forgotten her than I have her husband. Peace be with you all."

The following are the views of Dr. Emmons:

"FRANKLIN, *November* 2, 1819.
"REV. GARDINER SPRING, D.D.:

"DEAR NEPHEW: I know it is time for me to leave off spilling ink and blotting paper, but since you have provoked or flattered me to it, I will make a few remarks on the subject you propose.

"I have but very little to say respecting *Principle* and *Exercise,* because I never read Dr. Dwight's sermon upon the subject but once, and have it not by me, though I have tried to borrow it, and because I have published all that I know about the Exercise scheme. I recollect that Dr. Dwight allows that the essence of *matter* consists in its component properties; and that the essence of *mind* consists in its component properties. By these concessions, it appears to me that he has completely given up the common notion of a *substratum* in both matter and mind, and virtually adopted the doctrine which he meant to refute. I suppose that perception, reason, conscience, memory, and volition constitute the essence of the human mind; and I cannot conceive of any *substratum* in which these mental properties exist. Take away these mental properties of the mind, and I cannot conceive of any mind left. I am certain, however, that we cannot prove we have a mind which is distinct from, and the foundation of, all the mental powers and faculties of which we are *conscious*. I believe with Chevalier Ramsay, that ' we never ought to reason from what we do not know.' Since we know not that the mind consists in anything but the natural faculties and moral exercises of which we are conscious, we have no right to *suppose* that it essentially consists in any unknown substratum, nor to reason upon that *supposition*. Though Dugald Stewart does not deny that the properties of matter may reside in some unknown *substratum*, yet moral philosophers have nothing to do with that unknown something in their moral inquiries. In treating upon the mind, therefore, we ought to consider it as solely consisting in its *natural* faculties and *moral* exercises. The Scripture certainly expresses it in this light; and it is of the highest importance that theologians should represent it in this light. Unless they renounce the *Principle* and adopt the *Exercise* scheme, they never can reconcile the great and fundamental doctrines of the Gospel with each other. It is only on the supposition that the *heart* is distinct from the *natural* faculties of the soul, and consists altogether in free, voluntary, moral *exercises*, that any preacher of the Gospel can reconcile the *justice* of any divine commands given to sinners, with their total moral depravity; or can reconcile God's *secret* with his *revealed* will; or can reconcile God's universal invitations to sinners to accept of pardoning mercy, with his *electing* some to eternal life; or can recoucile God's giving so many cautions and warnings to saints against falling away, with his promise of *persevering* grace; or can reconcile *human* agency with *divine* agency in the free, voluntary actions of moral agents. I am very confident, sir, that you cannot write a 'Course of Sermons on Systematic Theology,' with any consistency, without adopting and establishing the *Exercise* scheme. No divine I ever read was able to remove the many *apparent* difficulties and inconsistencies everywhere to be found in the Scriptures, without adopting and reasoning upon the *Exercise* plan.

"Have you seen Stuart's Answer to Channing? Though I think he has displayed a good deal of ability, and a great deal of Biblical knowledge, yet I cannot agree with him in discarding the term *Person* in respect to the distinction between Father, Son, and Holy Ghost. We must use that term, or substitute another of the same import, or else give up the doctrine of the Trinity. Everybody knows that the names Father, Son, and Holy Ghost are in the Bible, but it can be of no importance to maintain this distinction of names, without we explain what they mean. I wish you would write what you and others think upon the subject, and you will gratify

"Your affectionate uncle,
"NATHAN'L EMMONS."

I have never entered deeply into this question. That fallen man is responsible for his sinful *nature*, as well as his sinful *acts*, I have not a doubt. Did I not believe this, I should be driven to the conclusion that God is the author of sin. As the judicial visitation for Adam's first sin, the native tendencies of the race are to evil and not to good. I never was an acute metaphysician, and I am too old to attempt to become so now. Yet I cannot help thinking, though I once thought otherwise, that there is something in man's moral character besides the acts of the will. Are not love, hatred, hope, fear, the spontaneous acts of the mind, instead of being produced by any efficient acts of the will? Is not their moral character derived from the character of the mind or heart from which they flow? The tree is known by its fruits. Is it not the heart that gives character to its exercises, rather than its exercises that give character to the heart? Do effects produce their causes, or do causes produce their effects? "Keep *thy heart* with all diligence, for *out of it* are the issues of life." Evil things come from *within*, and good things come from *within*. My own consciousness teaches me that there is something that lies deeper than the acts of my will.

CHAPTER VIII.

REVIVALS.

It was among the blessings of my childhood and youth to have heard much of those remarkable "outpourings" of the Holy Spirit which constituted the era of American Revivals. My parents often spoke of the "Great Awakening" under the preaching of Edwards, Whitefield, and the Tennents. From the time I entered College, in 1800, down to the year 1825, there was an uninterrupted series of these celestial visitations, spreading over different parts of the land. During the whole of these twenty-five years, there was not a month in which we could not point to some village, some city, some seminary of learning, and say: "Behold what hath God wrought!" There was a remarkable revival in Yale College, under the preaching of my beloved and venerated teacher, President Dwight, which commenced in the year 1802, and the influence of which was felt during the whole of my college life. While I was preparing for the ministry at Andover, and during the early years of my ministry in New York, I read with deep and growing interest everything I could find on the subject of revivals. Flemming's "Fulfilling of Scripture," Gillies' "Historical Collections," Brainerd's "Life," Edwards' "Narrative of Surprising Conversions," Edwards' "Thoughts on the Revival of Religion in New England," Edwards' "Humble Attempt to Promote the Spirit of Prayer for the Revival of Religion," and the various narratives of revivals as they appeared in the "Connecticut Evangelical Magazine," I devoured with eagerness.

Imbued as my mind was with the thoughts and emotions thus suggested, my great aim was to promote a revival among the people committed to my pastoral charge. Sparse clouds of mercy had been hovering over the congregation during the first four years of my ministry, and in the midst of the theological discussions before referred to ; and not a few, especially of those in middle life, had been brought into the kingdom of God.

The year 1814 was a year of great labor and deep solicitude. Many a time after preaching did I remain long in the pulpit, that I might not encounter the reproaches of the people of God for my heartless preaching, and many a time, as I left it, has my mind been so depressed that I have felt I could never preach another sermon. But I did not know to what extent the Spirit of God was carrying forward his own noiseless work. One thing encouraged me, and that was, as I toiled on from Sabbath to Sabbath, I enjoyed an unwonted enlargement and fervency in prayer, a greater facility in the selection of fitting themes for the pulpit, and more freedom and earnestness in declaring the whole counsel of God. God graciously interposed to relieve me from depression, and seemed to say to me: "Rise and stand upon thy feet; for I have appeared unto thee to make thee a minister and a witness unto the people to whom I now send thee, to open their eyes, and to turn them from darkness to light, and from the power of Satan unto God." I had been feeling after him in the dark. I had been floundering and plunging in the miry clay. They were not my own hopes that forsook me; these were bright and clear. My trouble was the want of success in my ministry. "Who hath believed our report, and to whom hath the arm of the Lord been revealed?" this was my burden. But now I could thank God and take courage. Though I felt as a worm and no man, I had more enlarged and delightful views of his truth, and my whole ministry from this hour received a new and cheered impulse. There was outward pressure enough to dishearten me, but the inward pressure was gone.

God was already beginning a precious work of grace among the people. He had taken it into his own hands, and was conducting it in his own quiet way, convincing the church and the world that it is "not by might, nor by power, but by his own Spirit," as the Author and Finisher of the whole. The spirit of grace and supplication was poured out upon the people, and they "looked on Him whom they had pierced." The weekly prayer-meeting and the weekly lecture were full of interest. Days of fasting and prayer were occasionally observed, and a Saturday evening prayer-meeting was established by the young men of the church, for the special purpose of imploring the divine presence and blessing upon the services of the approaching Lord's day. This meeting was for a long time held at the house of a widow-lady on the corner of Frankfort and Rose streets, and God blessed her, as he did "the house of Obed Edom where the Ark of God dwelt." Her four daughters were subjects of the work, two of whom died in the faith of the Gospel, and two of whom survive with their young blossoms to cheer the West. Our Sabbaths became deeply solemn and affecting. We watched for them as those who "watch for the morning." I verily believe we anticipated them with greater pleasure and more buoyant expectation, than that with which the sons and daughters of earth ever anticipated their brightest jubilee.

This was the first strongly-marked work of grace among my people. I take this notice of it for two reasons. God is wont to give every generation some inviting day of grace; to "set before them an open door." There were members in the congregation past the mid-day of life, who knew little of such seasons of awakening, and who had not become hardened by that resistance to the Holy Spirit which so often seals the damnation of scoffers. And this was chiefly the class that were the subjects of this blessed work.

Again: this season of mercy was an emphatic expression of God's goodness to the youthful minister. He had been but six short years in the ministry, but God foresaw that he was to occupy a place in his earthly sanctuary for more than half a century. It was a weary wilderness he was appointed to traverse, and the God of Israel refreshed him with some of the grapes of Eshcol. Poor a thing as I have been, and still continue to be, with devout gratitude I record it here, that it was this work of grace that made me what I am; which enlarged my heart, gave vigor to my thoughts, ready utterance to my tongue, new views of the great object of the ministry, made my work my joy, and stimulated me to reach forward to greater measures of usefulness. I loved preaching the Gospel before, but never as I have loved it since. But for this early season of mercy during the summer of 1814, I should have changed from place to place, and turned out what the Scotch call a " sticket minister." It was the Lord's doing, and marvellous in our eyes. The ingathering was not great, but it was the " finest of the wheat." Much of it has already been gathered into the garner of the great Husbandman, in full age, and full of grace. The Lord of the harvest sowed, that he might reap. It has been a pleasant sight to behold, while I have stood by the deathbed of these aged believers. " Mark the perfect man, and behold the upright, for the end of that man is peace." They are fallen asleep in Jesus. " They shall hunger no more, neither thirst any more; for the Lamb that is in the midst of the throne shall feed them, and shall lead unto living fountains of waters, and God shall wipe away all tears from their eyes." To the best of my knowledge, but one of this precious circle remains, and, like a ripe shock of corn, is becoming more meet for glory by her long experience of the divine goodness.

Those who have not passed through similar scenes,

cannot well appreciate the emotions of a youthful minister of Christ at the first ingathering. Even now, at the distance of fifty years, they are delightful memories. I look back upon them with that sort of melancholy pleasure with which the husbandman treads his bare and autumnal fields, after the harvest has been gathered in.

The winds of autumn had scarcely swept over the gleaned field, and the winter had just set in, when God was preparing us for another and more blessed harvest. "Instead of the fathers shall be the children." The commencement of the year 1815 was the dawning of a still brighter day. The last Sabbath of the "Old Year," and the evening services of that Sabbath, will be long remembered. The "New Year's Sermon," preached on the "last day of the Old Year," and printed under the quaint title of "Something Must be Done," has been widely circulated, and, by the divine blessing, I have reason to believe, was of some service beyond the limits of our own congregation. Among our own people, eight or ten persons, during the following week, were found to be anxiously inquiring for the way to Zion, with their faces thitherward; weeping Marys and bold young men, startled from the grave of trespasses and sins. The whole winter proved to be a "day of the right hand of the Most High." There was murmuring, indeed, lest the young minister *should carry things too far;* and there was open hostility. Nor were there wanting serious and conscientious apprehensions on the part of some of my honored brethren in the ministry, lest the work should savor more of fanaticism than sober thought, and ultimately show that it was the result of overheated and practised mechanism, rather than the work of God. But they were good men, and soon saw that their apprehensions were groundless. Amidst the greatest seriousness there was no outbreak and no disorder of any kind. The sacred influence was silent as the dew of heaven. There was PRAYER. There was solemn and earnest preaching. There was frequent pastoral visitation. There were private circles for religious conversation, and prayer, and praise, and these scarcely known beyond the individuals who composed them. There were no "new measures," no "anxious seats," and no public announcement of the names or the number of those who were striving to enter into the strait gate. Yet were there unexpected and unthought of instances of seriousness among the gay and frivolous, in the families of the rich and the poor, among the moral and immoral, and many were the triumphs of victorious grace.

The third Thursday of January, by a private arrangement, was set apart by about thirty members of the church as a day of fasting, humiliation, and prayer. It was at a private house in Church-street, just in the rear of St. Paul's; and such a day I never saw before, and have never seen since. Such self-abasement, such confession of sin, such earnestness and importunity in prayer, and such hope in God's almightiness, I have rarely witnessed. And what deserves to be recorded is, that as the devotions of the day were drawing to a close, there was a *strong and confident expectation* that the Holy Spirit was about largely to descend upon the people. And so it was. He was even then descending. That cry: "Where is thy hand, even thy right hand? Pluck it out of thy bosom," was heard in heaven, and echoed by our great High Priest. A delightful impulse was given to the work by this day of prayer. The promise was made good, "Before they call I will answer, and while they are yet speaking I will hear."

Our weekly lecture occurred on the evening of the same day; and I may say, it was the most solemn service of my ministry. The subject of the lecture was, "Marvel not that I said unto you, ye must be born again." God was with the hearers and the preacher; his Spirit moved them as "the trees of the wood are moved with the wind." There is good reason to believe that *more than one hundred persons* were deeply impressed with their lost condition as sinners, and their need of an interest in Christ, on that evening. It was not then with us as it is now. *Now* few attend our weekly lectures except the professed people of God; *then* the impenitent rushed to the house of prayer. Enemies were silenced; members of other churches came among us, some to spy out our liberty, and some to mark the character of the work for themselves, and all classes were constrained to confess, "This is the finger of God." Between one and two hundred attended the private meetings for religious instruction, and great solemnity pervaded the whole people. The work was rapid; awakening and conviction in many instances so short that older Christians began to doubt its genuineness. Yet some of the brightest and most enduring Christians among us were those whose conversion was as sudden as that of Saul of Tarsus. The gathered fruits of this protracted harvest were rich; consisting sometimes of thirty and forty, and at one communion season more than seventy, filling the broad aisle of the church—a lovely spectacle to God, angels, and men.

The "Old Session Room" is a memorable spot in the religious history of multitudes in this land. The citizens of New York well remember an English dentist of celebrity whose office was in the upper part of Cortlandt-street and near Broadway, whose name was Woofendale. He became a member of the Brick Church, and was a regular attendant on the weekly services of the "Old Session Room." I insert the following, received from his own hands, and himself the author.

"These lines were suggested by going to prayer-meeting at the lecture-room of the Brick Church on the evening of the 17th March; and seeing the light shine through the window, brought to mind the Star of Bethlehem.

"THE BETHEL STAR.

"Bright shines the Star at even-tide,
From little Bethel's holy wall;
It is a sure and heavenly guide,
It gives a kind and solemn call.

"A guide to those whose feet have strayed
  From wisdom's ways to ways of sin;
Their devious steps are here portray'd—
  Let every sinner come within.

" O sinner! did you know the grace
  That Christ our Saviour there bestows,
You'd haste to that dear heavenly place,
  And catch the blessing as it flows.

" Now, wretched sinner, come and try,
  For Heaven or Hell *must* be your doom;
Come haste! O haste! before you die;
  Come haste! O haste! while yet there's room.

" There's many a sinful, wretched soul
  Has bowed to Jesus in this place;
O come, and give your all in all,
  And he'll reward you with his grace.

" His grace can save your soul from death,
  His power *will* raise you from the tomb;
And with your last, your dying breath,
  You'll bless that Bethel for a home.

" Then shine, bright Star, from Bethel's wall,
  Shine upward to that blessed home
Where ransomed sinners at the call
  Shall rise TRIUMPHANT from the tomb."

There have been five seasons of the special outpouring of the Holy Spirit, during my ministry. They occurred between 1812 and 1834, more or less copious, but all seasons of refreshing. If the tree is known by its fruit, the results of these revivals were the fruit of the Spirit. The subjects of them have "run well," and with very few exceptions have turned out intelligent, active Christians.

I have ever felt a deep interest in revivals of pure and undefiled religion. The Church of God from the beginning has been enlarged, beautified, and perpetuated by them. My venerated instructor, the Rev. Dr. Griffin, who, from his settlement in New Hartford, through his happy pastorate in Newark, during his official services at Andover and Park-street, and his presidency at Williamstown College, lived almost incessantly under their blessed influence, and who, with the exception of Dr. Nettleton, was better acquainted with them than any other man, once said to me, "There never has been the time since 1792, in which the Spirit of God has not been poured out on some of the American churches. The spirit of missions as it first appeared in Great Britain, and the remarkable revivals in our own land, began together, and there has been no intermission in these 'days of the right hand of the Most High' down to the present hour." My old friend and class-mate, Dr. Humphrey, than whom, for his habits of observation, his practical wisdom, and his intellectual and spiritual culture, no man was better fitted for this service, has published a concise history of revivals from the days of Joshua, through the apostolic age; the Great Reformation in the sixteenth and seventeenth centuries; the remarkable awakening in Scotland, England, and the United States, in the eighteenth century, and the revival epoch from the commencement of the year 1800 down to the middle of the present century. His vigorous and classical pen has never been idle, and in my humble judgment has never been more *usefully* employed than in thus briefly retracing the ground so plentifully watered, and showing from historic records that " it has been God's method, under different dispensations and all along through the ages, to carry on his work by successive outpourings of his Spirit." I marvel not a little, that, after all our eyes have seen, and our ears have heard, there should be good men among us who look with suspicion upon these days of mercy, and who do not rather hail them, even in this midnight of our national tribulations, as the harbinger of that predicted period, when " the light of the moon shall be as the light of the sun, and the light of the sun shall be sevenfold, as the light of seven days." This is a ruined world; I should give up all for lost, unless God thus appear in his glory and build up Zion. There is no other helper; there is no other hope.

On the general subject of revivals, the following letters may be of some interest; to me they were timely and useful.

" LITCHFIELD, *July* 3, 1814.

" To THE REV. GARDINER SPRING:

" MY DEAR BROTHER: Your letter is very cheering to me, both on account of the information it contains, and the good it leads me to anticipate. For I think I perceive in it evidence that the Lord is with you and your people. I am only afraid that while the spirit is willing, the flesh will be too weak to sustain your exertions. You must call upon your praying people in your weekly meetings to make the prayers, that your strength may be reserved for preaching. I should have utterly failed last Winter, preaching four times a week, beside the Sabbath, had I not thus relieved myself. Economize your strength, Brother. Take heed to thyself, and contrive to do as much as possible with the least exertion. If the revival comes on, and if it do not, you must *extemporize*. It is easier, and will do more good. You will become animated as you progress, and find yourself wrought up to flights of sacred eloquence and holy pathos not else to be achieved. I know that you ought to premeditate and extemporize. It would be a wretched waste of strength to write your weekly discourses, except those for the Sabbath, and in those you would do well to leave places, particularly in the application, where you may lift a bolder wing than you can elevate in your study, without the ardor which ' crescit eundo.' I am not, however, writing to my pupil, though it might seem so, but to my friend, whose whole life, health, and prosperity in the ministry, interest me deeply.

"I hope you will come on in August. It is my intention to attend the next meeting of Synod, and thence to visit the churches on Long Island. The General Association of this State have recommended that each preparatory lecture be also a season for the catechetical instruction of the children, and also that it be devoted to special prayer for God's blessing

upon them. The reformation business respecting the Sabbath, and the petition to Congress, has gone well, and I think will go well in this State and through New England. I find good things among my people since my return.
"I am, affectionately, your Brother,
"LYMAN BEECHER."

The following from Dr. Humphrey I am not willing should be lost.

"FAIRFIELD, *November* 18, 1815.
"DEAR BROTHER:
"The months which have passed since I saw you have been months of great labor, and of mingled anxiety, hope, fear, and joy. The Lord hath done great things for us, whereof we are glad; and blessed be his holy name forever and ever. When I returned from Philadelphia, I found numbers of the young of my congregation in a very interesting state of mind. The work gradually increased from week to week, till the latter part of July, when it reached its height. At that time, and indeed for some weeks, both before and after, my house was the resort, often from morning till evening, of persons anxious to know what they should do to be saved. For the most part it was the still small voice; but in some cases it was the mighty rushing wind. We stood still and saw the salvation of God. Never did I witness such scenes before. Never had I dared to hope for what I have been permitted to see, under my poor ministry.

"The revival has been almost, though not altogether, confined to the young, and it has been in nearly all the principal families of my society. It began, as you know, in our Academy. A goodly number of the youth then belonging to it, are now the subjects, as we hope, of renewing grace. Many have wondered while they looked on, and a few have despised; but there has been no effectual opposition, and indeed none which would give the friends of Zion much uneasiness. The general belief has been from the beginning, 'This is the finger of God.'

"Twenty-three came forward and publicly joined themselves unto the Lord, the first Sabbath in this month. It was a most interesting day. Nothing like it was ever witnessed in this place before. Among the persons admitted were some who, but a few months ago, were among the gayest and most thoughtless youths in the town. It is the Lord's doing, and marvellous in our eyes. How animating when the fathers and mothers are falling asleep, to see those who are coming forward in life, dedicating themselves to God in an everlasting covenant!

"About thirty more will, I hope, soon be added to our church, as they give evidence of having passed from death unto life. But oh, what will become of those who are left? I tremble when I think of it. I almost seem to hear them exclaim, with an agonizing cry, as they sink into the arms of death, 'The harvest is past, the summer is ended, and we are not saved!' Brother, pray for us, that God will continue his work here, till every soul shall be united to Christ.

"There are two young men of my congregation, now clerks in your city, in whose welfare I feel deeply interested, Lewis B—— and Nathaniel L——. They were both awakened early, and the latter passed weeks in very great distress. They need a father and spiritual guide. Permit me to recommend them to your particular notice. I was glad to see, in a letter from the former, that he has already been introduced to you. He will readily make you acquainted with the other.

"Connecticut is still wonderfully favored by the outpourings of the Spirit. Among the towns recently visited, are Norfolk, Hartland, Colebrook, Salisbury, Berlin, Durham, &c. What shall we render unto the Lord for all his benefits?

"Remember me very particularly to Mrs. Spring, and believe me affectionately yours,

"H. Humphrey."

I have before adverted to my "birth-day" letters to my parents. The following is here introduced, as having more immediate reference to the subject of the present chapter. It was written during the revival of 1816, and with all the freedom of a son.

"New York, *Feb.* 24, 1816.

"Ever Dear and Honored Parents:

"I am thankful that I find leisure to pen a few thoughts on this memorable day. Notwithstanding the pressure of pastoral labor during the present week, I was enabled to finish my preparations for the Sabbath last evening, and have set apart this day to the purpose for which the 24th of February has been devoted for many years.

"And, my beloved parents, it is such a birth-day as I have never seen till now. The long-wished-for and long-prayed-for season has arrived. The God of Zion is indeed in the midst of my dear people. I can take my harp from the willows, and sing the Lord's song. I know you are looking for some communications respecting my own spiritual state; but I have better things to speak of. I have hardly time to think much of my own soul, except daily to cast myself on God, beg him to make and keep me humble, and so guide me that I may not give a wrong touch to the Ark at such a time as this. He has so evidently taken the work into his own hands, that all human dependencies are abandoned, and we seem to have nothing to do but stand still and see the salvation of God. To make an estimate of the numbers who are, in a greater or less degree, the subjects of the work, is what I dare not do. Much as we have seen and enjoyed for six weeks past, we hope it is but the foretaste of good things to come. Never have I felt so much the need of keeping near the throne of grace, and of having a continued interest in the prayers of my parents and of the people of God, as I do at this solemn season. I have often thought of the declaration in the Acts of the Apostles, 'And great fear came upon all the church, and as many as heard these things.'

"Yet the work has its opposers. There are those who laugh us to scorn; but He that sitteth in the heavens shall laugh *at them*. Some of God's own people in the city churches begin to say, 'This is innovation; we like the good old way better.' Others call it 'New Divinity,' and better suited to the latitude of New England; yet the work goes on. God is with us, and blessed be his name, notwithstanding all their prejudices, not a few of other churches are beginning to pray for the outpouring of the Spirit upon themselves. We have very solemn seasons, and we need them. You do not know how much I tremble. Call upon Christians among you to pray that God would not leave us. It seems to me, that by what he has already done, he has committed himself to do more. If he withdraws his Spirit now, what will become of his great name in our scoffing city? Oh, my father, my mother, will you not go into your closets, and say with Jacob, 'I will not let thee go, except thou bless me!' Oh, may the living and gracious Saviour be exalted in his own strength!

"I met the people on the morning of the last New Year's day, and told them that in all probability I was entering upon my last year's service in the earthly sanctuary. The whole house was in tears. We met for *one* hour of prayer; we could not separate till the expiration of *three*. The season will not soon be forgotten. I do not expect to live long; but the thought gives me little anxiety, except to be about my Master's business. You know not the joy it gives me, that my parents are bound to the same blessed mansions with their hell-deserving son.

"But I must close. Where is brother Samuel? I have just received a line from him, which looks as though he had found Him of whom Moses and the Prophets did write. If so, can he not be brought into the ministry? Means shall not be wanting. Where and how is sister Margaret? I have not heard from her, though I wrote to her soon after our fears about poor brother Lewis. I thank you for your approbation of the sermon. I intended to have re-written it before it went to the press. Pray for us all. We have had a sick winter, but one of great mercy. Why not *both* come on in May? We shall not see each other's faces many times this side the Holy City. We were not destined to live together here. Adieu, my dear parents. The Lord liveth, and blessed be our Rock!

"Your affectionate and dutiful son,

"GARDINER."

CHAPTER IX.

AFFECTING INCIDENTS.

THE following incidents are here introduced, not so much for their peculiarity as for the illustration they furnish of some one important truth. Although some of them have been narrated in a volume prepared several years since, and with some minuteness, in the Memoir of that Christian woman, Miss Hannah L. Murray, they deserve a place in this narrative.

HOPE NOT ESSENTIAL TO CONVERSION.

In this tragical conflict between the rebellious States of the South and the Government of the United States, the Government refuses to hold any intercourse with the rebels until they lay down their arms. This, we all see, is right, and just as it should be. They will make no treaty with *rebels*. The offended Majesty of heaven and earth acts upon the same principles of rectitude. He enters into no stipulations with his unrelenting enemies. Their own consciences, every right-minded being in the universe are witnesses that God is right, and they are wrong. He owes it to himself, he owes it to the rectitude of his government, he owes it to his mediatorial Son, he owes it to this rebel world, lenient and reconcilable as he is, never to propose any other terms of peace than those he has proposed, and never to be reconciled to men, until they first become reconciled to him. They must submit to him; he cannot, because he must not submit to them.

During the season of refreshing among my people, there were two sisters, the daughters of the late Perez Jones, then living in Cortlandt-street, near Broadway, who were the subjects of the work. They were very intelligent young women, of far more than ordinary culture, and proud examples of proficiency in my Catechetical and Bible Classes. Lucia, the younger, became the second wife of the Rev. Dr. Woods, of Andover; Louisa, the elder sister, was married to the Rev. Joseph Christmas, of Montreal, and subsequently the pastor of the Presbyterian Church in the Bowery, in the city of New York. Mrs. Woods is still living, and an ornament to her Christian profession. Mr. Christmas died in this city, in the thirty-fourth year of his age. Some imperfect sketches of this lovely and accomplished servant of God are contained in a discourse preached by the writer on the occasion of his funeral, entitled, "Moses on Nebo," and which was suggested by the character of this eminent young Leader of God's Israel.

During the revival, Miss Jones became interested, alarmed, and deeply convinced of sin. The work of the law was thorough, her convictions were intelligent, and, though resisted, she could not shake them off. The Spirit of God gave her a just view of her own character; she saw her sinfulness, and was made sensible that she was under the dominion of the carnal mind that is enmity against God. The commandment came, sin revived, and she died to all those reliant hopes and that moral deportment which had been her confidence. With this sense of sin fastened upon her conscience, she was thrown into deep distress. The past was black with sin; the present was hopeless; the future was all dark—darker and still darker, every step she took. Heaven—hell—oh, what solemn realities! She felt that she was the prisoner of justice, and it seemed to her that she was bound over to the curse. She struggled—with her own womanly valor she struggled—but she could not break her chains. She frequented all the lectures, the prayer-meetings, and the conference chamber; she had frequent interviews with me in my study; but there was no help for her in an arm of flesh. The poor girl seemed to herself to be actually going to hell, and felt that nothing she would ever do would prevent her going there. Often did I pray with her, and direct her to the Lamb of God that taketh away the sin of the world. I told her that she was without excuse; that she was every hour resisting the Holy Spirit; that it was vain for her to flee out of the hands of God; that if she continued in this wicked state of mind, she would inevitably be lost; and that if she sunk to hell, the blame would lie at her own door. But her heart revolted. She did not love God, she could not submit to him. Nothing afforded her any relief. That fair countenance was pale with something like despair. The arrows of the Almighty were within her, the poison whereof was drinking up her spirit. I felt that she was beyond the reach of help on this side heaven.

A day or two after, she came to my residence in Beekman-street, and inquired for Mrs. Spring, who had been familiar with her state of mind, and was no incompetent counsellor to the awakened and convinced. Mrs. Spring observed her altered and yet embarrassed countenance, and said, "*What is it, Louisa?*" "Oh, my dear Mrs. Spring, *I have lost all my convictions! I am as stupid as a block of marble. I am afraid I have grieved the Holy Spirit, and that he will never return.*" And she wept. Mrs. Spring replied, "*Louisa, I may not talk with you now; I must call my husband.* He desired not to be interrupted this morning, but *I know he would wish to see you.*" I went into the parlor, and Louisa was still weeping. "*What is it, Louisa?*" She did not answer at once, but at length said, "*I do not know, sir, but I have lost my convictions. I am very stupid.*" "But *have you no alarm?*" "*No, none except that I am so stupid.*" "But *do you wish to drop the subject of religion, and go back to the world?*" "*No; no, sir.*" "Have you *lost all sense of your sins?*" "*I have no sense of anything; I cannot feel the burden of my sins as I did.*" "Are you *quarrelling with God now, Louisa?*" "*No; I cannot quarrel with him; if he sends me to hell, I know it is just right.*" "And yet *you have no distress?*" "*No, none.*" I then smiled, and she, for the first time for weeks, assumed her wonted placidness. "*Give God the praise,*" I said, and said no more. She cast her eyes on the floor, and at length, with clasped hands and a heavenly smile, inquired, " *Oh, my dear pastor, do you think I am a new creature ?* " I simply replied, " *I do not know, Louisa, time will show ; the tree is known by its fruits ; this does not look to me like the work of man. Look to the fulness there is in Christ, my young friend. Remember him who said,* ' *When I am weak, then am I strong.*' *Remember Philip and the Eunuch ; go on your way, and rejoice as you go.*" She well knew the way of life, but I felt constrained to dwell upon it a few moments, and she received the word with joy. After a short prayer to Him who alone takes our feet from the horrible pit and the miry clay, I left her with Mrs. Spring, and retired to my study with renewed strength and zeal. This dear young woman I had the joy of receiving into the church, of uniting her in wedlock to one of our most beloved and honored brethren in the ministry, and of knowing that she was the adornment of her profession and her responsible position in the Church of God, and that she lived, and on the 9th of August, 1829, died in this city, in the precious faith of the Gospel.

UNITARIANISM DEMOLISHED.

Mr. Solomon Aiken was a gentleman from Massachusetts, deeply imbued with the principles of Unitarianism. He was a merchant of respectable standing in our city, of unblemished moral character, and, from his business connections, was the intimate friend of Mr. Abijah Fisher, one of our ruling elders, and with his family worshipped in the Brick Church. He heard the Gospel as he had not been accustomed to hear it, and, much to my surprise, neither withdrew from the congregation, nor abandoned his Unitarian views. I have reason to believe that he became attached to me personally; and while he had no partiality to the doctrines he heard, still remained a punctual attendant, and an interested hearer. It was a season of great solemnity in the congregation, and his friend Fisher intimated to me that a personal interview with Mr. Aiken would neither be unwelcome nor unseasonable. I called on him, and, without any allusion to his Unitarian errors, had a pleasant interview with him on the subject of personal religion. I found that the Spirit of God was striving with him. The world had lost its charms, and he had little interest even in his business affairs. His conscience was troubled, and I left him. A few days after this, he sent for me, and I found him anxious and filled with fear and trembling. The Spirit of God had convinced him of sin; he could no longer deny the Scriptural doctrine of human sinfulness, though he would fain betake himself to some refuge of lies. I remained with him alone for a long time. I said to him, "*Mr. Aiken, you are all wrong; you have been all wrong; the Spirit of God is striving with you; he will not always strive; and if you do not stop in this downward course, you will be lost.*" He replied, "*Oh, Dr. Spring, I have not told you all. Last night was a dreadful night. I could not sleep. The more I thought of myself, the more I felt that I must perish. I felt condemned, and that no created arm could rescue me from the doom that I deserved.* LAST NIGHT

ALL MY UNITARIANISM LEFT ME." "Mr. Aiken, *I am glad of it. You had last night a better teacher than you ever had before. Who teacheth like* HIM?—*so easily, so seasonably, so effectually? Give him the praise, and see to it that you do not turn a deaf ear to his instructions.*" "No, sir," said he, "*and I want you now to tell me what I shall do.*" "This one thing you *must do: repent and believe the Gospel. Believe on the Lord Jesus Christ, and thou shalt be saved. He came to seek and to save that which is lost. He is a divine Saviour, and is able to save to the uttermost all that come unto God by him. This is your present and imperious duty. You are a poor, guilty, perishing sinner; and to whom can you go but to this all-sufficient Saviour?*" "*But will you not tell me* HOW *I shall go to him?*" "Yes, I can tell you: you must *not go in your own strength; for your strength is weakness. You must not go in your own righteousness; for you have none. You must feel your need of Christ, and see that he is just the Saviour adapted to your wants. You must adore, and love, and trust him. Worm and sinner as you are, you must not exclude yourself from his invitations and promises. He loves to be believed and trusted. Go to him as your Saviour. Venture on him; venture wholly. Rest your hopes upon him. Commit to him your entire salvation, and in all holy obedience live devoted to his service.*" I prayed with him, and took my leave, rejoicing that another soul had been snatched as a brand from the burning, and that the proud edifice of Unitarianism was no better than Jonah's gourd which perished in a night.

UNIVERSALISM AND THE BED OF DEATH.

About forty years ago there was a man, living on the corner of William and Spruce streets, who was dying of consumption. His family worshipped in the Brick Church; his wife was an exemplary Christian he himself was a prominent member of the society of Free Masons, and rarely, if ever, worshipped anywhere. For obvious reasons, I withhold his name, but in this narrative designate him as Mr. B. I did not know of his illness, though I then resided in Beekman-street, and but a single block from his residence. I was made acquainted with his character and condition by his wife, who requested me to visit him, under color of a pastoral visit to the family. She told me he was a Universalist, and spoke of the Brick Church as "brimstone corner," and its pastor as the "hell-fire preacher." She did not wish me to inquire for her husband, lest he should refuse to see me; but she could not consent to his going out of the world without seeing his awful delusion. I went, and, so far as I now recollect, went the next day. I was received courteously by Mrs. B. in the ordinary sitting-room, and adjoining which, and on the same floor, was this dying man. The door of his room was open; and as I was conversing cheerfully with Mrs. B., the hollow cough of the sick man led me to remark, that I perceived some of her family were sick. "*Yes, sir,*" said she, "*my husband is very ill; he has been a long time confined to the house with consumption, and now he is, for the most part, confined to his bed.*" I expressed a regret that I had not known it earlier, more especially as he was so near to me that I could, with very little inconvenience, have seen him often. "*Perhaps he will be glad to see you now, sir; I will ask him.*" She returned, and invited me into his sick-room. He received me kindly, and I could not but perceive that his hour-glass was nearly run out. I was embarrassed. I did not think it wise to attack his principles, lest I should excite his hostility by provoking an unprofitable controversy. I merely said to him, "*I am sorry to see you so very ill, sir.*" "Yes, *I am very ill, and have been so for a long time.*" "Do you *suffer much?*" "No, *not a great deal, except from weakness, and this racking cough; it keeps me awake at night.*" "And *do you get no relief, and have you no hopes of recovery?*" His poor wife was listening with amazing interest, and he replied, with a stolid indifference, "No, *not much; I do not expect to recover.*" I was embarrassed no longer, and said to him, "*Is it indeed so, that you are going soon to* DIE, *and stand before God in judgment?* If I judge your case aright, that hour is not far distant. I hope, my dear sir, you are prepared for it." With most perfect coolness he replied, "*I am ready. I am satisfied my Maker will never send any of His creatures to hell. He wills not that any should perish. I never think of hell torments. I do not believe a word of it.*" I replied, "*It is well* to be satisfied at such an hour as this. We cannot trifle with God, nor with death, nor with eternity; nor may a man trifle with himself, without peril to his soul." He made no answer, but listened with prodigious interest. I remarked that I was sorry to see that he had adopted the delusion of the Universalists. "And now," said I, "do you really believe it?" "Yes, I do," was his prompt answer. "Are you satisfied with it? Are you sure it is true? I do not ask whether you wish it were true; nor whether you hope it is true; but are you *sure* it is true? The opinions of men are very apt to be influenced by their wishes. They shrink from the thought of everlasting retribution, and therefore they will not believe it. Wicked as it is, they often carry their delusion to the bed of death. But, my dear sir, what motive have you to practise this delusion upon yourself at this late hour? You may have been honest in your views of this solemn subject in the season of health and prosperity; all I ask is that you should be honest now, in this season of debility and tribulation. Do you now believe the doctrine of universal salvation to be true? and are you *sure* of it?" I perceived that these suggestions troubled him. He was pale and agitated. His steady, firm tone had forsaken him. His lips quivered, and there was a convulsive motion of his face that alarmed me. "Oh!" said he, all bathed in tears, and clasping his hands together, "Oh! sir, I am not sure of it! I am not sure of it!" He wept. Mrs. B. wept, and for a brief moment, we were all silent. Whether I prayed with him or not, I cannot now affirm. I left him with his own thoughts, resolving to see him soon, and not without hope that the word of God would become quick and powerful.

There was no time to lose. He had been the victim of a popular delusion that was making havoc of the souls of men; his refuge failed him; his time was short, and I hastened to his bedside on a second visit. He made me welcome, and though I rejoiced in the opportunity, much did I wish that some more wise and experienced counsellor could conduct the interview.

"I do not wish to alarm you, Mr. B., but I thought you would be willing to indulge me with a short interview this morning."

"Sir, I am glad to see you. Sit here by me, and say what you please. You will not offend me. I have given up my Universalism, and know that I am a great sinner. I have sat under the sound of that old church bell, and have ridiculed it, and despised the Sabbath. I have been a scoffer, and an ungodly man. I have no strong hopes now; indeed I have none at all. Instead of being sure that I shall be saved, it seems to me that I must be lost, and that I deserve to be damned."

"It may be you have not seen the worst of it yet. Your Universalism is not your only sin. There is wickedness that lies deeper than *that*. It is your corrupt and wicked heart that was the root of your Universalism, and that led you to cherish your hostility to God's justice."

"I know it: I have seen it, and feel condemned. This is my last call. Is there no hope for me?"

"I am glad you feel condemned, and I dare not say there is any hope for you, if you die out of Christ, and neglecting the great salvation. Listen to me a moment. You are condemned, and as a condemned sinner you lie at the footstool of sovereign mercy. God's holy law condemns you. You have cast that law behind your back; but you now feel the force of it, and it brings with it a knowledge of your sins, and a sense of your guilt and danger."

"I once thought the law of God a severe law, and that he was a hard master. I justified myself, and complained of God. But I was wrong: God is perfectly right. I was among the bold opposers of all religion, and thought it hard that God should damn men for breaking his law. But I was all wrong: God is perfectly right."

"You are right in this. Both the precept and the penalty of the law are just. Conscience feels this when the commandment comes home. The hearts of wicked men rise against it; they hate God, and they hate his law; but he shows them and makes them feel that the law is holy, just, and good. Now, my suffering friend, if you see these things to be so, and feel them, do you not perceive more clearly than ever, not only that all your past hopes are perished, but that you have no imaginary goodness on which you can rely, no righteousness of your own in which you can trust?"

"Indeed I do. I have been all wrong; everything, thoughts, words, actions, all wrong. *Words!* O how many wicked words have I spoken! It is all sin, nothing but sin. I have no righteousness; it is all sin; I have no hope from what I have done, nor from what I can do. Truly I feel embarrassed. I do not know where to go, nor which way to turn. I am cut off from every retreat. It seems to me I am actually going to hell, and that there is but a step between me and the everlasting burnings which I have so derided."

"I know, sir, there is nothing you will ever do that will prevent your going there. But have you never heard that the Son of Man came to seek and to save that which was lost; that when we were without strength, in due time Christ died for the ungodly? 'O Israel! thou hast destroyed thyself, but in *Me* is thy help.' Remember the thief on the cross. I know you are lost, but you are not lost beyond recovery. God's Spirit is inviting you to take refuge in Christ. The crucified One is saying to you, Come unto me, all ye that labor and are heavy laden, and I will give you rest. You need pardon; and he died, the just in the place of the unjust, that he might dispense it. You need righteousness; and he was made sin for us that we might be made the righteousness of God in him. Do not despair, my dying friend, there is balm in Gilead. I have no expectation that you will live a week. Behold, *now* is the accepted time. You have no security for a single day; and oh, that it may be said, This day is salvation come to this house!"

After prayer I left him, but saw him on the following day. He was near his end, but he was calm. He could speak but little, but expressed his hope in Christ. I had not much confidence in death-bed conversions, but I dare not suggest a thought that would obscure his hope. One circumstance at the closing interview encouraged me. He requested me to attend his funeral, intimated that his Universalist friends would be there, and desired me to tell them *from him* that *he had become convinced that* the Universalist doctrine was false, and that while it would do very well to live by, it would not do to die by. I engaged to do so, and told him that, God helping me, I would publish his recantation to the world.

I accordingly attended his funeral, which was very large, and composed of various characters, and some hard-visaged men. It was a " Free Mason's " funeral; and as we stood round the vault in the northeast angle of the old cemetery, the chaplain of the Lodge read their appointed burial-service, and closed with the memorable words, SO MOTE IT BE! The whole proceeding was sufficiently ridiculous, absolutely unmeaning, and in my judgment not far from impious. I did not interrupt it, but, abiding my time, felt nerved for an unembarrassed and bold deliverance of God's truth. I begged the attention of the audience, as I had a message from the deceased which he had requested me to deliver to them over his grave, and which I had promised to deliver. " There he lies, but being dead he yet speaketh. He did not die a Universalist, but in the full belief of that Gospel which proclaims to every creature, *He that believeth shall be saved, and he that believeth not shall be damned.* He wished me to say to you that he had no confidence in the soul-destroying doctrine that all men would be saved. It *is* a soul-destroying doctrine, my friends, and it is nothing else than the Devil's lie. It is the worst form of Infidelity, and the most subtle and alarming delusion of the age. It is the great Deceiver's gospel, and, before you are aware of it, will conduct you to the world of despair." As I proceeded, and with increased fervor, I perceived a confusion and hustling in the crowd, and heard the words *Damn him!* One of the ruling elders of the Brick Church, the late Richard Cunningham, who from the first stood near me, took my hand and said, "Don't be afraid, dear, they are chained. Go on." I went on, and was again assailed with the imprecation, *Go to hell!* "Gentlemen, I am glad that you have changed your minds. I perceive that you now believe there *is* a hell, else you would not *tell me* to go there. And when you say *Damn him*, I perceive that you no longer deny that there is a damning God in heaven. So your departed brother believed; but he believed also in Him who is the Saviour of the lost. I will not reciprocate your imprecation, and say to you, *Go to hell*, but rather pray that 'the grace of our Lord Jesus Christ may be with you all, Amen!'"

I have seen Universalists and Infidels die, and during a ministry of fifty-five years, I have not found a single instance of peace and joy in their near views of eternity; no, nothing but an accusing conscience and the terrors of apprehension. I have seen men die who were men of a mercurial temperament, men of pleasure and fun, men of taste and literature, lovers of the opera and the theatre, rather than the house of God; and I never saw an instance in which such persons died in peace. They died as they lived. Life was a blank, and death the king of terrors; a wasted life, an undone eternity.

THE PRIDE OF INTELLECT HUMBLED.

I have often found that those habits of thought and that self-reliant spirit which ensnared the soul, and which seemed to be the great obstacles to its conversion were the very idols at which the Spirit of God aimed its most deadly blows in the ordinary process of conviction. If it was radical error, the error was made the occasion of the most fearful alarm; if it was self-righteousness, it was the occasion of prolonged apprehension and agonizing despair. If it was the pride of intellect, it quarrelled with God's truth, it disdained divine teaching, it stood aloof from the ordinary means of grace, it demeaned itself loftily, until, by repeated mistakes and disappointments, it became conscious of ignorance, and learned to sit at the feet of Jesus.

Sabin Lethbridge was, in the high day of human life, a man of fine intellect and early culture, though never enjoying the advantages of a liberal education. He was a native of Franklin, Massachusetts, and was a parishioner of Dr. Emmons. He was an ultra Calvinist, and, though a punctual attendant on the ministrations of the pulpit, "wiser in his own conceit than seven men that can render a reason." He was present, with Mrs. Lethbridge, at one of our meetings for religious conversation, and after conversing with others, I passed him with civility, and took no further notice of him. At a subsequent meeting, for the same purpose, he came alone, and sat solitary in a distant part of the lecture-room. I sat down by him, and said, "Mr. Lethbridge, the servant that knew his Lord's will and did it not, was beaten with many stripes." "Oh, sir," said he, "I have come to ask you to teach me my catechism. My mind is all vacancy: I feel like a little child, and wish to be taught the way of life." I have no doubt that he was then a converted man, and had received the kingdom of God as a little child. His whole subsequent life showed it, and his death exhibited it in most beautiful coloring. He was prostrated by lingering consumption; and such sweet humility, such unconditional submission to the will of God, and such heavenly cheerfulness in the view of death, I have rarely seen. There was no triumph, but there was no gloom, in his chamber. We all felt sad when we visited him, but our sadness was out of place. He could not bear to see a gloomy countenance. I recollect well, that when on a certain occasion our mutual friend, Richard Cunningham, approached his bedside with his placid and cheerful countenance, Mr. Lethbridge gave him his hand, and said, " I thank God there is one man that can greet me with a smile." "*Almost home, Mr. Lethbridge!*" "*Yes, yes, almost home, Brother Cunningham!*" On another occasion, as I was conversing with him, Mrs. Lethbridge stood unseen at the head of the bed *weeping*. He happened to turn his eyes towards her, and said, " *O poh! I thought better of you than that.*" I never shall forget the scene when we were assembled at his funeral. It was a lovely scene. There was a calm serenity, a joyousness very unusual in the house of death. Expressive silence seemed to say, " This day is salvation come to this house."

A PLAIN TALK.

Dr. Nettleton once remarked to me, that in his interviews with different classes of men, he always endeavored to *fall in* with the operations of the Holy

Spirit on their own minds. The remark was of great service to me, and I saw at once the full bearing of it. If the Spirit of God was convincing them of sin, instead of giving them any relief from that impression, I labored to intensify it and make it deeper. If the Spirit of God was producing a deep sense of their dependence and helplessness, their obligations and inexcusableness, I endeavored to enforce these truths and make them felt. But what if I found instances in which it was obvious that, instead of being taught of God, they were under a different teaching, that the God of this world was blinding their minds, and that they were under the most fearful delusions? I then felt that I was called on to resist and overcome these counsels of the Devil.

This was the case in the instance which I am about to narrate. It was a season of great solemnity in the congregation: the Spirit of God was descending in copious effusions, and among others, the husband of the lady to whom this narrative refers, was a subject of the work. I felt a deep interest in her spiritual welfare, and was resolved to have a faithful conversation with her on the concerns of her soul. She was the daughter of an English clergyman, a lady of high intellectual culture, a widow in middle life, and who, on coming to this country, had become the wife of Sabin Lethbridge, whose conversion has been alluded to in a previous page. And she was by no means averse to religious conversation.

I found her thoughtless, asleep, and dead in sin, and I was convinced that she was the subject of some infatuating delusion. She gave me a cordial welcome, and I said to her, "Mrs. Lethbridge, do you mean to let your husband go to heaven without you? Why not go with him, and seek the better country, which is the heavenly?" "Oh, sir," she replied, "I think I shall go with him; I do not expect to be left behind. He has become a Christian, but I do not bid him farewell; I shall go with him yet." And here she was resting in perfect thoughtlessness. She was dreaming of heaven, and sunk down into a deep sleep. I thought I saw the snare, and was resolved, by God's help, to break up this pleasant dream. It was an unwelcome task, but I endeavored to show her that she had very little reason to believe that *she would ever be saved*, but many reasons to believe that she and her husband would part at the last day, and that she would go away into everlasting punishment.

"Mrs. Lethbridge, I am afraid you will be lost."

"What makes you think so, Dr. Spring?"

"Because you are not a Christian, and not likely to be."

"I know I am not a Christian; but what makes you think I shall never become one?"

"Because many are called, but few are chosen; it is not God's purpose to save all; and it seems to me, from the present state of your mind, that you are not among those whom He purposes to save. If you look around you, you perceive that the great mass of men are not Christians, and that those who live and die in sin, possess very much the character which you now possess. Very many of them once had the hope of being Christians, just as you now have, but they have gone to the bar of God with hopes no better than the spider's web. Your hopes of becoming a Christian are no better than theirs. When you come to the bed of death, you may find that this hope is not realized; and when you stand at the bar of God, you may find your husband at the right hand, while you are on the left. It is hard to give up this hope, I know. It is like the giving up of the ghost; but I would rather see you abandon it, and come to the conclusion that you are lost, than sleep on thus."

"I told you the truth, sir, when I said I am not a Christian; and I told you the truth, when I told you that I expected to be a Christian before I die. I cannot throw this hope away. I will not abandon it." Here she wept; and I could not but remind her of the Saviour's words, "There shall be weeping and gnashing of teeth, when ye shall see Abraham and Isaac and Jacob in the kingdom of God, and you yourselves thrust out." She continued to weep, and said to me,

"Dr. Spring, I am not worse than many others who have become Christians during the revival, and I do not see why you should say, there is so much reason to believe I shall never become a Christian."

"Listen calmly to me, Mrs. Lethbridge, and I will tell you the reason. I wish much to see you a child of God, and that you may live and die in the precious faith of the Gospel. This world, with all its joys and social endearments, will disappoint you. I do not wish to think of your being lost. I would have you go with your husband on his pilgrimage to the heavenly city. But the dividing line is drawn, and the hour of your final separation is not far away. You are not accompanying him, and you will not accompany him, because you 'will not come to Christ that you might have life.' He *commands* you to come; and you disregard His authority. When He speaks to the elements, to the deaf, to the blind, to the maimed, to the dead, they obey; but *you* will not obey Him. He *invites* you to come, but you make light of His invitations. He is inviting you now, but you refuse; the reply of your heart is, ' Somehow or other I expect to be saved, if I do not come now.' He has taken great pains to *instruct* you, from your childhood up to the present hour, and you repel all His teaching. You have long been the care of His providence; He has led you an orphan to this land, and here He has been a father to you; yet His goodness has not led you to repentance. You have been the daughter of sorrow; yet His judgments have only hardened you. You are now surrounded by the gracious influences of His Spirit, that are coming down like the rain of heaven, and every hour you live you are resisting the Holy Ghost. And you are past the middle of human life; others are dying around you, and you will soon drop into eternity. Your sun has passed its meridian, and is hastening behind the mountains. The night cometh, and your work is not even begun. Your day of grace and space for repentance is coming to its close, and the things which belong to your peace will ere long be hidden from your eyes. Are not these things so, and do they justify the expectation that you will become a Christian? Oh, Mrs. Lethbridge, I must be true to you, and ask you if they do not indicate great hardness of heart on your part? God's authority does not move you. His goodness, His love, His care, His winning invitations, do not move you. His judgments do not move you. His Spirit does not move you. And now, tell me, what more could He do to you, that He has not already done?"

"Oh, Dr. Spring, I do not know what to say. You corner me, let me turn which way I will."

"My dear friend," I replied, "your case is lamentable, but it is not hopeless. I have no apology for your prolonged impenitence, and no hope for you, if you cherish these delusions. But there is every hope, if you will abandon them, and repair to Him who came to seek and save that which is lost. He calls you now, by this interview, by the reflections of your own mind, and, notwithstanding all you have said, by the latent fear that you will be lost. Believe me, you will not find rest till you find it in Him who came to give rest to the weary and burdened soul."

"But," said she, "I *cannot* come." "Madam," I replied, "I have nothing to do with your excuses. You *must* come, or you must perish. 'If any man love not the Lord Jesus Christ, let him be anathema.'"

After a few words of prayer, I left her, trembling in my own heart, lest I had failed in the tenderness which became me, as the messenger of mercy. She afterwards thanked me for my faithfulness. The arrow had entered the joints of the harness. The fearful words never left her, "He that is unjust, let him be unjust still; and he that is filthy, let him be filthy still." By infinite grace, she was enabled to escape, as a bird out of the snare of the fowler. The next time I entered her parlor—it was in Cliff-street—I found her calm and peaceful, and rejoicing in hope. She became an intelligent and profited member of my Bible-class, lived a lovely Christian life, was the comforter of her husband on his dying-bed, and, not long after his departure, joined him on the Mount Zion above.

INSTANTANEOUS CONVERSION.

Every instance of conversion is an instantaneous work of omnipotent and effectual grace. There is a moment of time when the first ray of light enters the dungeon mind. There are preliminary processes of thought which precede regeneration itself; there is ordinarily, if not uniformly, a series of reflections and mental acts implying severe attention to the truth, so that the change is effected through the truth. But the change itself, the transition from darkness to light, the act of passing from death unto life, is not progressive, but sudden and instantaneous. The precise time may not be known; the evidence of it may be more or less gradually developed; but as respects the change itself, whether it consist in imparting a new nature or principle to the soul, or in imparting to it the first holy exercise, there is no intermediate space between the last moment when the carnal mind is enmity against God, and the first moment when the love of God is shed abroad in the heart by the Holy Ghost.

In a previous chapter on revivals of religion, it was remarked that, in many persons, the process of awakening and conviction was so rapid, and terminated so suddenly in conversion, that we were not without fears that the work was spurious, and would not manifest itself in a Christian character through life; and it was also added that these fears proved groundless. In the year 1804, and during the summer term of my junior year in Yale College, I was the guest of Lady Houston, of Savannah, then residing at New Haven, for the purpose of watching the education of her son, who was my class-mate. We occupied the same chamber, just opposite the south end of the South College, and pursued our studies together. *Sarah Houston*, the daughter of my youthful class-mate, during one of the seasons of the outpourings of God's Spirit upon us was a pupil in Mrs. Green's school, then in Murray street, and in the dwelling-house of the elder Dr. Mason, and a short distance from our place of worship. Mrs. Green was a lady of great dignity of character, and a truly Christian woman of the Baptist persuasion. She was assisted by her two daughters, worthy daughters of such a mother, who were members of the Brick Church, and who, with quite a number of their pupils, not only attended our Sabbath services, but our evening lectures. Miss Houston was one of this little company, and became one of the subjects of this work of grace; and so far as she was herself conscious of it, both her conviction and conversion began and were accomplished during a part of a single religious service. It was at a lecture on Friday evening, that was preparatory to the Lord's Supper, and at which a large number of young persons were received to our communion, on the public profession of their faith.

Her religious impressions began at the beginning of the long prayer, and steadily increased, till, at the close of the prayer, she was rejoicing in hope. At the close of the entire service, the Misses Green requested me to accompany them and their pupils to the school. I did so, and was introduced to Miss Houston, whom I had never known, and who, to my great joy, I found was the daughter of my old class-mate, and who was weeping. She welcomed me as her father's friend, and especially as her pastor. " Dr. Spring, I do not know what to say, nor what to think of myself. When you began that prayer, the first sentence of it sunk to my heart. I heard every word, from beginning to end ; and it seemed to me, my heart responded to every sentence. Your adoring thoughts of God, and those confessions of sin, and that supplication for mercy, and that casting of us all on the atoning blood of Christ, and that imploring petition, that the Holy Spirit of God would attend the services of the evening,—oh! sir, I went along with them all, and it seemed to me that you only spoke the feelings of my own heart. And when you came to the last sentence of thanksgiving and praise, and uttered those words, *Worthy is the Lamb that was slain, and has redeemed us unto God by His blood*, I felt that I could praise Him, and from the bottom of my heart say, Amen ! " I prayed with her. It was a scene of wonders. " When the Lord turned again the captivity of Zion, we were like them that dream. Then was our mouth filled with laughter, and our tongue with singing. Then said they among the heathen, the Lord hath done great things for them. The Lord *hath* done great things for us, whereof we are glad." I went home rejoicing, but with fear and trembling. It was a glorious day. God speaks, and it is done. The next morning Mrs. Green sent an urgent request for me to visit them. I did so, and as I entered the parlor, Miss Houston rose to meet me, burst into a flood of tears, and merely said, " Oh! sir, I sent for you to ask you, *if it is wicked for me to be so happy ?* "

Miss Houston subsequently became a member of the Brick Church, but not without first consulting her friends at the South. The following letter on this subject was addressed to me by her uncle.

" Savannah, *April* 27, 1831.

" Dear Sir :

" The interesting nature of the subject of the following communication will, I trust, be received as an apology for the freedom with which I address one to whom I am a perfect stranger.

" By letters received from my niece, Sarah Ann Houston, a pupil of Mrs. Green's school in your city, it appears she has been much engaged in the important subject of religion for some months. She now seems to think she has obtained a hope, expressed a desire of sealing her covenant with her Lord, and has solicited the approbation of her friends, to her making application for admission to membership in the church under your pastoral care.

" From the opinion I entertain of your prudence, together with the practical experience and consequent knowledge of the human heart which you must have acquired, from being so conversant with revivals of religion, and the numerous occasions you have had of examining persons presenting themselves for admission to the privileges of the church, I should be willing to submit the case to you, after mentioning some reasons which make it doubtful in my mind, whether it is proper to comply with the desire of my niece.

"In the first place, then, I consider it a general rule, that there is danger of bringing a reproach to the profession of religion, as well as it is frequently injurious to the spiritual welfare of the individual himself, to admit to the privileges of the church, one who has received his religious impressions under the excitement attendant on revivals of religion, until such excited feelings have subsided ; in which case a better opportunity is afforded of judging whether any effect has been produced that will give a reasonable hope of a real change of heart. If this opinion is entitled to any weight, I think it has additional force as respects Sarah Ann, from the particular circumstances in which she has been placed, since the time of her being first awakened, viz., secluded, as it were, from the world, living in a pious family, where, probably, she hears little conversation except what concerns the unparalleled revival with which New York has been blessed, and who, at such an interesting period, probably are much engaged themselves, and surrounded by young ladies possessing the tenderness of feeling so common with young people--many of whom most probably similarly affected with herself—all which must tend to keep up and increase the excitement. If, however, after conversing with Sarah Ann, you should be of opinion that her experience warrants the belief that her hopes are well founded, it deserves some consideration, whether it would be expedient that she should be received as a member of your church at this time, as she will be so soon removed out of the reach of its privileges and care, and whether it would not be better for her to make application to be received into the church in Trenton (where she will probably reside a part of her time for some years), the pastor of which I understand to be an amiable man, and respectable preacher of the word; or wait until her return to Georgia.

"Among the reasons she gives for desiring to join your church, is her attachment to you on account of your being the friend of her father in his youthful days; this, though an amiable feeling, and good ground for a preference, cannot have much weight, if other things make it inexpedient. Another reason she mentions is entitled to much consideration: it is that her joining the church would be a safeguard against the temptations to which she will be exposed on leaving school, and entering into society composed of various characters and dispositions; there is much force in this, which nothing can counterbalance but the danger of a premature profession of religion.

"I assure you, sir, there is nothing would give me more sincere pleasure than that my niece should be an open and sincere Christian; and with the foregoing observations, I should be willing to submit this matter entirely to your judgment, were I the only person to be consulted on the occasion. But she has other friends, who have equal, if not paramount, claims. I name, in particular, her Aunt Woodruff, who has had the chief care of her since she has been an orphan, feels something like a parental affection for her, and has always treated her as kindly as if she had been her own child. All of Sarah Ann's relatives who are professing Christians, except myself, are Episcopalians; they would not, however, oppose her becoming a Presbyterian, if they were satisfied her religious views were well founded.

"With the hope, dear sir, that you will excuse the liberty I take of troubling you with this letter, I subscribe myself,

"Respectfully, your obedient servant,
"PATRICK HOUSTON.
"To Rev. GARDINER SPRING, D.D."

Miss Houston was received to our communion on the 7th of July, 1831, and has given precious testimony that her life is hid with Christ in God. On a short visit to Savannah, many years after she left our city, I met her on the evening of the Lord's day, on which I arrived, at a religious service performed by the Rev. Dr. Stiles. She had recognized me in the audience, and introduced me to *Mr. Anderson*, her husband. She was an humble and active Christian, eminent in every good work, and anxiously employed in the religious instruction of the slaves. May the God of battles cover her with his feathers from the storm that desolates her beloved home.

MINISTERIAL COWARDICE.

The time was, in the history of the Brick Church, when there were *sixty men* whom I could call upon to lead in prayer, and who in little companies held weekly prayer-meetings in different neighborhoods of the congregation. I undertook, at this time, to visit the principal and more wealthy families, and with the special view of endeavoring to interest the more fashionable circles in seeking the kingdom of God. On the east side of Broadway, just north of Chambers-street, was a wealthy family from Georgia, which removed to New York as their permanent residence. Collin Read was a rough, ignorant, purse-proud Irishman; and Mrs. Read, his first wife, a woman educated as a Quaker, and of excellent common sense, and cultivated intellect, taste, and manners. Their adopted daughter, for they had no children of their own, *Frances Ballentine*, was a young lady of unusual personal attractions, the prospective heir of large possessions, and though punctual in her attendance upon the services of the sanctuary, had not, to my knowledge, a serious thought. I had resolved to visit the family, and to have a solemn and faithful interview with Miss Ballentine. I had many misgivings about it; I did not expect to meet a kind reception; I tried to excuse myself from the unwelcome service, but at length resolved to go. It was a painful struggle, but I went to the house, ascended the steps half way, and like a coward and poltroon, turned back and went home, and with a galled conscience and heavy heart. After some days I went a second time, put my hand upon the bell, and again acted the coward. I confessed my sin before God, and went a third time, resolved, whatever repulse I might meet with, not to come away with a bleeding conscience. I was introduced to the parlor, where Miss Ballentine was sitting, and alone. And what was my surprise, when, instead of receiving me coldly, she met me with unembarrassed cordiality, and as she took my hand, exclaimed, with tears : " Oh, Dr. Spring, I thought you were going *to pass me by*. I have desired much to see you, and tell you the state of my mind." I was ashamed ; I felt the reproof; and then thought that I would never again pass the door of affluence. This beloved young woman became a Christian, soon united with our communion, sickened with consumption, and died in all the serenity and sweetness of Christian faith, and the joyous anticipation of the rest that remaineth for the people of God. I visited her often, not more to instruct than to be instructed. It was a happy chamber, her chamber of debility and death. I have often thought and often spoken of the conversion, sickness, and death of Frances Ballentine. When she breathed her last, the weariness, the restlessness were over. The sun was going down ; it was like the " Cotter's Saturday Night," the weary laborer's hour of prayer, the quiet eve of holy time, the calm close of life's short week, ushering in the everlasting Sabbath. I shall not soon forget the hour, the place. There it was, in that memorable chamber, that this young bird of Paradise, just fledged from its beautiful but shattered lattice-work, flapped its wings, and soared aloft to begin its everlasting song.

THE STEAMER OLIVER ELLSWORTH.

A most painful event took place, of a very different character from the preceding, in the year 1827.

At the installation of my beloved brother, the Rev. Samuel Spring, as the pastor of the North Church, in Hartford, Conn., Mr. Stephen Lockwood and myself were commissioned to take part in the services. The original appointment was given to Mr. Abijah Fisher, Mr. Richard Cunningham being his alternate. Both Mr. Fisher and Mr. Cunningham were prevented from attending, and Mr. Lockwood was subsequently appointed, and accepted the appointment. On our return from Hartford, in the steamer "Oliver Ellsworth," and on a cold evening in March, and soon after we left Saybrook, I remarked to Mr. Lockwood, that I would take a walk on the deck and then go to my berth. My overcoat was on deck with other baggage, and as I was passing up the companion-way in order to get it, Mr. Lockwood ran before me, and was returning with the overcoat; and as he was passing the boiler, and directly in front of it, there was a tremendous explosion which shook the steamer from her mast-head to her keel. The alarm was fearful; the cries of the wounded, the rushing of the steam into the cabin, the rocking of the boat in the trough of a heavy and rough sea, officers and men staggering and at their wits' end, all created a scene more easily imagined than described. Those of us who were in the cabin were almost suffocated by the hot steam, and such was the pressure for the deck, that it was not possible for us to escape. A kind Providence led me to open a window in the cabin and thrust my head and chest out into the open air, until the steam had passed off, and I could venture on deck. The wounded and dying were there. Mr. Lockwood was there. "Where is Dr. Spring?" I heard those mournful words. "Oh, Sir, I am a dead man!" I was uninjured, and did what I could for him and others. But we knew not how soon we might go to the bottom. The steamer floated like a log on the ocean, and five or six miles from the shore. Our signals of distress were at length regarded, and we were towed back to Saybrook, where we passed a night of toil and anxiety; where on the next day three of the seamen died of their wounds, where I attended their funeral, and whence I returned to watch the last hours of my suffering and beloved friend. He remarked that he had been "breathing fire." I sent to New London for the best physician within reach, but it was all in vain. He knew he must die, and his mind was calm. He could scarcely speak, but gave me his last message to his family. We left Saybrook towards evening, and had not gone far when he breathed his last. It was a Sabbath morning when we reached New York, where a crowd of anxious friends were on the wharf, awaiting with mingled hope and fear the unknown result. It had been a terrible night, and it was a solemn Sabbath. I could not preach in the morning; in the afternoon, like one raised from the dead, and with his grave-clothes about him, I addressed an immense audience from the words, "Thou hast, in love to my soul, delivered it from going down to the pit of corruption." I shall never forget these scenes, nor that day. Mr. Lockwood was a man of great excellence of character, and highly esteemed in all the social relations; an irreparable loss to a greatly respected and beloved family, and an honored and useful office-bearer in the house of God. It was a mysterious providence that thus thrust *him* into that bursting furnace, in order to prevent *me* from rushing into it. Why was it thus? "Even so, Father, for so it seemed good in thy sight." What is the import of that affecting declaration, " I will give men for thee, and people for thy life?" A life *thus preserved*, ought, by a thousand bonds, to be all the Lord's.

THE CHOLERA.

In the year 1831 the Asiatic cholera desolated the city. It was a fearful season, during the months of July and August. It was no unusual occurrence for twenty, thirty, fifty of our citizens to be swept off in a day. When the number of deaths daily increased to beyond one hundred, the alarm was terrific. Medical skill was altogether at fault, and medical men, not a few, and among them my own family physician, abandoned their posts and fled to the country. My beloved wife was providentially at New Haven, at the bedside of her dying mother, and did not return until the pestilence had reached its height. No class was exempt from its ravages; rich and poor, parents and young children, were swept away with very little warning. The poor, and especially those that occupied the line of Centre-street, and were exposed to the miasma of the "Collect," filled the hospital, and were at length crowded into the "Hall of Records," near the Brick Church, and to whom I was called to minister the consolations of the Gospel. There they lay by scores, lining both sides of that wide Hall, in all the stages of that frightful disease, a most heart-sickening sight, most of them beyond the reach of religious influence. It had been my uniform habit to absent myself from the city during the summer months, and it was the expectation of my congregation that I would do so during the prevalence of this wasting pestilence. But I could not leave them in this hour of darkness. I announced to them from the pulpit that I should remain with them, and requested them to send for me at the first approach of danger. Never shall I forget the emotions which that announcement produced. They dropped their heads and wept like children. I appointed a daily prayer-meeting at six P. M. in the church, and the people flocked to it with earnestness, and those of every denomination and name. It was maintained for weeks, and greatly to our courage and hopes. I remained throughout the whole of the season, in much fear and weariness, and, with the exception of a single day, without even the premonitory symptoms of disease. Aside from my daughter Augusta, who was stricken down, but recovered, my own immediate family were all preserved, though our neighborhood was in mourning. My second son, Dr. Edward Spring, was a physician on Blackwell's Island, where he resided. Early one morning he came to my house in Bond-street, to ask my advice as to the duty of remaining at his post. The cholera had not then reached the Island, but the fit subjects of it were there in great numbers. He had no compensation for his services, and was under no obligation to remain. "Father," said he, "what shall I do? I can leave now without reproach." I replied: "You have chosen a profession that is full of dangers: never turn your back upon the storm. I will stick by you to the last, and so will your mother." He remained. The cholera visited the Island in great violence, but he was complimented as one of the most successful practitioners in the city. The poor inmates loved him; and when, towards the close of the season, he was stricken down, they bore him in their arms to the water-side, where, accompanied by his parents, he was taken home. It was on the morning of the Lord's day we first learned of his illness, and immediately after the morning service his mother and myself hastened to his side, with no other expectation than that he must die: but he was a young man of great courage. The convicts of the Island carried him home; and through the care of a kind Providence, his and our hopes were realized.

CHAPTER X.

FANATICISM IN REVIVALS.

There is no doubt that there was a powerful work of grace during the years 1826 and 1827, in Central and Western New York. It is no evidence of its spuriousness that it was inmingled with human imperfection, and sometimes accompanied by irregularities and extravagance which filled the minds of reflecting men with solicitude, and even gave the enemy occasion to blaspheme. It is true that the work was marked by ardent enthusiasm. Such is the nature of true religion; a Christian man may well suspect his religion, if he does not feel a deep interest in those seasons of refreshing which so deeply concern the glory of God, and the salvation of men. Spiritual declension is the abnormal state of the church, revivals the true, the normal state. They are not weak and impulsive minds alone, and those that are controlled by social sympathies' and animal excitement, that are the subjects; they are men of thought and acknowledged stability of character. When you see the church and her ministers waking up from prolonged spiritual declension, to renewed activity and zeal, to holy penitence and holy prayer and holy living; when backsliders are restored, and wandering Christians are brought back to duty and peace, and, notwithstanding all their wanderings, are brought again to God's holy temple; when those who have given their hearts to idols, in view of their criminal idolatry are tempted to cast away their confidence and their hopes, and give up all for lost; when the strong become weak and the confident begin to tremble, because He whose fan is in His hand comes to search Jerusalem with candles; when the more exemplary begin to feel that they have been stumbling-blocks to those that are without, and are humbled for the dishonor they have done to the Christian name; when they call to mind how they have forfeited the divine care, and are the more confounded because God is pacified towards them; and when, in addition to these tokens of the divine presence, mutual love and confidence are restored, and brethren dwell together in unity, and the world loses its power, and the realities of eternity obscure and shut out the vanities of time; when the beauty and brightness of a heaven-illumined piety shines as a light in the world, and the ordinances of God's house are honored, and indifference vanishes before the power of prayer; and the thoughtless are awakened, the prayerless become prayerful, and the unrepenting turn from the error of their ways to the wisdom of the just, and there is joy in heaven over the repenting; then and there the Omnipotent One is making bare his arm, and the whole scene testifies that of his rich and amazing grace, the God of heaven dwells with men, and in building up Zion appears in his glory.

It should not take us by surprise if scenes like these should be counterdrawn by the subtle adversary, artfully traced, and with a view to deceive and destroy. I have somewhere met with the remark, that the "chariot of the Gospel never has free course, but the Devil tries to be charioteer." There is nothing he is so much afraid of as the power of the Holy Ghost. When the sons of God come to present themselves before the Lord, Satan comes also among them. He would be deemed one of them, and therefore puts on the saintly garb; "for Satan also is transformed into an angel of light." Where he cannot arrest the showers of blessing, it has ever been one of his devices to dilute or poison the streams, and leave them to inundate the church and the world. When the Son of man sows good seed, the enemy comes and sows tares. Sometimes his subtlety appears by perverting the truths of the Gospel; sometimes by inmingling them with error, and sometimes by pushing them to those excesses of extravagance which neutralize their loveliness and power, and present religion only in a distorted and forbidding aspect.

With the obvious signs of the times in view, who does not see that this artful foe would enjoy his malignant triumph, if he could but prejudice the minds of good men against all *revivals of religion ?* This he does, not so much by opposing them, as by counterfeiting the genuine coin, and by *getting up* revivals that are spurious, and to his own liking. Revivals are always spurious when they are *got up* by man's device, and not *brought down* by the Spirit of God; when they are the result of mere animal excitement, and not the searching, discriminating, and humbling truths of the Gospel; and when the zeal and effort of the professed people of God are exerted in making men believe they are Christians, while they are dead in sin, and in bringing them into the church without " taking forth the precious from the vile." There may be great solemnity and tenderness under such influences, but " what is the chaff to the wheat?" What are alarmed fears, compared with a convicted conscience? What are the mere apprehensions of God's wrath, compared with enlightened views of the spirituality and obligations of his law, and a deep sense of the enmity of the heart towards him as the Supreme Lawgiver? What are the self-satisfied emotions arising from false confidences and false hopes, compared with the peace and joy of a broken heart? What are the visions of a highly-wrought imagination, compared with those spiritual views when it pleases God to reveal his Son to the desponding sinner, and Christ in him is the hope of glory? What is that piety that courts observation and wishes to be seen, that obtrudes itself on the notice of others, that talks of its own experience and attainments, that is bold and assuming, that wishes to be put forward, and that unblushingly exclaims with Jehu, " Come, see my zeal for the Lord!" compared with the spirit of the modest, retiring young convert, who esteems others better than himself, who looks on Him whom he has pierced, and mourns, and who, instead of being a pompous and splendid professor, goes to the communion of the saints, conscious that he is not worthy of the crumbs that fall from the Master's table?

There have been spurious revivals in my day, and the means of promoting them are the index of their character. In such seasons of excitement, great dependence is placed on the way and means of *getting them up*, and little of the impression that not a soul will be converted unless it be accomplished by the power of God. Whatever the words of the leaders may profess, their conduct proclaims, "Mine own arm hath done this!" There is a familiarity, a boldness, an irreverence in their prayers, which ill becomes worms of the dust in approaching Him before whom angels veil their faces. A pious and poor woman, in coming out from a religious service thus conducted, once said, "I cannot think what it is that makes our ministers *swear* so in their prayers." They count their converts, and when they survey their work, there is a triumph, a self-reliant exultation over it, which looks like the triumph of the Pagan monarch when he exclaimed, "Is not this great Babylon which I have built!" And hence it is that so many of the subjects of such a work, after the excitement is over, find that their own hearts have deceived them, that they are no longer affected by solemn preaching and solemn prayers, that their past emotions were nothing more than the operations of nature, and that when these natural causes have exhausted their power, there is no religion left.

This state of things produced no small discussion on the subject of revivals at the West, and discussions not always of the most amiable kind. Ministers lost their confidence in one another, as they approved or disapproved the course pursued by their brethren. There was contention where there ought to have been harmony; Christians were influenced by the evil surmisings of men of corrupt minds; they became alienated from one another, there was no more union in prayer, and the gracious Spirit was grieved away. Dissension in regard to the Scriptural method of promoting revivals became general, and the solicitude of the churches was diverted from the great concern of laboring for the souls of men, by their different views about the way in which they should labor. Some were advocates for those injudicious and extravagant presentations of the truth that *aimed* at stirring up the enmity of the natural heart; while others, not less faithful and fearless, favored those presentations in the simplicity of the Gospel and in the meekness of wisdom. Some advocated the setting apart seats for those who were awakened and anxious, and called them up to "be prayed for" in the presence of the congregation; while others chose to visit them at their own private residences, or to meet them in retired circles for personal conference and prayer.

There were errors in doctrine also which greatly facilitated these new measures; errors that were so artfully and insidiously presented as allied to important truth, as not to be easily detected. Men were instructed that all that is necessary in order to become Christians, is to *resolve to become Christians*, and that the purpose and determination to become Christians, are themselves the religion of the Gospel. But the question here arises, What are the motives which lead to such a resolution, and does it, or does it not, arise from supreme love to God? "*I go, sir*, and went not," is not piety. There may be no holiness in such a purpose, and no right motive, and no heavenly influence. A naked purpose to be a Christian is not love, it is not repentance, it is not faith, it is not obedience, it is not a saving change of heart. The Bible calls upon men, not merely to *resolve* to dismiss their hostility to God, but actually to abjure it, and *to be* reconciled to him. It was the teaching of some that the renovation of the heart, instead of being the work of the Holy Spirit, is the creature's work, and that the power of the Spirit consists in *persuading the sinner* himself to perform it.

The principal advocate of these new measures and these Pelagian errors, was the Rev. Charles G. Finney. I scarcely know why, but very unexpected efforts were made by ministers and laymen, whom I loved and respected, to give him my countenance and coöperation during his expected visit to New York. In addition to an appeal from my deceased and valued friend, David L. Dodge, the two following communications show the honesty and earnestness of this desire.

"ROME, N. Y., *Feb.* 22, 1826.

" REV. AND BELOVED SIR:

" It is with feelings of no ordinary interest that I address one, who, I may truly say, for years has held so high a place in my affection. When I have been in the enjoyment of religion, it is you, sir, under God, to whom I am indebted for that enjoyment; when in affliction and darkness of mind, how often have I wished and resolved to write to Dr. Spring, and was deterred by the reflection that he could have no time to devote to me.

"We have had a glorious revival of religion in our town this winter, and I hope it will continue until all shall be brought to repentance. From the child of nine years old, to the old man of sixty or seventy, all descriptions of persons have been made the subjects of a saving change; some of the most abandoned, and in some instances almost whole families, have been converted. Mr. Finney has taught, as he was moved by the Holy Ghost, to look to the promise of God, and rest there. Without any regard to the character of the individual or the individuals, he pleads God's promise to give the Holy Spirit to them that ask him. The prayer of faith has been much dwelt upon this winter; and many Christians, I believe, have had new views on the subject. In many cases, the answers to prayer have been wonderful and astonishing. Ought not Christians and ministers to endeavor to emulate the faith of the apostles and primitive Christians in praying for the outpouring of the Spirit? and will it not be in this way that the latter-day glory of the church, the millennial day, will be ushered in? I do not know the number of converts in our town; it may be four hundred. Two evenings since, when those were requested to come forward who had obtained hopes within about thirty-six hours, between twenty and thirty presented themselves. Usually every other evening the ministers made the request, that they might see who they were, and shake hands with them.

"Dear sir, may I ask an interest in your prayers, that I may never live to dishonor my Saviour's cause as I have done, and be so much like Martha, careful and troubled about many things. Mr. Finney is at Utica, and a few mercy drops have fallen there, an earnest, I hope, of a plentiful shower. The most fervent prayers are offered for Utica. Mr. Finney is prayed for wherever he goes. Our communion will be the second Sabbath in March; Mr. Finney will be here. There is a glorious revival in ———, where Mr. Smith is settled. He came to Rome, and got the Spirit, and carried it home with him. The instances have been many in which parents have brought their children to Rome for this purpose, and they have been awakened or converted. It reminds us of the days when our Saviour was on the earth. Pardon the familiarity with which I have written, and believe me yours in those bonds which I trust death will not rend asunder. I think you may say of me as St. Paul did of his spiritual children, 'You are my daughter in Christ.'

"CATHARINE HUNTINGTON."

The following is from a greatly beloved Brother, and one with whom I enjoyed many, *many* hours of delightful fellowship, while he was pastor of the Spring-street Church in this city, and who was called to a Professorship in the Auburn Theological Seminary.

"AUBURN, *April* 9, 1831.
"DEAR BROTHER:

"Mr. Baxter Sayre, from your city, is in this place, and has come with an invitation to Mr. Finney to visit

New York. It does not appear that he has a request from the ministers generally. He does not wish to come against the feelings of his brethren in the ministry, and many of us in this country do not think it advisable that he should come unless he should be kindly received by them. Feelings of ministers and people, in this quarter, are greatly changed with respect to Mr. F. He is now viewed as an active, zealous, skilful, and successful ministering servant of the Lord Jesus Christ, and the pastors of churches throughout this district of country are anxious to have him as a fellow-laborer, with their people. Those who have been opposed to him in times past, are ready to acknowledge their faults, or are silent on the subject.

"On the great subject of the present revivals, I do think, my dear brother, that there should be a full understanding between Christians at the East and the West. I fear that the revivals at the West are not as yet viewed in a proper light by many of our brethren at the East. The impression that has gone abroad, that the two precious servants of Christ, Mr. Nettleton and Mr. Finney, do not agree in their views respecting revivals, has had a great tendency to make many Christians think that there is a great difference between revivals at the East and at the West. Of course, Christians at the East, and friends of Mr. Nettleton, have thought unfavorably of the great and good work that has been witnessed in our Western churches, and *vice versa.* Now, Brother Spring, can you not do something towards having a perfect understanding between Mr. Nettleton and Mr. Finney? Things ought not to continue as they are. There must not be a separation between the East and the West. Will it not be best to have an understanding between these two brethren, and to have them invited to your city as fellow-laborers? And can you not effect this? The impression is, that you have more influence with Mr. Nettleton than any other man. Thousands in this country, remember, my dear Gardiner, have their eyes turned towards you; and also remember, that the friends of revivals here are, as a general thing, the friends of Mr. Finney. I wish, for the general good, that you would bring Mr. Nettleton and Mr. Finney together. And I wish, if consistent with your feelings, that you would evince an approbation of Mr. Finney. This would be highly gratifying to your friends here.

"Attempts, Brother Spring, will be made to get Mr. Finney to visit New York. Many are engaged in it, and will not be turned from their purpose. Can you not consistently express your approbation of such a measure, and unite in an invitation to him? I wish you would converse with Mr. A. Tappan on this subject, who is much engaged in getting Mr. Finney to come to the city. I have written to him on the subject, and stated the reasons why many of us advise Mr. Finney to delay his visit.

"Your brother,
"M. L. R. PERRINE."

There is no man in the ministry who had more of my love and confidence than dear Brother Perrine. I had no predilection for Mr. Finney, nor for his doctrines, nor measures; yet I confess to some hesitation, on receiving this letter. I did not unite in the request to Mr. Finney to visit our city; but I greatly desired that this divisive spirit might be healed. Instead of widening the breach, and blowing up the flame of contention, I determined to judge for myself, and to pursue a course that should not alienate the confidence of my Western brethren. It seemed to me due to Mr. Finney that he *should be heard*, and I heard him. Nor was anything exceptionable in his sermon, except a vulgarity that indicated a want of culture, and a coarseness unbecoming the Christian Pulpit. Not a little to the dissatisfaction of some of my brethren, I afterwards introduced him to the pulpit of the Brick Church. I did it with fear and trembling, but I was satisfied with the result. He preached to a large audience, with much power, and more sophistry, and not without evident intentions of converting me and my people to all his extravagances. His subject was, "The Prayer of Faith." It was a well-arranged discourse, and, so far as I can remember at this distance of time, he dwelt largely upon the fact, that there is such a thing as the effectual, fervent prayer of a righteous man; that such prayer is prevalent, and avails much; and that it is *always* answered by the *specified* blessing prayed for. His last proposition startled me, and I saw that it might lead to the wildest fanaticism. I could not admit his strongly-expressed inference, that if our prayers for specified blessings are not infallibly answered, either *God is not true to His word, or we do not pray in faith.*

I confess, with shame, that I have not that measure of confidence in God as the hearer of prayer, which his character and word justify and demand. It has been habitually my joy to have free access to his throne, though I have not always believed that I should receive the very things that I asked for. I have felt that infinite love and infinite wisdom are on the throne; that I could not hope for too much from God; and have felt satisfied to leave my petitions at his feet. The declaration of the Saviour, "And all things whatsoever ye shall ask in prayer, believing, ye shall receive," once troubled me. I asked myself, what is the prayer of faith? It seemed to me to consist in an earnest desire to obtain the blessings sought after; a persevering importunity in seeking them; a deep sense of unworthiness of the least of God's mercies; a tranquil submission of my own will to the will of God; access to the throne in the new and living way by the great High Priest of the Christian profession; and confidence in God as the hearer of prayer, and in his willingness to bestow and perform above all we are able to ask or even to think. There *are* specified blessings which God has promised to bestow in answer to prayer. They are pardon, grace, wisdom, and perseverance to his heavenly kingdom. The promise here is absolute, and we may rely upon it; if we do not receive them, it will prove that we never prayed for them in the "faith which is of the operation of God." All true believers have confidence in a prayer-hearing God. And "this is the confidence we have in him, that if *we ask anything according to his will*, he heareth us;" and that when "the Spirit maketh intercession for the saints" it is "according to *the will of God.*" In one view, it is always true that believing prayer is answered by the specified blessing prayed for, because it is always *submissive* prayer. The prayer that God's will may be done, and not our own, is always answered. God's will *is done*, and that is the very thing the believer prays for. And this shows us, that when we pray in faith, without referring the whole matter to the will of God, we have no assurance that the very thing we pray for will be bestowed. Moses prayed earnestly that he might go over with the Israelites into the promised land; but God refused his prayer. The Saviour prayed that the bitter cup might pass from him; but justice put it into his hand, and as he drank it, he cried, " My God, my God, why hast thou *forsaken* me." Paul besought the Lord thrice, that the thorn in the flesh might be removed, and his prayer was answered, not by giving him the very thing he prayed for, but something far better, and in the enjoyment of which he gloried more than he would have done in the removal of the thorn.

My own embarrassment on this subject arose from not discriminating between the faith that was peculiar to the age of miracles, and the faith that is given to the church of God, under all dispensations, and in every age. The Saviour's declaration, on which so much reliance is placed by the advocates of the prayer of faith, obviously refers to the faith of miracles. It was addressed to the disciples, to whom authority was given to preach the Gospel, to cast out devils, to heal all manner of diseases, and who were invested with miraculous power. The miracle of the withered fig-tree, which excited the wonder of the disciples, led Him to say, "Have faith in God. I say unto you, that what things soever ye desire when ye pray, believe that ye shall receive them, and ye shall have them." The promise related to miraculous gifts, and the faith rested on the promise. It was not the faith that received Jesus Christ, and rested on him alone for salvation; there is no evidence that Judas did not exercise it, and work miracles, as well as the other apostles; it was simply the peculiar faith that believed in the promise of divine assistance to work miracles. In the sermon in the fifth volume of Dr. Emmons' Works, there is a series of remarks which makes it evident to my own mind, that neither ministers nor churches at the present day have any right to apply the promise; and that to do so, is only running into the grossest delusions. I have known some persons in our own city who persuaded themselves that this promise was applicable to them, and who acted under the influence of this delusion. There are men and women still alive and among us, who remember the circumstances of the death of *Mrs. Pierson*, around whose lifeless body her husband assembled a company of *believers*, with the assurance that if they prayed in faith, she would be restored to life. Their feelings were greatly excited, their impressions of their success peculiar and strong. They prayed, and prayed again, and prayed *in faith*. But they were disappointed. There was none to answer, neither was there any that regarded. She slept the sleep of death; they were constrained to follow her to the grave. St. Paul speaks of a faith that "could remove mountains;" but he tells us that, without

Christian love, it is nothing. The Holy Ghost, in respect to his supernatural gifts, may be given without that charity which is the fruit of the Spirit. The faith of miracles did not extend beyond the age of miracles. If, in the rapid progress of the Redeemer's kingdom, and in its encounters with the Prince and powers of darkness, the age of miracles should return, the faith of miracles will return with it. To look for them now is the wildest fanaticism, and leads to that dependence upon men and machinery which " sows the wind and reaps the whirlwind."

I know not how the following letter, from the Rev. Dr. Richards, of the Auburn Seminary, came into my possession. I found it among a mass of neglected papers, and think it ought to be preserved. It is without date, and is marked on the envelope, " Dr. Richards to Mr. Nettleton." I presume it was put into my hands by Mr. Nettleton.

" My Dear Brother:

" I concur with Brother Prime in thinking it desirable that some measures should be taken to get what we deem correct views, fully before the public. Were I, however, to judge of the whole case, by what appears to me to be taking place in the western section of this State, I should say there is no ground to fear. Your letter to Oneida County and to a student in our Seminary, has had a visible and decided effect. Mr. Williston's sermon, and the pastoral letter from Oneida Association, have done much to correct the prevailing errors, and are destined to do still more; while your review of Mr. Finney's sermon has gone to the very core of the business, and will surely be effective in dissipating much of the illusion which is connected with these mournful innovations. They call it *severe*, but I call it *just*, and as timely as it is just. I think you may greatly felicitate yourself for having written just such a thing. In my opinion, the cause of truth demanded it.

"The sermon of Mr. Finney was founded upon a principle which, if admitted, would sanction every species of wildness and enthusiasm; or, if it did not *directly sanction*, it would furnish a *defence*, for the greatest extravagance that ever disgraced the religious world.

"The notice which has been taken of your review in the Troy and Utica papers, need not, I should suppose, alarm you. Depend upon it, they feel the weakness of their cause. Much, I know, is said, and no small stir made, to keep up the spirits of the friends of the new measures; but we, who have been looking on, can clearly perceive that their cause and their resolutions are both at a stand.

"Perhaps I am too much influenced by what I observe in my own neighborhood; but there are two facts of a general character which speak pretty distinctly on this subject. One is, that numbers of the ministers who were for a season carried away with these novelties, are silently returning to their old habits, both in their preaching and their intercourse with their people; and the other, that they are unwilling to allow that any such facts have existed, as have been made the subject of public criticism and remark. The truth is, they perceive these things to be indispensable, and that the good sense of the community will not long endure them. Instead, therefore, of replying to the arguments of their opponents, and defending what all the world believed at the time to exist, they allege that their brethren who have complained are strangely deluded in point of fact; some abused by false report from people at a distance, and others by their own imaginations, fancying they saw and heard things which really never happened, or which never happened in the manner and circumstances related.

"Can there be any mistake in supposing that they begin to feel that the waters are running low? A highly respectable man in Utica told me, three weeks since, that he had no idea that it would be possible to get up again the things that have gone by—so sensible were the influential people of the deleterious effects of what had already happened. Still, pride of character would not admit of open retraction, nor could this be done, without awakening the distrust and perhaps resentment of the more enthusiastic and less informed.

"A curious state of things also exists in Auburn, but prudence forbids that I should be very communicative. I will only say it is a state which cannot possibly last. A great deal is done and said to keep up appearances, but the ebbing tide is fast leaving the shore. The professors and students, with the exception of three or four (and the confidence of those is much abated), are of one mind on the subject of revivals; and with us concur the opinions of the Presbytery to which we are attached, and all the ministers and churches to the West. I know of not more than three or four ministers in the bounds of the two synods of Geneva and Genesee, that I should suspect of embracing the views of Mr. Finney.

"Still, no man should sleep at his post. It would be desirable to spread correct views before the public, and to take such measures to warn the churches against approaching danger, as might be both seasonable and effective. But how shall this be done? My opinion and that of my associates is, that the most promising expedient would be for Mr. Weeks, or Mr. Prime, or some other able and leisure hand, to make a statement of facts capable of being proved in a court of justice, accompanied with such remarks as would fully disclose the unhappy and dangerous character of the spirit which has been displayed, and the measures adopted in different sections of our country —something, in short, like what President Edwards has done in his third and fourth part of a history of a revival in New England in 1740. Anything short of this, in the present stage of the business, will accomplish but little. Our wish would be, that this statement should be preceded by a candid and full allowance of all the good which has been accomplished in these revivals, and of all the zeal and faithfulness which have been exhibited by its immediate promoters; that the spirit of Christ should eminently characterize the performance, that it might be seen that there is a plain distinction between those who mourn over what has been wrong in this business, and those who are enemies to all revivals.

"Say what you will of irregularity or extravagance, and the facts are called in question. A statement, we think, ought to be made once for all, founded on such evidence that it could not, without great disingenuousness, be gainsaid. Not that we propose anything like taking or exhibiting testimony, as in a court of record, but selecting facts after full investigation, and let them go forth to the world under the solemn assurance that they are not founded on vague report, but on evidence of an unquestionable character. A pamphlet of fifty or a hundred pages, we should think, would be all-sufficient. When it should be prepared, let it be submitted to a number of respectable clergymen, and let them severally or jointly lend to it the sanction of their names. We have many reasons for thinking that such a measure would be more safe, as well as more effective, than carrying on a petty warfare in any periodical journal. It would raise a louder note of warning, and prolong its tones to a later period, than anything so partial and ephemeral as are most of our newspaper communications, and their public journals. Such a work might be reviewed, and extracts occasionally taken from it, and published in the *Spectator*, *New York Observer*, and other papers, as particular circumstances might demand.

"We feel deeply indebted to you and Dr. Porter for your recent communications, and shall be able, I doubt not, to turn them to a good account. True, there are flying reports that Dr. Porter, Dr. Beecher, Mr. Williston, and I know not who, are going over to the new measures; but they are empty, and can do no harm. We think it best to put them down in a private way, rather than to contradict them by any public testimony.

"May God preserve your life and health, my dear Brother, and let nothing discourage you; your voice has been lifted up, and it will be heard, notwithstanding the murmurings and janglings and wrath of those who oppose.

"Affectionately yours,
"J. RICHARDS."

The following letter also, from my departed and venerated Brother, the Rev. Dr. Porter, of Catskill, refers to the same subject.

"CATSKILL, *May* 28, 1827.
"REV. GARDINER SPRING, D.D.:

"DEAR SIR: Mr. Nettleton came to this place on Friday last—is feeble, but considerably better than he was a few weeks ago; possesses all his strength and clearness of thought; preached yesterday twice with great power, and to the astonishment of those who heard him, and, I hope, to the saving benefit of souls.

"I think it a happy circumstance, in the providence of God, that his letter to yourself came out in the *Observer*. I have read Mr. Finney's sermon, and to my mind it is clear as the noon-day sun, that Mr. Nettleton's remarks, though one or two of them, at first view, may seem severe, are unexceptionably correct and in point; and that the irregularities and confusion introduced into revivals at the West, and some other places, grow directly out of the principle which the discourse is intended to vindicate. The sermon is a comment, and, I think, a very perfect one, on the proceedings in the religious meetings in question. The facts are well attested and abundant, which go to show that the allusions in Mr. Nettleton's letter, and also in the pastoral letter of Oneida Association, so far from coloring too highly what has actually transpired, are but a faint picture of a management, which, if it should prevail, cannot fail to tarnish the character of religious revivals, and render them disreputable in the view of the religious public, and such as the best and most enlightened Christians can never approbate, but must deplore. In a doubtful case, I would speak with doubt. But in this case, I do not hesitate to say, there is cause for alarm. I have been looking at this species of management for a year. I have seen what appeared to me extremely imprudent and exceptionable, and have learned more, from various sources entitled to the fullest confidence. In my humble judgment, the watchmen of Zion could no longer justify themselves to Christ, without lifting up their voice.

"Mr. Nettleton, at length—whose praise is in all the churches, and I know not who could be a fitter person—has published his views. Now, my dear brother, shall not the stated pastors, and those in particular to whom God has given an extensive influence, step into the front ranks, and with boldness, and with the meekness and gentleness of Christ, show their love to Him, by watching against the wiles of the adversary, and defending the church He has bought with His own blood, and against the storm that is gathering over her head, threatening to mar her beauty, and despoil her of her ornaments, and bring her to the very dust in lamentation and woe.

"I have written, my dear sir, more for my own sake than yours. I have written, if I know my own heart, from an imperious sense of duty, to express my views, and give my testimony against what appears to me to be an evil which we have great cause to fear and reason to deprecate; and in favor of what demands our seasonable and best efforts to maintain and defend.

"I am, dear sir, yours in the fullest confidence,
"DAVID PORTER."

Looking back through almost forty years upon the irregularities of the West, I have not hesitated to condemn them. The new measures require no real self-denial nor humility, but give full scope and employment to the opposite emotions, and under specious names feed those false affections which are so often regarded as genuine religion. If I mistake not, it is their tendency to justify and encourage these spurious emotions, which gives the new measures their popularity. It is a sad mistake when the *quantity* of religious emotions, rather than their *quality*, is made the measure of piety. The fiery, the furious, the *martial* has little sympathy with Him who was meek and lowly in heart. I am afraid of that kind of religion which enlists the passions of those who fall under its influence to such a degree, that they seem incapable any longer of reasoning, or of anything which requires calm and deliberate thought. The tone of evangelical truth has been sinking fast in the West for five or six years, and never so rapidly as when these revivals were in progress. Upon a deliberate view of this whole subject, I cannot but remark, that the character of revivals should be guarded with the greatest care, and not be put at hazard by the hasty introduction of men or measures, which, by a large majority of the most experienced friends of revivals, is considered so calamitous.

CHAPTER XI.

DOMESTIC MISSIONS.

No nation now on the earth is more indebted to the care and bounty of Divine Providence, than the people of these States. Descended from an intelligent and pious ancestry, enjoying civil and religious institutions not equalled by any of the European nations, protected in the midst of dangers, and supported in darkness and distress, multiplied in population, rich in all the resources of material wealth, and distinguished for their spiritual growth and advancement, the American people have a high destiny, and were planted in this land for great and important purposes. Nor were our forefathers unmindful of the designs of God's providence, nor of the obligations of their sacred trust in Christianizing this western world. This was the great field of their benevolent exertions. It was a vast field, extending from the British dominions on the North, to the Gulf of Mexico on the South, and from the iron-bound coast of New England on the East, to the Alleghany and Oregon mountains on the West. Since that period it has extended to the Pacific Ocean, where the heralds of salvation from these lands look across to pagan shores. The great valley of the Mississippi alone contains one million and three hundred and fifty square miles—more than two-thirds of the United States, and one twenty-eighth part of the entire land-surface of the earth. It has immense alluvial lands of great variety and richness of soil, great beauty and fertility, and is watered by the Mississippi, the Ohio, the St. Francis, the Arkansas, the White River, the Missouri, and the Red River, which are some of the finest in the world.

It deserves to be recorded, that in the year 1698, a voluntary society was formed in England, called the "*Society for Promoting Christian Knowledge,*" the object of which was to disseminate the knowledge of the Gospel in foreign parts, and principally among the British plantations in America. In the year 1781 this society obtained a charter from William III., by which they were incorporated and invested with full powers for carrying into effect their benevolent design, " in promoting the real and practical knowledge of the true religion, by such methods as appeared to them, from time to time, to be most conducive to that end." This venerable society enjoys the glory of being the first laborer in this western world. The early settlers in this country were cheered by their efforts; their correspondence with them was a welcome impulse to their own infant enterprises, and they hailed them as honored fellow-laborers in the work of converting this barren land into a fruitful field.

God had raised up the Puritans of New England, and girded them for this spiritual war. They were not only men of valor, but strictness and even severity of manners; qualifications that are very apt to be characteristic even of good men, when their religion puts them in peril. Their first efforts were directed towards evangelizing the native Indians, that brave and ill-used race, now melting away before the Anglo-Saxons, like snow beneath a vertical sun. Antecedent to the period to which these reminiscences refer, there were Elliot and the Mayhews, Seargeant and the Brainerds, the elder Wheelock and Kirkland, men whose names are embalmed in the memory of these aboriginal tribes, and whose life and services, whose steady zeal and untiring disinterestedness, commend them to our reverence and love.

The earliest recollections I have of home missions, are associated with the efforts of my honored father in the formation of the Massachusetts Missionary Society, and the origin and support of the Massachusetts Missionary Magazine. That society was formed in Boston on the 28th of May, 1799, and was duly organized by the appointment of Dr. Emmons as president, Dr. Austin as secretary, Deacon Simpkins as treasurer, and Rev. Messrs. Sanford, Hopkins, Weld, Spring, Niles, Barker, Crane, Austin, and Strong, trustees. The Massachusetts Missionary Magazine was commenced in the year 1803, and the profits of it were devoted to "the support of missionaries in the new settlements, and among the Indians in North America." It was extended to five volumes, from May, 1803, to May, 1808. I was acquainted with its commencement and progress, and with the leading contributors to its pages. They were Dr. Emmons, Dr. Sanford, Dr. Daniel Hopkins, Mr. Samuel Niles,

Dr. Holmes, Dr. Parish, and my father; and comprised the theologians of the Hopkinsian and Calvinistic schools, uniting their efforts, as they were accustomed to do, "to edify Christians, and inform the rising generation." The "*Religious Conference between Clerus and his Young Friends*," begun in the first volume, and continued in ten successive numbers; "*The Character of Dr. Samuel Hopkins*," "*Questions to Exercise the Minds of Children*," "*The Rural Assembly*," in the same volume; "*Conference between a Calvinist and Methodist*," "*Dialogues between Agnostes and Philalethes*," in three successive numbers in the second volume; "*The Ninth of Romans*," in two numbers in the third volume, were written by my father. Five successive numbers on the "*Divine Immutability*," in the first volume, were from the pen of Dr. Emmons. He was a large contributor to this magazine, and, if I mistake not, wrote over the signature of Theophilus. The "*Letters from Pascal to Julia*," in the first and second volumes—more than twenty in number—were written by Dr. Austin, of Worcester. I have received many important hints, and no small amount of instruction, from this valuable publication. The discussions in some of our modern quarterlies about the *Conditioned* and the *Absolute*, and *Hard Matter*, neither instruct nor edify me half so much as the doctrinal discussions and practical treatises of the earlier magazines.

Though small in its beginnings, the Massachusetts Missionary Society did good service in the home-field. The Rev. Messrs. Avery, Cram, Sawyer, Alexander, Wines, and Sewall, some of them in western New

York, others in the district of Maine, others in Vermont and Pennsylvania, extending their ministrations to the Indian tribes and Upper Canada, though often disheartened, persevered in their work with a resolution and zeal worthy of their high calling, and compensated with marked tokens of the divine favor. That great region which lies West of the Hudson, and reaches to Lake Erie, was then a desert; now few, if any, portions of the American Church have more strength and vigor, or are more abundant in the fruits of holiness.

The *Missionary Society of Connecticut* was formed in June, 1798, a year in advance of the Massachusetts society, and was patronized by the first civilians in the State, the leading clergymen, and the great body of the churches.

This society was largely patronized. The *Connecticut Evangelical Magazine*, one of the best publications, and established in 1800, consecrated all the profits arising from the sale of it to the formation of a permanent fund, the annual interest of which was appropriated to the cause of missions. It was sustained, in vigor, by such men as Dr. Strong, Dr. Backus, Dr. Perkins, Dr. Hart, Dr. Smalley, Dr. Trumbul, Dr. Dwight, Dr. Lewis, the younger Edwards, the late Governor Treadwell, and their associates. The late Dr. Strong himself furnished no less than *eighty* original communications for these instructive volumes. By the courtesy of the printer, I have received the entire list of his communications, and of the subjects which employed his pen. They were plain thoughts on great subjects, and well fitted to instruct and interest all classes of readers, promote the spirituality of ministers and people, and save the souls of men. Noble men were the conductors of this magazine, and not the least among them was this Nathan Strong, of Hartford. I know of nothing in any of the fugitive publications of the present day, that stands abreast with the theology and the piety of the old *Connecticut Evangelical Magazine.*

The field of operations of the Connecticut society was the Indian tribes bordering on Lake Erie, the western and northern parts of Vermont, the settlements on the Delaware and Susquehanna rivers in the State of Pennsylvania, and adjacent regions in the State of New York, and also the region northwest of the Ohio River called the Western Reserve. In the year 1814, this society had in its service forty-three missionaries, some laboring in New Hampshire, some in Vermont, some in northern and western New York, and some in the north counties of Pennsylvania, New Connecticut, and other parts of the State of Ohio. Liberal as was this supply, not only was the harvest great and the laborers few, but on the same field it was not possible for the laborers to overtake the labor. And still the work goes on, an honor to old Connecticut, and the pledge that this society will not be " weary in well doing."

We give all due honor to the churches in New England in this effort. Our Puritan fathers and brethren have greatly exceeded us in the *amount and success* of missionary effort; while it was to the Presbyterian Church that the providence of God awarded the honor of first breaking up the fallow ground.

Under the colonial government, and as early as the year 1709, the *General Presbytery* made an appeal to the churches in London through Sir Edmond Harison, to extend their liberality to the destitute in this land; and the following year the Presbytery made the same appeal to the Presbytery of Dublin. The first fund created was in the year 1717, and in 1718 the Synod made a second appeal to the churches in Ireland, and in the same year another appeal to the dissenting ministers in London. In 1719 the first appropriation of funds received from Glasgow was made to the Presbyterian congregation in New York, and a yearly collection was appointed throughout all the churches of the Synod. The first appointment of itinerant missionaries was made in the year 1722, and to the destitute in the State of Virginia. In 1732 these efforts were so seriously obstructed by illegal prosecutions, that an appeal was made to Governor Gooch, of Virginia, to protect the missionaries, to which he gave a favorable answer, promising the countenance of the government upon the condition of their good behavior, and their conformity to the Act of Toleration in England. In 1753 the celebrated Samuel Davis, then in London, was authorized by the Synod to use his influence in obtaining a redress of these grievances. In 1764 the Synod extended their operations into North Carolina, and in 1776 they sent a missionary from New England into the western frontiers of New York, New Jersey, and Pennsylvania. In 1752, the Presbytery of New York ordained and commissioned a missionary to the Indians; and in 1756 they employed Mr. John Brainerd in this service, who continued his faithful labors until his death, in 1781. In 1761 they established a mission among the Oneidas, under the care of the Rev. Sampson Occum, an Indian of the Mohegan tribe, educated by Dr. Wheelock. In 1763 they appointed an exploring expedition to the West, and directed Dr. Allison, Dr. Witherspoon, Dr. Rodgers, Mr. Brainerd, and Mr. Ewing, to devise and report a plan for their more extended operations. In 1801 they established the Sandusky mission, and in 1805 the Synod of Pittsburgh reported to the General Assembly that they had commenced operations on the Alleghany and Lake Erie shore, among the Wyandots and Senecas. In 1803 they established a mission among the Catawbas, and in 1805 among the Cherokees. In 1802 the Assembly appointed the *Standing Committee of Missions*, to superintend the missionary business, and to whom the Presbyteries were to make their report; and in 1816 this committee was constituted a commission, under the style of the *Board of Missions*, who, in 1827, in addition to the powers already granted them, were authorized to manage, appoint, and direct the whole concerns and business of the Assembly's missions, and report annually their doings to the Assembly. Under this arrangement, the missions of the General Assembly were conducted with efficiency and success, extending the boundaries of the church, organizing new congregations, and establishing churches in the neglected and waste places of the land. As the results of their efforts, between the years 1830 and 1850, the increase of missionaries was from one hundred and one, to five hundred and seventy; the increase of funds from $12,000 to $79,000; the organization of nine hundred and forty-three new churches, the erection of fourteen hundred and eighty-four houses of worship, and the addition of over forty thousand souls, on the profession of their faith, to the missionary churches. To the God of Zion be all the praise!

Among the important coadjutors in this work were the *New York Missionary Society*, the *New Jersey Missionary Society*, the *Young Men's Missionary Society of New York*, the *Evangelical Missionary Society*, the *Presbyterian Board of Domestic Missions*, and the *American Home Missionary Society*. The selected field of the New York society was the Indian territory in the remote West; while that of the New Jersey society was in territories nearer home. The Young Men's Missionary Society of this city rose from small beginnings, but by very considerable accessions to its members and its resources, and by the enthusiastic spirit which animated it, gave a powerful impulse to the good cause, and promised to be one of the important agencies in the missionary work. It was composed of the young men from all our evangelical churches; its officers were men of intelligence, enterprise, and honored Christian character, and its practical influence upon the young men of our city was of the most desirable kind. But the age of bigotry and dogmatism had not passed away. While I was a member of its Board of Directors in the year 1817, and cheerfully united with my fellow-laborers in the appointment of all well-qualified missionaries of evangelical views, it was not difficult to perceive that the

Board were unduly influenced by their apprehensions of the theological errors of some of their own number, as well as of some who were proposed to be employed in their service. The controversy between Hopkinsians and Calvinists was then at its height, and the Board adopted a principle in the appointment of its missionaries which was not only unwise and uncalled for, but utterly subversive of the missionary enterprise. The nomination of the Rev. Samuel H. Cox, who was strongly recommended by myself and Eleazer Lord, Esq., as a young man of brilliant talents, exemplary piety, and sound in the faith, and as strongly opposed by the Rev. Dr. Matthews and others, brought the subject fully and fairly before the Board; and after a thorough investigation of the views of the candidate upon the doctrines of original sin, the nature of true religion, the extent of the Atonement, and the sinner's inability, Mr. Cox was rejected. An appeal from this decision was made to the society itself, constituted, as it was, of men of evangelical views, though differing in their construction of some Calvinistic doctrines. The meetings of the society were held in the session-room of the old Brick Church, where, for several successive evenings, the questions and the doctrines involved were freely and abundantly discussed. It was a most exciting scene. The principal advocates of the decision of the Board were the Rev. Dr. Matthews, the Rev. Dr. McLeland, and Thomas Warner, Esq., and the principal opposers of that decision, George Griffin, Theodore Sedgewick, Eleazer Lord, Esqs., and the Rev. Dr. Spring. We traversed the whole disputed territory, and, with some discourteous interruptions from Dr. Matthews, were listened to with patient earnestness. It was purely a theological discussion, and such an one as I have never listened to before, nor since; and threw more light upon the minds of the masses, in relation to the doctrines of the Reformers, than could have been easily thrown in any other way, and in the same time. It formed a memorable epoch in the history of the Presbyterian Church. A few men, advanced in years, are still living among us who have more than once testified to the importance of this discussion in forming their doctrinal opinions. It was a season of deep interest to the clergy of our city and land; some of them fearing, and others hoping for, an open division in our evangelical churches. No small influence was exerted against us by the talent, standing, and piety of some of our fathers in the ministry, and the result was, the society vindicated the action of the Board in the rejection of the candidate. We were in the minority; and immediately after the meeting at which these discussions were concluded, proceeded to organize a new society. As a matter of history, the following document is here inserted, presenting more fully the *facts* which led to this result.

" Defence to ourselves, if not to the public, demands an explanation of the origin and design of the NEW YORK EVANGELICAL MISSIONARY SOCIETY OF YOUNG MEN. An event of so much notoriety as the secession of more than one hundred young men from an institution whose professed object is the propagation of the Gospel of Jesus Christ, cannot, at first view, be regarded but with sentiments of regret. At an age of the world when the various denominations of Christendom begin to feel that they have attached too much importance to the things in which they differ, and not enough to those in which they agree; when the dissemination of the Gospel is the great and common cause which unites the affections, the prayers, and the exertions of the great family of believers; and in the promotion of which they already begin to find a grave for their party spirit and sectarian prejudices; nothing but considerations of commanding influence can justify a disjunction of missionary labors. Charity suffereth long; but there is a point beyond which Christian forbearance cannot be extended, and when the wisdom that cometh from above demands a struggle, not only to extend the Redeemer's kingdom abroad, but to maintain its independence at home.

"Considerations of this imperative character did exist, and led to the organization of this infant institution. On the 23d of January, 1809, a number of young men of different religious denominations in the city of New York, formed themselves into a society for the purpose of raising a fund to aid in promoting the objects of the New York Missionary Society. So unexpected was the success, and so hopeful the promise of this institution, that, on the 14th of February, 1816, it resolved on the future management of its own funds, independently of the parent society. It was no longer the Assistant New York Missionary Society, but the Young Men's Missionary Society of New York.

"Though it was expected that this institution would consecrate its efforts to the great work of disseminating the Gospel, without descending to the littleness of party distinction, circumstances of no equivocal import very early indicated that there were some unhappy jealousies in the Board of Directors on the subject of Christian theology. A studious effort to avoid bringing the points of difference into view, together with the spirit of mutual conciliation and confidence, which appeared to be gradually increasing, it was hoped, would repress everything like secret alienation, as well as remove the possibility of open rupture. But in this respect the fondest hopes were defeated. These miserable jealousies had never slept. At their recent session on the 11th of November last, Mr. Samuel Hanson Cox, without his own knowledge, was nominated to the Board as a suitable candidate for the missionary service. Mr. Cox was himself a member of the Missionary Society, and in October last was licensed to preach the Gospel by the unanimous vote of the Presbytery of New York. The minority were at no loss to determine that this nomination was not grateful to the majority of the Board. As the most compendious method of overruling it, and with the impression that the funds of the society would not authorize the appointment of more than one missionary in addition to the one in actual employment, the Rev. Arthur J. Stansbury, of the Associate Reformed Church, was introduced to the Board as a rival candidate. With the hope of avoiding concussion, and with the desire to evince an exemption from party prejudice, the mover of the resolution nominating Mr. Cox, begged leave to insert the name of Mr. Stansbury in conjunction with that of Mr. Cox, thus placing the candidates of either side on equal ground. But the ifficulty was neither removed nor diminished. The apprehension was too well grounded that the objec to be secured by the majority was not the appointment of Mr. Stansbury, so much as the rejection of Mr. Cox. The appearance of this determination, while it did not allay the fears of the minority, excited equal surprise and regret. Nothing but the thorny field of controversy now lay before them. Still reluctant, however, to hazard the interests of a society hitherto so prosperous, anxious to avert the probable issues of a public conflict, and most unwilling to embarrass the Redeemer's cause by dissensions among his professed followers, the minority were happy to have it understood that the subject be informally referred to the *Committee of Missions.*

"That committee were convened on the following Monday. The name of Mr. Cox was mentioned with diffidence and solicitude. No objection was made to his talents or piety. It was too well known to be disputed, that, in both these particulars, he enjoyed no small share of public confidence. The majority of the committee had, however, unhappily associated with the name of Mr. Cox certain religious sentiments which they deemed *unsound*, and which they supposed to be inconsistent with the character of a useful missionary. It was not to be concealed that, in the great outlines of truth, his views accorded rather with those entertained by Calvin, Edwards,

Bellamy, Scott, Smalley, Dwight, Pierce, Ryland, Fuller, and, indeed, with the great body of the Christian world in this period of enlightened piety, than with the incoherent and unintelligible dogmas with which local intolerance seems resolved to burden the Church of Christ. If not to believe that we actually sinned in Eden, six thousand years before we were born; if not to believe that the inability of the unregenerate to comply with the terms of salvation is the same as their inability to pluck the sun from his orbit; if not to believe that the depravity of man destroys his accountability; if not to believe that the Atonement is made exclusively for the elect; if not to believe that the elect are invested with a title to eternal life, on principles of distributive justice, while destitute of renewing and sanctifying grace; if not to believe that the Christian's love of God is founded in selfishness, as completely as the miser's love of gold; if want of assent to these repulsive notions disqualifies a man for the missionary service, then, doubtless, Mr. Cox is disqualified. But if a cordial adherence to the truth that through the sin of Adam all mankind are sinners from the first moment of their own existence; that the inability of the unregenerate, though absolute, inculpates rather than excuses them; that, notwithstanding his apostasy, man is still a free agent, and accountable for his character; that the Atonement is unlimited in its nature, and limited only in its application; that the salvation of the elect is not of debt, but of grace; that all holy affection, though caused by the divine Spirit, is founded on the divine excellence rather than the divine favor; if a firm belief and cordial reception of these glorious truths qualifies a man for the ministry of reconciliation, then the minority have every reason to concur in the unanimous opinion of the Presbytery of New York that Mr. Cox is qualified.

"Notwithstanding this diversity of sentiment, it has been well understood that there was no reluctance on the part of the minority to coöperate with the majority in any measures to advance the missionary cause. While the minority loved the truth, and designed to maintain it, it was far from their purpose and their wishes that the spirit of theological controversy should creep into the missionary society, or these differences in doctrine ever be recognized in their appointment of missionaries. Nor can they be accused of a single departure from this catholic principle. In the appointment of Mr. Cox, they asked no more than they were willing to give. Presuming that questions of similar import might hereafter agitate the society, unless the present case should be avowedly decided as a precedent, the committee agreed, without a dissenting voice, to decide upon the present nomination as involving the principle, whether *any man holding Mr. Cox's sentiments should be eligible to their employment?* With this important question before them, they separated without a decision, agreeing solemnly and prayerfully to review the whole subject, and convene for their final decision on the following Friday.

"On Friday all were present, except one in the minority. There was much inquiry and some discussion. After having received a full development of

Mr. Cox's views from a member of their own Board, the committee resolved, '*That it is* inexpedient to recommend Mr. Cox to the Board of Directors as a missionary.' The ground of this resolution was but one —that the religious sentiments of Mr. Cox savored so much of error, and contained so visibly the germ of heresy, that the committee felt bound to withhold from him their sanction as a missionary of the cross. The votes were four for and two against this resolution; when it was resolved *unanimously*, That it is inexpedient to recommend to the Board the Rev. Arthur J. Stansbury as a missionary.

" The evening of the same day was to convene the Board of Directors to receive the report of this committee. On the reading of this report it was moved, That, notwithstanding the decision of the Committee of Missions, Mr. Samuel H. Cox be appointed a missionary in the service of the society for the term of six months. After discussing this resolution at considerable length, the Board determined to follow the example of the Committee of Missions, and defer their decision to a further meeting. On Friday of the next week they met, when all the directors were present. Either with the hope of avoiding a full discussion of the resolution on the table, or with the expectation that the minority would resist the proposal, it was moved by the majority that the further consideration of the proposition respecting the employment of Mr. Cox be deferred, in order to consider the recommendation of the Committee of Missions respecting Mr. Stansbury. Whatever might have been the views of the minority of such a course of measures, they determined not to oppose them, and therefore cordially united with the majority in engaging Mr. Stansbury as their missionary. The contrast between the conduct pursued by the minority and that persisted in by the majority, must strike every Christian eye, and impress itself on every Christian heart.

" Not without the hope that the liberal sentiments of the minority in this appointment would soften the rigor of the majority, the motion was renewed for the appointment of Mr. Cox. Very considerable discussion ensued. The minority used every effort to ward off and lighten the shock. They entreated the majority to avoid the hazard of a rash decision. They entreated them to regard the honor and prosperity of the common cause. They entreated them not to lose sight of the grand object of the institution, and forget the claims of the perishing. But it was all in vain. A tide had set in, which could not be turned out of its course; a torrent which it was hopeless to resist; a deluge of intolerance which threatened to sweep away every mound, and in its progress to desolate the fairest portions of the Redeemer's heritage. The lamentable decision was passed, negativing the appointment of Mr. Cox as a missionary, and virtually recognizing the principle that no man of similar views could be patronized by the Board. The votes on this question stood twelve to six. Two members of the Board, at heart with the minority, from considerations of peculiar delicacy which did them honor, declined voting, who, from considerations of high attachment to truth and justice which have done them greater honor, have since connected themselves with the newly-organized institution, and accepted a seat in its direction.

"There is something in the retrospect of what is wrong that goads the mind. After all the promptness with which it is accomplished, the aspect of evil, after it is done, is ugly and distressing. The deed was performed, and it was fondly hoped that some misgivings of heart were discoverable on the part of the majority. The inquiry was made by the minority, and reiterated by the less determined of the majority, Is there no way in which this breach can be healed? Lest it should be imagined by some of the majority, and lest the intimation should possibly be suggested at some future period, that the minority were contending for an individual, rather than for those whom he represented, and were more attached to the name of Mr. Cox than to the principle involved in their discussion, they submitted the proposition on the spot, though not by a formal resolution, to unite with the majority in declaring it to be inexpedient to appoint Mr. Cox, provided the majority would yield the principle that a licentiate or minister in good standing, holding Mr. Cox's sentiments, should not be considered as an outlaw from the missionary service. The proposition was rejected with a tone of such decision by the leaders of the majority, that there was no other alternative than for the minority either silently to withdraw from the society, or bring the whole subject before them at their annual meeting, which was just at hand. To the latter course they were urged, as well by a multitude of counsellors, as by every correct sentiment of duty to themselves and the Church of God. Especially did they consider the claims of the society imperative, because of the fourteen congregations of which it was composed, no less than six of its directors were from the Reformed Dutch church in Garden-street. Whatever might be the views of the great body of the society of the points of faith discussed in the Board, the minority did not believe that they would justify the directors in making these differences the governing principle of their conduct in the appointment of missionaries. At the close of the annual meeting, therefore, a brief statement of what had transpired in the Board, was succeeded by the following

" ' Resolution : Whereas, it appears that some unhappy differences of opinion concerning certain religious doctrines have existed in the minds of the directors of this society, and that these differences, though involving nothing inconsistent with the constitution or object of this society, have unduly influenced the minds of the directors in their appointment of missionaries, therefore, Resolved, *That the society disapprove such measures as have been pursued by the Board, recognizing the differences above named as the governing principle of their conduct, and most earnestly recommend to them, in their proceedings as directors, to leave out of view all those disagreements in sentiment which may have a tendency to weaken the union and paralyze the efforts of this once harmonious association.*' After much altercation, and unwearied effort to avoid the discussion by *motions of amendment*, by the introduction of *substitutes*, and by one unmanly effort at *an indefinite postponement*, the minority were permitted to enter upon the discussion, having stricken out of the original resolution the clause openly disapproving the conduct of the directors. The points of difference in religious opinion were necessarily brought into view, opposed by the one party, and defended by the other. In the course of the argument, the minority freely referred to the sacred Scriptures in justification of their views; feeling it their duty to maintain the principles they avowed by unequivocal declarations of the word of God, rather than by denouncing the opinions of other men, or by appealing to human authorities. The course they pursued, however, did not pass without reprehension. They were not a little surprised and mortified to hear a reverend gentleman of the majority express his hope that if any person should introduce arguments from the Bible in support of his positions, he should be considered out of order; adding, that if this course were admitted, the discussion might be protracted through the winter. Nor was their mortification diminished, to hear another reverend gentleman of the majority concur in this extraordinary proposal. Safe as such a measure would have proved to the majority, and little as they wished to be encumbered with Scripture testimony, happily no question was formally taken on the subject. The period had not yet arrived when, by a solemn vote of a religious assembly, quotations from Scripture should be declared 'out of order,' in the discussion of a theological question.

"After several long evenings, the strength and patience of the society were exhausted. As the discussion drew towards a close, and it was seen that a division in the society would inevitably be the result of a vote sustaining the conduct of the directors, the minority resolved to make one more effort to save from impending ruin an institution reared by united labors, and cemented by united prayers and tears. They expressed their willingness to strip the resolution on the table of everything that should have a retrospective influence; they were anxious to overlook all that was past, provided they could have some pledge of toleration for the time to come. Unwilling to relinquish this last, though almost forlorn hope, they begged the privilege of submitting a resolution simply recognizing the principle that licentiates or ministers of the Gospel in good standing in the church of Christ, and acknowledged to be sound in the faith by a Judicatory of the Dutch Reformed, Associate Reformed, or Presbyterian churches, and who possess, in the judgment of the directors, the other proper qualifications as missionaries, shall be indiscriminately employed by the society. More than this the minority consented not to ask; less, it was thought, the majority could not give. The only question then was, whether, irrespective of their differences of sentiment, the society would, upon principles that were impartial and honorable, combine their efforts in the missionary cause.

"It was the joy of the minority to be permitted to live in an age of the world which calls upon them to unite with men, differing, indeed, from them in important articles of faith, but according with them in the great designs of glory to God and good-will to men. The heathen were perishing in their blood. It was no time to foster the spirit of alienation and bigotry. The fields were whitening to the harvest. From every desert and every mountain the cry was reverberating, ' Thrust ye in the sickle ! ' A sphere of action was opening upon the rising generation, such as the world never saw. The minority hoped that the majority would tread back their ground with the magnanimity of Christian heroism ; or, if they revolted at this, that they would welcome this last proposal—would rejoice to strike their hands with ours in this holy league ; and wherever else we might admit them, eternally banish all our differences of sentiment from this hitherto harmonious society.

" But what were their feelings when the proposition—in a manner how little resembling the Christian spirit, will never be forgotten—was repelled as *cowardly*, and promptly, though reluctantly, withdrawn. Their utmost fears were now realized, and the hope of conciliation forever extinguished. There remained the sweet conviction, that an invisible and almighty hand would yet be discovered and exalted in this unsearchable providence, and that there was One on the throne who was able to redeem the pledge, ' *The wrath of man shall praise the Lord, and the remainder of wrath he will restrain.*'

" The yeas and nays being called for, the question was decided against the resolution by a majority of one hundred and eighty-two to ninety-one. Two hundred and fourteen members of the Society were absent, and a very considerable number of those present declined voting. By this ruthful blow was this fair temple cloven to its base. If solicitude, and entreaty, and tears, could have availed, it would have stood firm and risen high. But the blow that severed it laid the deep and broad foundation for an edifice whose triumphal arch and lofty dome will be seen from afar. Abundant thanksgiving is due to the great Head of the Church, that we have been carried through the conflict, and that in the darkest season the pillar and the cloud were before us. '*Not unto us, O Lord, not unto us, but to thy name give glory, for thy mercy and thy truth's sake!*' It has been an event which in prospect we deplored, and which in its approaches has been resisted by every expedient which truth and charity could dictate. It has been a struggle for all that is dear in religious liberty. It has been a conflict for Gospel truth. It has been the birth-pang of the daughter of Zion for the souls of the heathen. But the agony is over. We are troubled on every side, but not distressed; we are perplexed, but not in despair; *persecuted*, but not forsaken; cast down, but not destroyed. Though disfranchised, we inherit; though excommunicated, we commune; though amputated from the body, we hold the Head. While the earth is the Lord's and the fulness thereof, our purpose is to breathe his vital air, and display a banner because of the truth. This will we do if God permit. It is of little purpose that we should be thought to have gained the victory; it is sufficient to have gained a release from that spirit of intolerant bigotry to which we are willing to bid adieu forever."

Immediately after the meeting at which the discussions above mentioned were concluded, the minority proceeded to organize the "New York Evangelical Missionary Society of Young Men." It was a large meeting when the constitution was adopted, while a few weeks afterwards the society numbered more than four hundred members. The Board of Directors at their first meeting unanimously resolved to employ Mr. Samuel H. Cox as their Missionary. It was a noble Board, and nobly and successfully were they devoted to their work. The City and State of New York were the field early selected by them, and were occupied by most devoted men. It was my privilege, as the Secretary, to correspond with the missionaries, and to address the communities to which they were sent; and much as it added to my labors, it is with thankfulness that I look back to the part I was called to perform in originating and sustaining this society. It was an honor to be a fellow-worker with them, and to greet them as fellow-workers with me, not only in the missionary cause, but in every good word and work. They gathered around me, encouraged and strengthened me, and gave a hallowed influence to the church of which I was pastor and so many of them were members. Little did I think that so many of those beloved young men would be called to the rest that remaineth for the people of God, and leave me alone to give this brief notice of what He has wrought by them. To the best of my knowledge, there is but a solitary one of that Board of Directors now remaining, and he is an old man. Nor can I now recollect but one of our missionaries who is now on the earth. The lovely man whom we early employed in this city, at what was then called *Corlears Hook*, after having laid the foundation of two large congregations in one of the most destitute parts of the city, finished his honored course in the State of Ohio as the President of the Miami University. Well do I remember that Brother. For a series of years we met for prayer on the afternoon of every Saturday, his study and my own alternating the privilege. They were sweet seasons. And they were instructive seasons, when by the interchange of subjects and thoughts we both felt invigorated for the services of the sanctuary. I would speak of other departed missionaries; but though I may not linger in the land of darkness, I could not pass the graveyard without stopping at the sepulchre of Elihu W. Baldwin.

The American Home Missionary Society has long and deservedly held, and still holds, a wide place in the confidence of the churches. Its object from the beginning has been, and still is, *to assist congregations that are unable to support the Gospel ministry, and to send the Gospel to the destitute within the United States.* It was composed of the friends of missions in the Congregational, Presbyterian, and Dutch Reformed churches in all parts of the country, and was designed to be a national institution. Several preliminary consultations on the subject of forming such a society were held at Andover and Boston, attended by some of the most eminent ministers in New England, at the last of which it was *unanimously resolved*, That in the opinion of this meeting it is expedient to attempt the formation of a *National Domestic Missionary Society.* Local societies there were in the New England States. The *United Domestic Mission-*

ary Society of New York, formed in May, 1822, by delegates from ten smaller and local societies, and in no sense a denominational institution, was prosecuting its work with great efficiency, and from the well-known character of its committee, were prepared for the adoption of any well-devised arrangement that should secure a more united and combined effort for the spread of the Gospel among the destitute. At the request of the meeting in Boston, the Executive Committee of this society addressed a circular to a large number of the churches, inviting them to convene at the session-room of the Brick Presbyterian Church in the city of New York, for the purpose of forming an American Home Missionary Society. This circular was signed by Absalom Peters, Corresponding Secretary; Peter Hawes, Treasurer; Stephen Lockwood, Recording Secretary; and by John D. Keese, Chairman; Gardiner Spring, Jas. M. Matthews, Thomas McAuley, Elihu W. Baldwin, John Nitchie, Eleazer Lord, Knowles Taylor, Archibald Falconer, and Thomas Webster, Executive Committee. The response to this invitation was a large assemblage in convention of one hundred and twenty-six ministers and laymen from thirteen States and Territories of the Union,—men of high character in church and state, and from four different Christian denominations. The Rev. Dr. Day, of Yale College, was appointed Chairman of the Convention, and Rev. Drs. De Witt and Chester Secretaries. A constitution, previously prepared under the direction of the United Domestic Missionary Society, was read, and, on motion of Hon. Chancellor Kent, seconded by Rev. Dr.

VOL. 1.—12

Bates, of Middlebury College, was discussed, amended, and approved as the Constitution of the American Home Missionary Society; and on motion of Dr. Blythe, of Kentucky, seconded by Rev. Dr. Richards, of Auburn Seminary, it was recommended to the United Domestic Missionary Society to "adopt the same, and become the American Home Missionary Society." It did become so by its own action on the 12th of May, 1826, adopting the recommendation of the Convention, and becoming the *American Home Missionary Society* under the constitution thus recommended. In all this happy arrangement the Presbyterian Church, as a body, were heart and hand with their brethren of the Dutch, the Scotch, and the Congregational Churches. The late venerable Dr. Miller and Dr. Alexander, of Princeton Seminary, in a letter addressed to the Corresponding Secretary, dated Princeton, March 6, 1826, say: "We rejoice to hear that there is a plan in contemplation for forming a Domestic Missionary Society on a much larger scale than has heretofore existed. Our prayer is that the God of all grace may rouse the spirit of the nation on this subject." Few societies, if any, in this land were ever formed under brighter auspices, or enjoyed larger measures of the divine favor. Its executive officers for the first year were: Treasurer, Peter Hawes, Esq., New York; Auditor, Arthur Tappan, Esq., New York; Corresponding Secretary, Rev. Absalom Peters, New York; Recording Secretary, Stephen Lockwood, Esq., New York. At a meeting of the Directors, May 13, 1826, the Executive Committee were appointed, viz., John D. Keese, Chairman; Rev. Gardiner Spring,

D.D., Rev. James M. Matthews, D.D., Rev. Elihu W. Baldwin, Rev. Matthias Bruen, Messrs. Thomas Webster, John Nitchie, Archibald Falconer, Knowles Taylor, Eleazer Lord. Members *ex-officio*, Peter Hawes, Esq., Treas., Rev. Absalom Peters, Corresponding Secretary, Stephen Lockwood, Esq., Recording Secretary.

The United Domestic Missionary Society continued its operations but four short years, and was then merged in the American Home Missionary Society. At the close of their fourth annual report, the United Society say:

"It has been our privilege to be made the organs of assembling in this city, the present week, a numerous and respectable convention of the friends of Domestic Missions from all parts of the United States, for the purpose of forming an 'American Home Missionary.' The unanimous and highly auspicious result of their deliberations will be laid before this Society at the present meeting. We have only to add, that should you adopt the recommendation of that Convention, the present is the last report which the Society, in its present form, will be called on to accept from their Committee. Were it to be the close of your efforts in the same cause, we would call the people of the land to mourning. But it is happily otherwise. The United Domestic Missionary Society will here *lay down its life, to take it again*. We come to the close of our fourth year, therefore, with such feelings as surviving friends are wont to cherish when they stand over the grave of a good man, and there, in remembrance of all that was holy in the acts of his life, and in anticipation of all that is to be glorious in his future existence, are heard to say, '*It was gain for him to die.*' The Society which we have served has finished its probation. The experiment has been fairly tried, and the result is a conviction pervading the mind of the nation, that it is an instrument of God's own choosing for the salvation of the American people, and that it is worthy to be elevated to a higher sphere, to be introduced into a wider field, and, to be clothed with greater efficiency in its glorious work, that all the people of the land, in the length of it, and in the breadth of it, may rejoice and be glad in the Lord."

Some there are who may express some surprise at these commendations of the American Home Missionary Society, arising from the fact, that some few years after its organization, I became the advocate of the General Assembly's Board of Domestic Missions, as a separate and distinct organization. I can only now say, that it was not that I loved the American Home Missionary Society less, but that I loved the Assembly's Board more. It is said that the course I have pursued in favor of our own Board is hostile to the American Home Missionary Society. Why is it thus said? It is a poisonous suggestion, and has implanted many a root of bitterness. It is a most ungenerous suggestion; nay, it is worse: nothing has less to support it; nothing is more untrue. It is true, emphatically so, that I have been, and am, the friend of the Assembly's Board, but not in indifference, much less in hostility, to the American Home Missionary Society. I hope and pray that both may have their full share in the blessed work of sending the Gospel along the hills and plains of this land of promise. Both these institutions may have their imperfections, and both have their excellencies. The excellence of the American Society lies in its popular element, and in its energy; its faults, from my Presbyterian stand-point, are its tendencies to Congregationalism, and its exposure to loose doctrine. The excellence of the Assembly's Board lies in its attachment to our confession of faith and its efforts to extend the influence of Presbyterianism. But which is the greater mistake, to insist, it may be too rigorously, on the exclusive appointment of missionaries, who, *imo corde*, adopt the standards of the Presbyterian Church, or to scatter throughout the infant churches of the West, the innovations of the New Haven theology? If I were an eye-witness of the evils that are reported as the consequence of the conflicting interests of the two Boards, I might judge differently. But as the whole matter now presents itself to my mind, it is in every view unwise for these two institutions to encourage conflicting interests in an enterprise of such moment. For myself, I say, let the American Society plant Congregational churches, and let the Assembly's Board plant Presbyterian churches, both as rapidly and as successfully as they can; and the missionary field will be the gainers by it. 'Let not Ephraim envy Judah, nor Judah vex Ephraim.' There remaineth land enough to be possessed, nor should the conquest of it be retarded, because the tribes of Israel advance under different standards. I have seen the time when earnest efforts were made by some Presbyterians to frown upon the American Society, and I resisted them; and I have seen the time when some of the friends of that Society would have strangled the Assembly's Board, and when, at no small loss of their confidence, I boldly resisted them, both in the Presbytery of New York and on the floor of the General Assembly. I was aiding and abetting in the formation of the American Society, and was one of its Executive Committee; but when a proposition was submitted to that Committee for the union of that Society with the Assembly's Board, I was opposed to it, and expressed my views before the Committee. Though the measure was carried in the Committee, I did not vote for it, nor did I vote at all; and after the measure was decided by a large majority, I never gave it my concurrence. At a meeting of the Presbytery of New York, a discussion took place which related to the operations of the Assembly's Board. During that discussion, the remark was made and repeated, that the Board was pursuing a course calculated to impede the benevolent operations of the age, and that it was doing more harm than good. I took part in that discussion, and advocated the cause of the Board. I was a Presbyterian, and in favor of measures to extend the bounds of the Presbyterian Church. It was no new thing for different sections of the Church of God, in their organized capacity, to engage in the work of missions. There was safety in so doing, and I was grieved to observe a state of feeling that seemed to array one Society against the other; that the field was large enough for both; and that these remarks were in accordance with sentiments of strong attachment to the

Home Missionary Society. Such was the state of the churches, and such their prejudices, that it was impossible for the Home Society or the Assembly's Board to have access to all the congregations, and that if either attempted the work alone, the whole country could not be roused to action. We must take men as they are, and we must take *good* men as they are. Considering their imperfections, the work of Home Missions ought to be in more hands than one. And especially were these convictions strengthened by the incursions of error from the New Haven school. The standards of the Presbyterian Church were, under God, the strong bulwark against those growing errors, and just at this crisis to embarrass the operations of the Assembly's Board, would be fraught with injury to generations to come. I love the confession of faith of the Presbyterian Church, and always loved it. I have not altered in my preaching; my publications speak for themselves. I do not concur in all the peculiarities of old Calvinism, nor did I ever; nor do I agree with any of the New Haven theology. If I must choose between old Calvinism and New Haven theology, give me old Calvinism. Old-fashioned Calvinists and old-fashioned Hopkinsians are not far apart; the more closely they are united in opposing modern errors, the better. These sentiments were uttered more than thirty years ago. So far as they respect the importance of sustaining the Assembly's Board of Missions, they have now, if my information is correct, the hearty concurrence of large numbers of our New-School brethren who have coöperated with the American Home Missionary Society. This Society, the last year, employed 802 missionaries, and its receipts for the same period were well nigh $157,000, while the resources of the year, including the balance in the treasury, were $268,539. Verily, "a little one has become a thousand."

The *Board of Domestic Missions* of the General Assembly of the Presbyterian Church was formed in the year 1816, and was the outgrowth of a *Committee of Missions* appointed by the Assembly in the year 1790, and of the *Standing Committee of Missions* appointed in 1802. It consists of an Executive Committee who conduct its missionary operations, and a Board of Trustees for the conduct of its financial affairs; both appointed by the Assembly, and required to make their annual report to that body. It has struggled with difficulties, and more especially those which have arisen from the partiality of not a few of its ministers and churches, towards the American Home Missionary Society, and from the excision of so many of the churches in Western New York, and the consequent secession of our brethren of the New School. But the great Head of the Church has vouchsafed to it signal tokens of his favor. Though for many years a member of the Executive Committee, located as it is in Philadelphia, I have not been familiar with its business transactions, and have no information in relation to them but what is accessible to all from its Annual Report. From "the handful of corn on the top of the mountains," in the year 1790, it has reached the waving and rich harvest of 1865, "the fruit whereof already shakes like Lebanon, and they of the city are become like the grass of the earth."

To my mind this is a beautiful view of the progress of the missionary enterprise to the destitute of our own land. To say nothing of the noble enterprise of the Methodist Episcopal Church, and of our Baptist brethren, we see the whole family of Presbyterians and Congregationalists, a solid and bright phalanx, moving onward to the subjugation of the powers of darkness. Never was the cause of Domestic Missions more important than at the existing crisis of our national history, and never was the demand upon the churches and their ministry to come up to the help of the Lord against the mighty, more imperative. If we hesitate now, the floodgates of iniquity will let in upon us torrents of evil, that can neither be resisted nor diverted, and Rome with all her millions and her cruelty will triumph, either in the apostasy or the blood of our children. There is no hope for this nation but in the power of religious principle. We might as well blot the sun from the firmament, and look for light and heat from the world of nature, as to ignore the influence of Protestant Christianity, and look for national prosperity from popular institutions. Our Government must rest on the strong foundations of religion and morality, or we must be swept away with the nations that forget God. The character of our apostate race, the whole current of national experience, the teaching of the wisest statesmen, and even the brightest days of the most free and prosperous governments, both before and since the Christian era, demonstrate the inefficacy of all human laws apart from the sanction of a heaven-born religion. The great God is not shut up in eternal solitude, but is everywhere, surveying the nations of the earth, and by his own invisible and omnipotent hand adjusting the political machinery of the nations, and putting his fingers on the electrical wires that control the world. His government is not one of impulse or of policy, but of principle. His expostulations with the nations and their rulers come to us in the authoritative language, "Be wise now, therefore, O ye kings; be instructed, ye judges of the earth. Kiss *the Son* lest he be angry and ye perish from the way when his wrath is kindled but a little." His right hand is even now teaching him terrible things, opening the seals of the Book of Providence, which none could open but the Lion of the tribe of Judah; and with these astounding judgments, sending forth throughout the land the heralds of his great salvation, and with them his Holy Spirit, realizing his triumphs in the history of Missions. We have but to look at this heterogeneous population of thirty millions, in order to be convinced that the conflict with the powers of darkness has just begun. The seed of the serpent are not only bent on evil, but desperately bent upon it, because their time is short. The Devil well knows that the Son of God sets him at defiance, and means to tread him under his feet; and he is therefore coming in great wrath, if for no other end than to gratify his pride, his envy, his malice, and his revenge against the Son of God. But let the church of God take courage. The ascended Saviour, the first Domestic Missionary, the Captain of her salvation, has girded his sword upon his thigh, and is going forth conquering and to conquer. He did not look upon this

Western World with indifference when he directed our fathers, a choice vine, to the iron-bound coast of New England, and dispersed their descendants from the Atlantic to the Pacific; nor does he turn a deaf ear to their Macedonian cry, as it now echoes from woodland and prairie, "Come over and help us!" He has a deep interest in the purity and enlargement of his kingdom in this favored land; nor, with all my solicitude and apprehension, do I believe that he will suffer the boar out of the wood to waste the vineyard which his right hand has here planted, nor the wild beast of the field to devour it. I have no doubt he has high and comprehensive purposes to answer, by the combined efforts, prayers, and munificence of the American church; only let us not be recreant to our trust. Our pious ancestors would reprove us; our civil and religious liberties would reprove us; our enlargement and prosperity as a nation would reprove us; our tranquil Sabbaths would reprove us; and future generations will rise up to bear testimony against us, if, through our parsimony and supineness, the problem remain a doubtful one, whether, or not, these United States shall be a Christian nation. Daniel Webster once remarked, that "human liberty may yet perhaps be obliged to repose its principal hopes on the intelligence and vigor of the Saxon race." We live in an age when momentous problems are agitating the nations, and when our relation to them, as the most popular government, is not only deeply interesting to ourselves, but to the civilized world. Our cause and our name are already on the page of history, and I would fain hope that our children and their children may read them legibly inscribed in the annals of the combined and harmonious efforts of our evangelical churches, in sending the Gospel to the destitute.

CHAPTER XII.

FOREIGN MISSIONS.

THE enterprise of Foreign Missions, by the American churches, was commenced while I was pursuing my course of study with a view to the Gospel ministry. The institutions with which I have been associated in the great work, are the AMERICAN BOARD OF COMMISSIONERS FOR FOREIGN MISSIONS, and the BOARD OF FOREIGN MISSIONS *of the General Assembly of the Presbyterian Church.* With their origin and progress it has been my privilege to be somewhat familiar.

In the pleasant service of preparing the Memoirs of Samuel J. Mills, I became intimately acquainted with his early devotion to the missionary cause, and his interest and agency in the promotion of Foreign Missions. That gracious Saviour who has pity on the heathen, early set apart this young man as a missionary to the unevangelized world. Soon after his conversion, and when quite a youth, he once remarked to his father that "he could not conceive of any course of life in which to pass the rest of his days, that would prove so pleasant, as to go and communicate the Gospel of salvation to the poor heathen." It was a heart yearning over perishing millions, that led him to acquire an education for the Christian ministry. Nor did he ever lose sight of his darling object. With this view he became a member of Williamstown College, where some of those beloved men whom the American church has sent to heathen lands will not forget his instrumentality in their conversion and missionary spirit. Though one of the most modest of men, he once said to a Brother in the ministry of a kindred spirit, "Brother Cornelius, though you and I are very little beings, we must not rest satisfied until we have made our influence extend to the remotest corner of this ruined world." Hitherto, the attention of the American churches had been exclusively turned to Domestic Missions; but the time had come when they were to act a distinguished part in the conversion of six hundred millions, beyond the destitute in their own land.

While Mills was a member of College, he became acquainted with several young men of a kindred spirit, who formed an association, the object of which was to "effect in the persons of its members a mission to the heathen." I was a member of the Andover Seminary in the year 1809, and until the close of the winter session in 1810. Mills was there; Hall, Judson, Newell, and Nott were there. And there it was that the Foreign Missionary enterprise, originating in the minds of Mills and his youthful associates, began to assume some tangible form. In the month of June of the same year, the General Association of Massachusetts held its annual meeting at Bradford, a few miles only from Andover, and whose sessions I attended as a spectator. At that meeting Judson, Nott, Mills, and Newell laid their views on the subject of missions to the heathen in a respectful and earnest memorial before the Association, who, after a prayerful consideration, adopted the outlines of a plan for the spread of the Gospel in heathen lands, which resulted in the formation of the *American Board of Commissioners for Foreign Missions.*

The Rev. Dr. Worcester and my honored father were members of this Board, and on the adjournment of the Association, they rode together in the same chaise, setting their faces towards *Salem*. Such was their interest in the cause of Missions, and such the responsibility of their appointment, that they turned aside from the road into a grove, where they united in prayer for the Divine direction and blessing. On returning to the road they changed their route, and directed their course towards Boston, and to the residence of Jeremiah Evarts, Esq., in whose parlor the incipient arrangements for the future operations of the Board were made. On his return to Newburyport, my father, on the Sabbath morning, gave a brief narrative of the devotement of the young men, the measures adopted by the General Association, and the consultation of the gentlemen at Boston, and also gave notice that he would preach on the subject in the afternoon, and that after the sermon a collection would be taken up for missions to the heathen.

In the days of my youth, the town of Newburyport was an active, commercial village of great enterprise and wealth. My father's congregation had a large share of the wealth of the place, and a large share of its mercantile marine, composed of sea-captains and native mariners. At the close of the service, one of the old and rich sea-captains remarked, as he came out from the church, "the Doctor has given us a grand sermon, and he has preached all the jack-knives out of the sailors' pockets." On returning to my father's house, and laying out the collection on the parlor table, there was gold, and silver, and copper, and not a few jack-knives. The sailors had little else to give. There was an envelope, too, carefully folded, which was found to contain a *gold ring*, and the following lines:

> "I give, but oh, my gift's so small,
> 'Tis like not giving you at all;
> In future, if by God I'm blest,
> I'll pay him tenfold interest."

I know not now the amount of the collection, and only know that such men as William Bartlett, Moses Brown, John Pettingell, Thomas Thompson, Charles Coffin, John Pearson, and Captains Tappan and Holland, contributed something besides *jack-knives*. And this, the *first* collection in the United States for Foreign Missions, was taken up in the North Church, in Newburyport, where, by my father's hands, I was baptized. I have, for more considerations than these, been strongly attached to this Board of Commissioners. I look upon it as a noble and most effective institution, surpassed by none in the world, conducted with great wisdom and energy, embodying the popular element to a degree that should make our own denominational Boards ashamed of their inertness, and giving to the heathen world a band of missionaries and a richness of blessing that call for universal thanksgiving and praise.

The following communication to my father, from one of the first missionaries, never before published, refers to some of the discouragements of the noble pioneers in this enterprise:

"CALCUTTA, *July* 30, 1812.

"REV. AND DEAR SIR:

"I have this day taken leave of our Serampore friends, and put my baggage on board a ship which to-morrow sails for the Isle of France. Only one of us can be accommodated in this vessel, so that I go alone, while Brother Judson waits here the arrival of the Harmony.

"The reasons which determined me to adopt this measure are the following, viz., *the Government will not permit us to settle in any part of the Company's dominions.* We have been ordered in the most *peremptory* manner to return to America in the same vessel in which we came, or to depart *immediately* to some place out of the territories of the British and their allies. By the intercession of our friends, however, we have obtained permission to go to the Isle of France, which is not a part of the Company's territories, but is attached to the Crown of Great Britain.

"Being compelled to leave *British India*, the great and most promising field of missions, we were, in effect, excluded from the whole of this quarter of the world. China, and the Eastern peninsula of India (which comprehend the whole of this part of the world, not under the English), are both in such a state as forbids the attempt to establish a mission in either of those places at present. Mr. Morrison, who has for several years been endeavoring to gain a footing among the Chinese, may more properly be considered a prisoner in Macao than a missionary to China. He is not permitted to reside in Canton but six months in the year, and then in the capacity of Chinese interpreter to the East India Company. He writes that if the Chinese knew his object, they would no doubt put him to death. During that half of the year in which vessels are not allowed to trade in Canton, he is obliged to retire to Macao; and even then he is unsafe; he never preaches, nor speaks of Christianity.

"With respect to India beyond the Ganges, the prospect is but very little, if any better. The London Society have tried it and left it. The Baptist Missionaries have tried it, and all but one have quit the ground. Mr. F. Carey is still in Rangoon, but he is unwilling to continue there. He wrote but a short time since ' that he had no prospect of doing any good for many, many years to come, except in the business of translating the Scriptures, which he could do better in Bengal than there.'

"But the great difficulty in the way of a mission to Birmah and the adjacent countries, is the extreme danger to which the lives of missionaries in those parts are exposed. Females especially are subjected to continual fear of death, or what is worse than death. The Birmans have no law to restrain the indulgence of their passions; but lasciviousness is rather encouraged than discountenanced, and European females are sought after rather than the native females. Men may go without ceremony into the apartments of females and do what they please, and there is no redress. There are a multitude of civil officers in Birmah who have the power of life and death; and capital punishments, even that dreadful one of crucifixion, are inflicted for the most slight, and even imaginary offences. Drinking spirit, or whitewashing the walls of a house, is a capital crime. Doctor Carey told me that not long since the Commander-in-Chief of the Birman army ordered five hundred men to be buried alive, and was instantly obeyed. You will imagine that they had committed high treason against the Emperor; but they had committed no crime at all; they were buried alive merely because their General had a dislike to the officer who sent them to him!

"The information and advice which we have received from our Baptist brethren respecting Birmah have discouraged Brother Judson and me from prosecuting the Birman mission; and from the manner in which our brethren in the Harmony speak of it, we apprehend that they, too, have nearly given it up. We have received letters from them from the Isle of France. We learn from them that the Governor of that place is a friend to missionaries; that he will not only not oppose them, but will afford them his aid and protection. There are about twenty thousand souls on this Island, who are entirely destitute of religious instruction; and adjacent to this, and within six days' sail, is the large and populous Island of Madagascar, equal almost in extent to the United States, and containing from three to four millions of souls. The Governor of the Isle of France is particularly desirous that a mission should be sent to Madagascar, and has even applied to the London Society to turn their attention to that place. Dr. Vander Kemp was designated for this station, but we learn with regret that he has finished his work and gone to receive his reward. It is somewhat uncertain whether the other brethren will return to the Isle of France or not. They may be obliged to do it, but possibly they may obtain permission to go from here directly to Ceylon, but not very probable. I have written to Dr. Worcester by the Francis, and also by the present opportunity. Wish I had time to write more fully, but I must go on board to-day, and I have much to do.

"Dear sir, pray for us and comfort us by your letters. I hope soon to inform you that I am fixed somewhere, and have begun the glorious work which you have assigned us. It will ever be my most earnest wish to meet the approbation of the Board.

"I remain, Rev. and dear sir,
"Your most obed't and humble serv't,
"SAM'L NEWELL.
"Rev. Dr. SPRING."

I take pleasure in recording my poor testimony in favor of the American Board. At its first meeting but five persons were present, and at its second but seven. The receipts the first year were but a thousand dollars. Now its meetings are like the going up of the tribes of Jerusalem; and its annual receipts, four years ago, three hundred and fifty thousand dollars.

Then it had no missions, and it was not known that any heathen country would be opened to them. Now its "missions belt the globe, so that the sun does not set upon them." It is with joyous thankfulness that I now add, as these pages are going through the press, that at the annual meeting of the Board in Chicago, the present year, 1865, its receipts were $537,763; and its missionaries more than 1,000. I know of no missionary enterprise more worthy of confidence and generous patronage than this venerable Board. The encomium of the Earl of Shaftesbury, more than once referred to, is an encomium which the Board richly deserves. "I do not believe," says he, "that in the whole history of missions, I do not believe that in the history of diplomacy, or in the history of any negotiation between man and man, we can find anything to equal the wisdom, the soundness, and the pure evangelical truth of the body of men who constitute the American Mission. They are a marvellous combination of common sense and piety."

I was chosen one of its corporate members in 1824, and have attended as many of its anniversaries as I could, consistently with my obligations to our own Presbyterian Board. I have been censured for my seeming indifference to it; but I trust I shall not be censured for my humble efforts as a Presbyterian, to encourage the Presbyterian church in these United States to take part in the same blessed and glorious work.

The BOARD OF FOREIGN MISSIONS OF THE PRESBYTERIAN CHURCH was formally organized by the direction of the General Assembly in the city of Baltimore, in the month of October, 1837. Different Synods had previously enterprised this work, and with commendable zeal and success. The *Central Board of Foreign Missions*, comprising the Synods of North Carolina and Virginia, and which had hitherto coöperated with the American Board, not influenced by any feelings of unkindness or dissatisfaction towards that venerable institution, but from the conviction that it was their duty to aid and sustain the Presbyterian church in the effort she is making in her distinctive character to obey the last command of her ascended Lord, became auxiliary to the Board of the General Assembly. The Synod of Pittsburgh had for several years been devoted to the extension of the Gospel among the heathen, and themselves established a Board of Foreign Missions, under the title of the *Western Foreign Missionary Society*. It is due to that Synod to say, that they were deeply imbued with the missionary spirit, and that it was through their untiring influence the Assembly's Board was formed. The organization of that Board was a consummation towards which they had long looked with hope; and when it was effected, and the supreme judicatory of the church was prepared to adopt the Western Society as its own, that Society promptly transferred all its funds, missions, and papers, to the Assembly's Board. The Synod of Philadelphia also, which had been united with the Synod of Pittsburgh in sustaining the Western Society, concurred in the action of the Synod of Pittsburgh, and thus perfected the union of the hitherto local institutions. At their first meeting in Baltimore, the Board was organized by appointing the Rev.

Ashbel Green, Chairman, and the Revs. Nicholas Murray and John M. Krebs, Secretaries. It consists of forty ministers and forty laymen, who make their annual report to the Assembly, and of an Executive Committee of not more than nine members besides the Corresponding Secretary and Treasurer, whose conduct of all the affairs of the Missions is subject to the revision and control of the Board of Directors. The principal seat of its operations is the city of New York. At the time of the transfer of the Western Society, that Society had under their care four stations in Northern India, one in Smyrna, one in China, one in Western Africa, and two among the Western Indians. Their receipts for the year ending October, 1837, were forty thousand dollars, and the balance on hand and brought to the Assembly's treasury, was nearly six thousand dollars. The blessing of thousands ready to perish be on the Western Foreign Missionary Society, and on the head of the Rev. E. O. Swift, of Alleghany, and the Hon. Walter Lowry, through whose agency this delightful coöperation was effected!

The principles on which the Assembly's Board have conducted their affairs are in some respects different from those of the American Board. They are strictly *denominational*. Its aim is to send out Presbyterian missionaries, and to establish Presbyterian churches and presbyteries in heathen lands, that shall be, in their ecclesiastical relations, responsible to the General Assembly in the United States. Not that we claim to be exclusively *the true church*, but that we adopt the polity of the Presbyterian church as the wisest polity, and eminently so in heathen lands. We have confidence in the great Head of the Church, and look for his blessing on this arrangement, while we give the right hand of fellowship to Christian institutions of every name, and thank God for all their zeal, liberality, and success. It is also the law of the Board that *their expenses shall never exceed their income.* I cannot affirm that this policy is still adhered to; while I was a member of the Executive Committee, they never involved themselves in debt. I have no doubt the same wise policy is adopted under the present and effective administration. The Board and the Committee thus throw the responsibility of sustaining the missions upon the church, where it ought to rest. It is not to be denied that a rigorous adherence to this rule has occasionally embarrassed their operations. Men of promise have been detained at home, and new appointments have sometimes been withheld, for want of funds. Yet the work has gone forward; the liberality of affluent individuals, and the rigid economy of the executive officers, have supplied the deficiency, and the cry of the heathen has not been unheeded. The Board has now been in existence twenty-seven years. The receipts for the year ending April, 1864, were nearly $222,000, leaving a balance in the treasury of more than seven hundred dollars. Their missions are established among the Indian tribes of this continent; in South America; in Western Africa; in India; in China; in Japan; among the Chinese in California; in Papal Europe and among the Jews; employing the press as well as the pulpit, and establishing schools for the rising generation. The total of missionaries now occupying these different missions from our own Board is three hundred and eleven, and the receipts for the last year nearly two hundred and sixty-two thousand dollars.

As early as November, 1837, the Presbyterian Board commissioned two beloved missionaries to China, and in November, 1841, they sent forth an additional Brother to labor in that immense field. I find among the accumulated papers in my study a document entitled "An Address delivered in the Garden-street Church, Nov. 28, 1841, on the departure of a Missionary to China," by myself. I give place to it in these reminiscences as a curiosity, and as an index of the onward course of the cause of missions from that day to the present. Such an address, at the present advanced progress of the work, would be like a matured believer "going back to the first principles of the oracles of God." It is as follows :

"We have assembled this evening, not to set apart a beloved Brother to the office of preaching the Gospel—that service, as a Missionary Board, we have no authority to perform; it belongs to the church of God; and in the present instance has been recently done by the laying on of the hands of the Presbytery and by solemn prayer. We have met under the authority of the church, and by her appointment, to designate his particular field of labor; to give him his instructions as to the service he is to perform; to unite with him and with one another in commending him to the God of all grace; and to give him this affectionate and fraternal farewell of the churches in whose bosom he has been nurtured, and whose faces he will probably see no more until we all stand before the Son of Man.

"The cause of missions is of divine origin. At the first propagation of Christianity, all the ministers of the Gospel were missionaries. And, to a greater or less extent, many of them will continue to be so for ages to come. Natural science may refine human depravity, and civil government check, and in part control, it; but the whole history of the most enlightened, as well as the best governed communities, demonstrates the utter powerlessness of these influences without the Gospel. This great truth, so abundantly revealed in the Scriptures, and so clearly unfolded by the providence of God, is the apology of the Christian church for engaging in the great work of missions to the heathen.

"The missionary cause needs *impulse* rather than light; and the impulse of principles which *every* Christian believes, but which *no* Christian carries out in his life.

"One of the truths which we all have need to feel more deeply is, that *this benighted world is to be brought to the saving knowledge of Jesus Christ*. It is not surprising that men who do not believe this truth take no interest in sending the Gospel to the heathen. Nor ought it to surprise us that men who but *partially* believe it should be but *partially* devoted to this cause. Let a man lay it down as one of the established maxims of his life, and habitually regard it as one of the great principles of all his conduct, that THE WORLD IS TO BE CONVERTED TO CHRIST, and the aspirations and thoughts of his mind will preserve an habitual tendency towards this great object.

He may experience his sorrows and griefs; he may have seasons of darkness, and be the subject of not a few alternations of feeling; but like the magnetic needle amid the variations of the passing storm, the direction of his mind will remain fixed and unaltered. Multitudes scoff at the idea of the world's conversion to Christianity. Infidelity treats the prediction with contempt; Paganism points to her six hundred millions as yet untouched by the boasted prophecy; Mahometanism defies it; and Judaism smiles at the attempt as hopeless. And a languid, hesitating Christianity trembles before the magnitude and difficulties of the enterprise as a consummation more to be desired than confidently expected. But there is no more obvious truth revealed in the Word of God than this. It is not more certain that God is on the throne, than that the 'whole earth shall be filled with his glory.' It is not more certain that Jesus Christ is the atoning, interceding, and reigning Saviour, than that 'the heathen are given to him for his inheritance, and the uttermost parts of the earth for his possession.' It is not more certain that the Holy Spirit is the sanctifier, than that 'it shall come to pass in the latter days that God shall pour it out upon all flesh.' The unchanging God will never repent of these purposes of love. Doubt and uncertainty in the minds of men are of little avail when opposed to the truth of God. Hesitation and timidity have no place where 'the mouth of the Lord hath spoken it.' I would sooner believe that the whole Pagan world would be converted in a day, than question the veracity of God. This great fact, then, should be deeply impressed on our minds;

should enter into all our plans of individual effort; and should become one of the great principles of action to the Christian church. It would be impossible for us to give this truth its proper influence, and at the same time live in the neglect of those systematic and unwearied efforts which it necessarily involves. The reason why so many who do not deny this truth act as though it were not true, is that it has never sunk into their bosoms, and forms no part of their habitual thought and moral feeling. Every truly Christian mind is sincerely devoted to God and his cause; and it is impossible to account for the apathy of the church on the subject of missions to the heathen, except through a wavering belief of this important truth. Has this plain fact, my friends, no correlative obligations? May men believe it without feeling its power? This truth, like every other truth in the Bible, was revealed to be believed, loved, obeyed; to enlighten the understanding, penetrate the conscience, touch the heart, open the hands, move the prayers, and control the life. Give this truth its proper efficacy, and your interest in the cause of missions will not depend upon accidental and occasional excitement, but flow from those associations of thought that are congenial with the pursuits of every renewed heart, and find its aliment and its joy in all that affords enjoyment to a spiritual mind.

"Another truth, which, if I mistake not, we all have need to feel more deeply, is that *the success of the missionary enterprise depends upon the Spirit of God.* We believe this truth in relation to the success of the Gospel in Christian lands; and yet we all know the difference between having it recorded in our confession of faith and written upon the tablet of our hearts. A cold and lifeless recognition of this truth, by a minister of the Gospel in Christian lands, will produce a calm and tranquil acquiescence in an unprofitable ministry; a languid and spiritless exhibition of the Gospel; indifference to an interest in the prayers of God's people; and, if he is a pious man and is enabled to keep his eye steadily on the great objects of his ministry, will ultimately produce that deep depression and dejection of mind which not unfrequently tempt him to doubt if he has not mistaken his calling. The *church* that embodies this truth in her creed and gives it no place in her affections, instead of being fellow-workers together with God and his ministers, warmed by love and invigorated by faith, encouraged and impelled to watchfulness and prayer by hope, is like the ' salt that has lost its savour,' and ' savours not the things that be of God, but the things that be of men.' But where the ministry and the church *believe* and *feel* this truth, and *act under its influence, there* is God's own chosen instrumentality for the success of the Gospel. Where the divine prerogative in the conversion of men is understood and appreciated, the appropriate and subordinate duty of his people and his ministers never fails to be understood and appreciated. The whole history of the church shows no one fact more clearly than this, that men who deny the special influences of the Spirit in conversion, have themselves, notwithstanding all their reliance upon human effort, *done the least* for the conversion of men. There is so much in a humble, confiding, prayerful reliance on the faithfulness, condescension, and omnipotence of the Spirit of truth and grace as a motive to diligence, and a source of comfort; so much as the great antidote to discouragement and despondency; and as furnishing the only assurance of success, that it is among the last truths in the Bible that we can afford to dispense with in our efforts for the *conversion of the heathen.* Without this confidence in everlasting strength, we should have no hope for the nations that forget God. Upon all their land shall come up thorns and briars, 'until the Spirit be poured from on high.' Leviathan is not tamed by any other power. If the only reason we have to hope for the conversion of another sinner from the error of his ways in these Christian lands, is in the renovating influence of the Holy Spirit, where must be our hope for the heathen, if not in this renovating and sanctifying power? Six thousand years more will roll their tardy course over the nations, and the heathen world will remain just as it is now, if the Spirit of God do not make their wilderness a fruitful field. Asia will still remain in her idolatry and luxury; China, with three-and-thirty hundred millions, will still be sunk in bondage; and Africa will still be covered with impenetrable darkness. We know nothing of the future prospects of the heathen, except as God has promised to pour out upon them his Spirit. Here our minds rest with confidence. While we see and feel that the work transcends the power of man, we at the same time see and feel that with God all things are possible. The exceeding riches of his grace are to be unfolded to the heathen.

They *have* been unfolded, and they will be more and more, till a 'little one shall become a thousand, and a small one a strong nation.' We need, in the great work of sending the Gospel to the nations, to make much of this truth; to become imbued with it; and to have our habits of thinking and feeling, and all our plans and efforts, receive from it their coloring, and that humble and yet elevated character that glories not except in the cross of Christ and the power of his grace. *Well, well* may we repose on the truth that 'God's arm is not shortened that it cannot save, neither is his ear heavy that he cannot hear.' He has long borne with the heathen world, but the day of his forbearance is not past. He is not weary of these poor degraded nations; but is even now searching out among the 'many vessels of mercy afore prepared unto glory.' We address ourselves to this work, not because *we* are sufficient for it, but because our sufficiency is of God. We are cheered and animated in it, not only because we are weak and he is strong, but because our weakness is the occasion, the very signal, for the exercise of his promised power.

"There is another thought also with which it becomes us to be deeply imbued in conducting the work of missions to the heathen; and that is, *the importance of possessing the enlarged and public spirit of the Gospel*. Men are not their own property. Christian men *profess* not to belong to themselves. God is their owner, and has an inalienable right to all they have and are. 'None of us liveth to himself, and none of us dieth to himself; but whether we live, we live unto the Lord, and whether we die, we die unto the Lord; so that whether we live or die, we are the Lord's.' Elected by his grace, called into being by his power, redeemed by his Son, sanctified by his Spirit, adopted into his family, and dedicated by solemn covenant to him, the great end and aim of their existence is to 'glorify him in their bodies and spirits, which are his.' They belong not to the domestic circle; not to the individual church of which they are members; not merely to the nation of which they are citizens; but to Jesus Christ, to his kingdom, to his world. It has been said of distinguished statesmen and patriots that 'they lived for all ages, and all countries; they lived for future time.' Emphatically may this be said of every true Christian; nay, he lives less for time than for eternity. The living Christian is all for God; a living sacrifice which lives to God. This was eminently the enlarged and noble spirit of Jesus Christ, and that which elevated him so immeasurably above all the rest of that apostate race whose nature he condescended to assume. Portions of this exalted spirit have been possessed by all his true disciples; it was possessed by the apostles and early Christians, and by none more than by the great missionary to the heathen, whose grand object was that 'Jesus Christ might be magnified in his body, whether it be by life or death.'

"I do not know any way by which this spirit may be more successfully cultivated than by an enlightened and ardent attachment to the cause of missions. For what is the object of the missionary enterprise? It is to publish the Gospel of the Lord Jesus among all nations; it is to destroy every false system of religion from the face of the earth; it is to turn the whole world to the service and favor of the only true God. Now, this is the very object the church needs to elevate her spirit and character. Let the importance of this object be seen and felt; let it be truly desired and sought; and Christians will be raised above their own selfish interests, and will possess a vigor and elevation of purpose, a constancy and strength of effort, which receive their impress from the great object they are pursuing. In no other department of Christian labor is this elevated spirit so imperatively demanded. The magnitude of the enterprise demands it; its dangers and difficulties demand it; its encouragements and its successes demand it. There is little doubt but the noblest specimens of the Christian character will be elicited in the progress of the missionary cause. Those periods in the annals of the church during which she has been indifferent to the progress of the Gospel, and has made no aggressions upon the heathen world, will be found to be what the middle and dark ages were in the annals of the human intellect. Whatever enlarges the heart, elevates the intellectual character. It gives clear and comprehensive views, and furnishes the mind more richly than it otherwise would be furnished. The sublimity of a man's motives gives weight and sublimity to his thoughts, and his intellect becomes fertile, inventive, and bold, from the sacred and high direction it receives. The operations of the mind that lives and labors, and prays and suffers, for the universal diffusion of the Gospel, and the salvation of the world, cannot but rise above tameness and mediocrity.

There is an exhaustless energy in that generosity of intellect which seeks the highest interests of man. One reason why philosophy, poetry, genius, taste, learning, and commercial enterprise have so often failed to elevate the character of their votaries, is, that instead of being baptized with a heaven-born spirit, and laboring for the glory of God and the good of mankind, they have labored for wealth, admiration, and fame. There must be an inward power that moves the mind to stronger, more enduring, and more elevated motives; and a power that is found only in that communicative goodness which regards other interests more than its own. It is this *enlarged and public spirit* which the church needs, to elevate her character. And as she will find no such original impulse to this spirit as in the missionary enterprise, so to no cause is this spirit more indebted for its sustenance and growth. It is an enterprise which cannot live without great self-denial, great moral courage, great devotement, and great enlargement of heart. The thought should be ever present to our minds, that the cause of missions is not the cause of those who conduct it, but the cause of God and a perishing world. It becomes us more constantly to feel that it is a cause identified with ourselves; and that if this great work prospers, *we* prosper; and if this declines and wanes, we ourselves also are covered with a cloud.

"There is still another thought that has a strong and practical bearing upon the extended and permanent success of the missionary enterprise, and that is, *the importance of a growing and unsolicited liberality in the churches.* May it not be questioned if the churches have not fallen into an error on this subject, which, however unavoidable in the infancy of this undertaking, ought no longer to exist ? It is an error by no means chargeable upon the different Boards who have the direction of the undertaking, but one for which the churches themselves are alone responsible. The churches *give* to this great object only under the pressure of what are appropriately called *begging sermons.* The consequence is, that a large number of able and faithful ministers of the Gospel, themselves imbued with a missionary spirit, and who would otherwise occupy important posts of labor in heathen lands, are necessarily detained at home as *agents* in the churches, to solicit their bounty, at an expense of not far from twenty-five per cent. of what they collect, and the whole of which belongs of right to the heathen, because it is given and most sacredly devoted by the donors to that object. I hold this to be *morally wrong,* unless it be indispensably *necessary ;* and it cannot be indispensably necessary if the churches *do their duty.* Is it, then, one of the received axioms of Christianity that *the churches will not do their duty ?* My brethren, ' I speak this to our shame.' Has it come to this, after thirty years' experience in the work of missions, that from eighty to a hundred thousand dollars must be subtracted annually from funds devoted to the heathen, by different departments of the American church, simply for the purpose of inducing the churches to do what obviously ought to be done without any such effort and any such expenditure ? It is not more certain that the cause of missions to the heathen cannot be sustained without pecuniary means, than that it cannot be long and effectually sustained without a spirit of liberality that is founded in *principle*. The churches need more sober and scriptural views on the great duty of *giving* the Gospel to the heathen. There is sound judgment, there is an enlightened conscience, as well as transient zeal, in true Christian liberality; and where these are wanting, that steady and glowing fire of holy love which dissolves the heart, opens the hands, and melts the gold of avarice, will be gradually extinguished. The time has already come when men professing godliness will be suspicious of their faith and hope in Christ, if they bring not their annual free-will offering for this great cause to Him who, unthought of and unsolicited, 'though he was rich, for their sakes became poor, that they, through his poverty, might be rich.' Where is the Christian in this land who ever thought of making himself *poor* for Christ? Where is the Christian that ever fixed his eye on that precept, '*Sell* that ye have, and give alms?' Where is the Christian that remembers the words of the Lord Jesus, how he said, 'It is more blessed to give than to receive?' The Saviour did not reproach the poor widow who cast into the treasury 'even all her living.' I am persuaded we have all to learn much on this subject. We must look upon the duty of giving, for the purpose of sending the Gospel to the nations, as a permanent duty. We must do it habitually. We must do it as long as we live. We must no more neglect it than we would neglect the worship of God in our closets, in our families, or in his sanctuary.

Your agents will be found in your beneficiaries, in the poor heathen, in the wants of a dying world, in the solicitations of your divine Benefactor, when uttered from lips which he has appointed to proclaim to you *all* his word. Men must give more from love to God and regard to his authority. Their liberality, like their faith, must be full of Christ. 'Whatsoever ye do, in word, or in *deed*, do all in the name of the Lord Jesus, giving thanks to God and the Father by him.' Give, thankful for the opportunity and the privilege. There can be little doubt that the time is soon coming when the churches must be brought to the test of a system of *unsolicited* liberality, and if they cannot abide the test, they will see the cause of missions decline, and feel that the fearful responsibility is their own.

"I should do injustice to the place I am appointed to occupy this evening, if I did not, on behalf of the committee, say a few words in relation to that field of labor to which our beloved young brother is destined, and for which he is so soon to take his departure.

"The immense empire of China, containing more than one third of the entire population of our globe, seems to be just opening to the Gospel. The emigrant Chinese, amounting at least to one million, are already open to it. Little can be done to evangelize the world, so long as this vast empire is neglected. That devoted man, Robert Philip, of London, and the author of several works known to many of my audience, in a letter not long since addressed to the speaker, says, 'It is time, my dear Brother, to *strike the gong* for China.' This is now the watchword for the Christian army. There are now about fifteen missionary stations, and from twenty to thirty missionaries, in this extensive field from Protestant churches, while the church of Rome stands ready to occupy it by hundreds. The Board of Foreign Missions of the Presbyterian Church, whom we represent this evening, as early as November, 1837, gave, in this house, instructions to two missionaries destined to this field. Since that period they have sent three others, with their wives, to occupy the same ground. They have already begun to form an extended chain of missionary stations, each of which furnishes facilities for reaching far into the heart of the empire, both by preaching the Gospel, printing and distributing Bibles, tracts, and other religious books, and conducting schools for children and youth. However unrighteous the war, there is reason to believe that the recent successes of the British arms in China will be overruled, in the providence of God, for the rapid propagation of the Gospel in that empire. It would be no marvel if that mighty empire should be shaken by terrible convulsions, in order to accomplish the purposes of redeeming mercy. It is a dark land, and in its moral state, 'without form, and void, and darkness is upon the face of the deep.' If the divine predictions, under the effusion of the seventh vial, are not yet accomplished, great and important changes are ere long to take place in the nations of the East. The word has gone forth from heaven, ' Remove the diadem and take off the crown : this shall not be the same. Exalt him that is low, and abase him that is high. I will overturn, overturn, overturn, and it shall be no more, until he come whose right it is, and I will give it him.' In this interesting aspect of human affairs, it becomes the church of God in all lands to be in readiness to plant the standard of her ascended Prince. We solicit your sympathy and prayers, my Christian friends, in His name whose truth we propagate, and whose honor you regard as your ' chief joy.'

"It is in this interesting aspect of human affairs, that we commission you, my young brother, to go to that dark land. You cannot think too highly of your station, or of the importance of your object. You have anticipated trials, but you have no occasion for dismay. You will often be remembered at these altars; and when *we* forget you, you well know there is One who never forgets. You will have your reward, if not here. You may not live to see God's temple rise in beauty in that dark land; but go you, and be ready to build. And though you should live to see but a single idol-temple fall, and should yourself fall beneath its ruins, you will not have labored in vain. Go, my Brother, with a deep sense of your own guilt, and misery, and weakness, and with a firm reliance on Jesus Christ as your righteousness, strength, and joy, daily holding communion with God, and sincerely and cheerfully obeying his will, and he will never leave you—never forsake you. The God of peace be ever with you, dear Brother. Amen."

I wish I could say that the missionary cause is, or

ever has been, as near my heart as it should be. When Judson, and Newell, and Nott, my fellow-students at Andover, were so absorbed in it that they lost sight of every other vocation, it was no easy matter to resist its claims on my own heart. I thought of them. I once thought even of becoming a missionary to the heathen. But it was the dream of the moment. I had not piety enough to look at so self-denying a question. I had too many natural imperfections of character to " endure hardness " in such a vocation. I felt as if I should be no honor to the cause of missions. But when Hall and Newell sent that thrilling appeal from the heathen world to the American churches, I felt ashamed that I had not shared their toils and perils; I felt that I had mistaken my calling, and ought never to have been a minister of the Gospel. Conscience pressed me with the inquiry, Do you love the Saviour at all? If you love him, do you love him enough to obey his last command, and preach his Gospel to the heathen? How can you love him, if you care not for the sheep scattered upon the mountains in the cloudy and dark day? I was sad. I was afraid my selfish heart had deceived me. There is an omniscient eye, and a throne of judgment; I know it well. Oh! how will earthly interests disappear! and popular applause, and worldly comfort—what are they, when weighed in the balance of the last day? How sweet the thought, then, to have loved the Saviour enough to have borne his precious name to the perishing millions of the pagan world! And, blessed be God, there are those whom he calls to the home-work, even though they shrink from the discouragements of the foreign field. There are sheep and lambs to be sought out and fed in every clime. Yet the thought still recurs, why was I not a missionary to the heathen? And it brings down my lofty look. If here, at the close of a prolonged ministry, I feel condemned for spiritual barrenness at home, what would it have been, exposed to the trials and snares of heathen lands, where there is no Christian fellowship, no restraining and exhilarating means of grace, and so few sources of encouragement and comfort in those regions of drought and darkness?

CHAPTER XIII.

THE ANDOVER THEOLOGICAL SEMINARY.

THERE are *some facts* in relation to the Theological Seminary at Andover, with which I am probably quite as well acquainted as any other man. It is due to my father's character, and it is but a just tribute to historic verity, that they should be known and understood.

My father, from having for a series of years himself been a theological teacher, felt a deep interest in the more thorough training of young men for the Gospel ministry. From three to six or seven students in divinity were, from time to time, members of his family; and I well remember the hours daily set apart for their recitations. I could mention the names of many of them; and as I now look back upon their useful and honored course, I confess to the occasional doubt, whether or not the church has, on the whole, been the gainer by the more scholastic and erudite course pursued in our theological seminaries. My father felt the deficiency of the old system of instruction, and early set himself, with his characteristic decision, earnestness, and enthusiasm, to supply the defect by the introduction of a system that should combine the advantages of a literary course with a familiar acquaintance with the responsibilities of the pastoral office. In theology he was a thorough-going Hopkinsian; in church government he was not only a thorough-going Congregationalist, but a thorough-going Independent. I have often heard him say that the decision of *the church* is absolute and final; that while an ecclesiastical council might give their *advice* in cases of difficulty, it is not binding except as matter of advice; and that there is no appeal to any tribunal under heaven, from the decision of *the church*. In accordance with these views, he himself was a *member* of the church of which he was the pastor, and considered himself amenable to their judgment. In form of government and church discipline, he was a follower of the Independents in the time of Queen Elizabeth, and regarded every separate society of Christian worshippers as having sufficient power to perform everything relating to religious government within itself, and in no respect subject or accountable to other churches. He regarded himself as a "*jure divino*" Puritan. His favorite authors on church government were Robinson's Apology, the Savoy Confession, the writings of Dr. Glass, and the Cambridge Platform. The three volumes of Glass he presented to me, and they are now in my library.

It was with these views that his thoughts were directed to the formation of a theological seminary. His first wish was that it should be located at Franklin, Mass., within the bounds of the Mendon Association, and under the direction of Dr. Emmons, as professor of theology.

Failing in this, his next effort was that it should be established under the instruction of Rev. Leonard Woods. Mr. Woods was a young man of similar views with his own, and the pastor of a rural church in Newbury Newtown. But though overruled in this, he did not less earnestly pursue his darling object. In the year 1807, while I was a teacher in the Island of Bermuda, he gave me an account of his success, and of the liberality of two of his parishioners, William Bartlett and Moses Brown, and John Norris of Salem, who were associated with him in originating the institution. I am perfectly confident that, from the commencement, it was the design of these its founders that it should be established upon the principles of Hopkinsian theology. His letters to different gentlemen in New England and out of it, his expressed views to his family, and his unceasing efforts to establish the Board of Visitors on a basis that should secure this object, all indicate both his zeal and his fears. When it was ascertained that Andover would take the place of Franklin and Newbury, my father's thoughts were turned towards Mr. Woods as the first professor. That overruling and wise Providence, whose eye was upon this infant enterprise, had directed the trustees of Philips Academy to the same man. My father's choice was their choice. So that, much as he had been opposed to any coalition with the arrangements at Andover, his favorite design of an institution entirely distinct from Philips Academy was reluctantly abandoned. Mr. Woods, the candidate both of the Hopkinsians and the Calvinists, was known to belong to the Hopkinsian school, but had wisely commended himself to the old Calvinists, and had their entire confidence. It might gratify the friends of truth, were his letters to the Rev. Dr. Morse and the Rev. Dr. Pearson, on this subject, given to the world; we doubt not they would honor his charity and his ingenuousness. My father's course in this matter was straightforward. He would not, and he did not, abandon the effort of a distinct and separate institution, until he had first received from Mr. Woods the most unequivocal assurances, that if he were chosen the professor of theology, he would occupy the theological chair as a Hopkinsian. My father wrote him several letters, in order to bring out his views and determination, and, I have no doubt, though inaccessible to me, they are in the keeping of Dr. Woods' family. The following letters from him to my father, will rectify some misapprehensions in the minds of many good men, in relation to this whole matter. They came into my possession with my father's private papers, nor have I ever allowed them to go out of my hands, except into the hands of the Rev. Leonard Woods, the President of Bowdoin College.

"NEWBURY, *February* 13, 1808.
"REVEREND AND MOST BELOVED SIR:
"Your letter of the 7th inst. affected me, as it did Mrs. Woods. The covenant and coöperation which you propose, are altogether congenial with my feelings and views. And were I not afraid to trust my

heart, which has so often been deceitful and treacherous, I would say, '*it shall be a covenant of salt.*' May the grace of Christ help me to harmonize with you in promoting the '*consistency*' and '*the sacred influence of truth.*' I am satisfied that all the opposition which we have reason to expect, will arise either from the hostility of the unrenewed heart against God, or from the ignorance and prejudice of good men. How opposition, arising from each of these sources, should be treated, is a question of great importance, on which I have much need of instruction. I know not that there is *any difference* between us as to the *matter* of *divine truth*, or the *principles of theology*. And I don't feel now, as though I could decide on *one single point* differently from you, as far as my researches have gone. What I shall wish to be the great subject of our conversation and correspondence, is this: how can the evidence of the consistent theory of evangelical truth be most clearly, prudently, and effectually stated? How can objectors be most satisfactorily convinced? How can their arguments be exposed to the greatest advantage? What is the happy, the sacred art of leading young minds, from step to step, into the knowledge of the inspired system, and of furnishing them with the whole armor necessary for good soldiers? In short, how can we best subserve the interests of the ministry, and, through them, the interests of Zion? Oh! that we may be 'illuminees, in the proper, sublime sense.' I perfectly agree with you, that in becoming all things to all men, we are 'not to move one inch from our theoretic ground.' But what firmness and wisdom are needful! When I think of the host of prejudices in the public mind, and begin to ask, how shall I get along with them, and render myself acceptable to all sides, I am distracted and lost. But, blessed be God, there is ' a better way.' We have only *One* to please, and he infinitely and unchangeably wise and good. We have only one cause to promote, one Master to serve, one foundation to stand upon, and one set of weapons to use. If we mind our business, the elements will fight for us, and God will give success. What if there is a tremendous storm at present? I never knew a storm which did not cease after a while. The fiercest wind will abate, the thickest vapors be scattered, and we shall enjoy a serene sky. Even malice and envy will shoot all the darts in its quivers, or, finding shooting in vain, will desist.

"When you speak of my increasing forty years, and of your decreasing ten, you bring into view a most affecting subject—a subject so solemn and tender, that I cannot say anything suitable upon it. Oh! this transient shadow! How quickly will it be gone! And yet, how much have we to do! My leanness, my indolence, discourages me. I desire to relinquish every pursuit and enjoyment, to give up every plan and every interest, that will interfere with the great object, or, indeed, that will not promote it. Your hints about the Panoplist do not wound in the least degree. They will be duly attended to.

"Your remarks near the close are perfectly just—certainly as to me. I thought, last spring, I should be praying the rest of my life. But in the midst of our perplexities and cares, I have been too little with

Christ. I need fasting and prayer. Probably we have all too much neglected the throne of grace.

"To-day I spent several hours very pleasantly with Dr. Parish. He appears perfectly disposed to be friendly, and to coöperate with us. But, alas! the unhappiness between him and Dr. M. is great. I lament it, especially at this period. I long to hear whether Dr. Pearson has been along, and how the business progresses.

"Accept, with Mrs. Spring, our united love and esteem, and believe me yours in the most pleasing and indissoluble bonds,

"Leonard Woods.

"Reverend Dr. Spring."

"Newbury, *May* 1, Sabbath evening.

"Beloved Sir:

"I have been absent on a journey to Dover and Portsmouth most of the time since I saw you, which has prevented my design of writing to you before now. But let me say, dear sir, I have never written to you with such feelings as now agitate my breast. Present circumstances lead my thoughts to past scenes. I remember the time when I first entered your house, and embraced your friendly hand. I call to mind the concern you have manifested for my comfort and usefulness. How many instances of your paternal and brotherly kindness have I experienced. What aid have I derived from you respecting the knowledge of the truth, and the duties of the ministry! I have enjoyed no such friendship with any minister. To no other have I felt myself at liberty to open my heart with such freedom. In no other have I found that which invited such confidence. With no other have I tasted to so high a degree the pleasures of mutual love and tenderness. One of the best comforts in my present situation, and what I have prized as one of my greatest advantages, has been the growing intercourse which I have been permitted to have with you. I say these things from the fulness of my heart. Yea, this is not half of what my heart, full of dutiful, grateful feelings, prompts me to say. I have recorded your friendship as one of the most precious blessings of Divine Providence. In this state of mind, how affecting is your letter, just received! I am ready to weep, when I read what you say in the postscript, 'You and I are unhappy now, not to harmonize.' Beloved sir, though I have often heard, often read, and often affirmed myself, that friendship is precarious and changeable, I have indulged, and still indulge, the pleasing hope that our friendship will never be interrupted. I am confident it will not, unless my conduct shall be such as justly to forfeit your esteem. Whether my conduct in the affair now before us be such, I know not. If it be so, my present feeling is, that I should have no hard thoughts of you, should you entirely cast me off.

"*Monday.* But to come to the point in hand. I assure you, dear sir, I *never felt more strongly attached to Hopkinsianism than now. I am more and more convinced that this system of religious sentiment and administration is the nearest of all existing systems to the apostolic standard;* and in the hands of wisdom and prudence, the most likely by far to do good to the souls of men. I have *embraced the system with deliberation*, and *in full view of all the evils to which Hopkinsians are liable.* I knew what I was doing as to my popularity. I counted the cost. And when, from time to time, I learn the effects, I repent not of my choice. Now, surely, with these views and impressions respecting the importance of Hopkinsian theology, I could not engage in any undertaking which, in my apprehension, is unfriendly to it. Nay, I think I should not engage, if I did not expect *ultimately* to subserve the interests of Hopkinsian truth. I say *ultimately*, for such is the nature of the undertaking, that I cannot do it *professedly.* Yet in this I see no dishonesty, no underhand dealing, no duplicity. For we are not obliged, whenever we begin to write or to speak, to declare ourselves Hopkinsians. I appeal to your conduct. In your late address to the public, you did not think it prudent to take the signature of *Hopkins*, but of *Calvinus*, although you glory in the name of Hopkinsian, rather than Calvinist. Although you meant ultimately to subserve the Hopkinsian cause, you said little or nothing which brought into view the distinguishing features of Hopkinsianism. So, in your preaching in my desk, in consequence of peculiar circumstances, you did not, for a time, deliver those sermons which display Hopkinsian peculiarities in the clearest light; certainly not those peculiarities against which the prejudices of the people were the most inveterate. The good effect of your measures is now apparent in the influence you have acquired over the minds of my people. You have most successfully promoted the cause which is so dear to your heart. My aim is to imitate your example. I mean to do all I can to promote the cause of gospel truth in its most distinguishing form. I mean to advocate the religion *in substance* which distinguished New England; which religion you have so highly applauded in your late publications. If this cannot be done decidedly and in earnest, I retreat.

"I am, reverend and dear sir, yours in the warmest attachment,

"LEONARD WOODS."

The last page of this letter has reference to another and irrelevant matter. Justice to Dr. Woods also demands the insertion of the following, dated

"ANDOVER, *July* 30, 1816.

"REVEREND AND BELOVED SIR:

"I always sit down to write to you with respectful and tender emotions. I should charge myself with strange insensibility, had I not such emotions now. We do, indeed, sympathize with you in this scene of affliction. Your beloved daughter was dear *to us*. We have long known her; and have felt how much her amiable, interesting character could attract the heart. We have known her dutiful affection to her parents, and the strong hold she has had upon your feelings. Oh! it is a painful stroke. The God of all grace and comfort give you and Mrs. Spring all needed support. You have reason to trust in God; and you will remember what tranquillity of mind he has heretofore granted you both, in time of trouble. You will think, too, with lively sensations, how his grace has abounded, as we hope, in the sanctification of some of your children, and how all-sufficient that same grace is for the salvation of all the rest. Be assured, dear mourning parents, that there are many hearts here, as well as elsewhere, that will not cease to feel tender condolence towards you, and to beseech God to afford you the best of all blessings, *his gracious presence*.

"I am glad you have opened your heart on the subject of *our church*, because it gives me opportunity to open mine. I am sure, if you knew all that is in my heart, you would not feel anything but candor and tenderness towards me. I never differ from you without the pain of cutting off a right hand. The struggle of my mind, in the one or two instances in which I have felt it my duty to act in opposition to you, has come the nearest to breaking me down, of any event which ever took place. From some men with whom I have been brought into connection, I look for difficulty. I expect hard treatment; and I can bear it. But I can't bear it from you, because I know the warm affection of your heart. From the first moment that I saw you, you have been a father to me. You have cherished me with paternal fondness, and have, more than any other man, or all others, been the instrument of bringing me to this elevated and important station—a station whose duties I greatly love, though I tremble at its responsibility. I go back now, in my thoughts, to scenes through which we have together passed, and my heart grows warm within me.

"But I must check my wanderings. I will, however, say, that one of my best supports and encouragements in my arduous station has been, and is, that I have enjoyed your friendship and your approbation. Whatever I do that gratifies you, is doubly pleasant to me. I say this, respecting myself and my colleagues. There is no man on earth whom we are so desirous to please, and so unwilling to offend. When you come here and mix with us in the Seminary, and feel at home, and show yourself well satisfied with the state of the institution, we are elated. Your *satisfaction* is our *joy*. If in anything we differ from you, we do it with a full confidence in the integrity of your heart, and so without any withdrawment of affection. There ought to be no disunion or strife between you and us. It would be unnatural, unnecessary, and hurtful to the last degree. It must not be. It cannot be. If you knew our views on the subject of the church, I am certain your feelings would be at rest. But you have some misapprehension, or wrong impression, which must be corrected. It is with this view I now write. And I do think, if you take into calm and sober consideration the following things, you will be convinced that no just charge can be brought against us in this affair.

" 1. The constitution and the associate statutes, the latter of which you had an agency in forming, and both of which trustees and visitors are most solemnly bound to observe and govern themselves by, leave the particular form of the church in the Seminary undefined. But they say what looks towards the subject in several articles. See Constitution, Art. II.; Asso. Stat., Arts. II. and XXIII. In these statutes it is expressly provided that the professors shall be Congregational or Presbyterian, and the students likewise. And you have proved that you understood them in their obvious sense, and meant to proceed accordingly, by thinking of Dr. Romeyn, Dr. Miller, etc., for a professor of sacred rhetoric, and finally fixing upon Dr. Griffin. You never made any objection to them because they were Presbyterians. On the contrary, you rather chose, by selecting a Presbyterian professor, to give a more enlarged character, and more extended influence, to the Seminary. You always showed the same feeling as to students. And it never entered into my heart, till lately, that you cared anything about the distinction, or meant ever to contend for one denomination, or oppose the other, certainly so far as the Seminary is concerned. Now I say, according to all these statutes, and these proceedings, we never expected to be pressed on this subject. We did suppose ourselves perfectly at liberty, according to the unalterable principles of the constitution and statutes, to be either Presbyterians or Congregationalists. We did suppose that you, and everybody else, connected with the Seminary, would be willing we should be at liberty. And now, if we had all felt it to be our duty to join ourselves with a Presbytery, no man would have any right, as we supposed, to call us to account. As professors, we are bound by the statutes. So are both Boards. If we are to be blamed by either of the Boards, we do expect it will be for violating some of the statutes. We have always considered the government of the Seminary to be the government of laws. The course, we have thought, was plainly marked out for us and for others. If a professor were to become an Episcopalian or a Baptist, he must, of course, be put out of office. But a Congregationalist or Presbyterian he *may* be. You have said it, and all the founders have said it, and you can't unsay it, to the end of the world, that a professor here is to be 'a Congregationalist or a Presbyterian.' But,

"2. *We have not become Presbyterians.* At the first consultation with the committee of the trustees, we gave our united voice in favor of a Congregational church, on the general principles of the Cambridge platform. At the same time, we gave it distinctly as our judgment, that, considering the statutes, and the state of our country, it ought not to be so rigidly and exclusively Congregational as to be at *war* with Presbyterianism. Indeed, we have all along been convinced that the democracy, which has sometimes cleaved to Congregationalism, is hostile to the interests of the church. But, from the nature of the Seminary, and the express provisions of the statutes, whatever be the case elsewhere, we have thought that the church *here* ought to be formed upon so liberal a basis, that Presbyterian students, as well as professors, might, without difficulty, be connected with it. Else there will be a schism produced within the Seminary in direct contradiction to the statutes.

"Still, I say, we have been uniformly in favor of a Congregational church, and when Dr. Pearson's feelings were strongest on the subject of a minister's membership in his church, we were desirous to waive that subject wholly, and proceed to form the church upon Congregational principles.

"3. When Dr. Pearson handed us the report of the committee, leaving out certain exceptionable things in the platform, and acknowledging the rest as our general basis, we were satisfied; and Dr. Pearson told us *you* were satisfied. All we have done is to insist upon the principle, which is practically acknowledged by all our churches, that the final censure of a minister ought to proceed from an ecclesiastical council, not from his church. We did suppose all difficulties were removed, and that all concerned were prepared to proceed, with love and unity, to form a church.

"If you consider these things, you will, I think, perceive that there is no ground of complaint against us for the part we have acted in this affair.

"But I cannot stop here. I do think we have just cause of complaint against others, and, I am grieved to say it, against Dr. Spring. The subjects of complaint are these:

"1. You have brought charges against us contrary to *fact*. You say, we oppose the formation of a church in the Seminary on Congregational principles. This we never have done, and are not disposed to do.

"2. You charge us with acting from motives which we abhor. Your hints imply that we have 'the hearts of aspiring clergymen;'—that we are to be classed, not only with 'Presbyterians and Episcopalians,' but with 'Papists, and *others of the same elevated spirit;*' that we are looking for 'clerical superiority,' and that we wish to be exempted from discipline, etc. I will say nothing in reply to these things, except what may be necessary to correct a mistake as to matter-of-fact; viz., that we have, from the beginning, wished ministers to be under the inspection and discipline of an ecclesiastical council, purely because that inspection would be more faithful, and that discipline more just and effectual, than that of a single church. We wish ministers to be under stricter discipline, and more impartial discipline, and more effectual discipline, than is common; while you charge us with wishing to free them from discipline, and give them 'clerical superiority,' 'the benefit of the clergy,' etc. If these charges had come from the laxest men of the Unitarian school, we should have regarded them as the idle wind. But from *you* we did not look for them. From *you* they cannot come without *wounding*.

"3. You attempt to compel us to act, not only against our consciences, but against the statutes. We consider the statutes as containing the terms of a public contract between you and us. That contract says we may be 'Congregationalists or Presbyterians.' You say we must be not only Congregationalists in general, but Congregationalists of the strictest order; that is, Independents, and in such a sense as to be absolutely exclusive of Presbyterians; *ex*clusive of Presbyterians when the statutes are *in*clusive of Presbyterians. I say, therefore, that you urge us against the letter and spirit of the statutes, even if we were Presbyterians; much more now, when we are in favor of a milder form of Congregationalism.

"4. You press us to a measure which would be intolerable to the feelings of most of our students,— which would excite a prejudice against the Seminary generally through the United States, and thus turn the current against it, and do much to diminish its influence and usefulness.

"These, sir, are the complaints which we think we have a right to make. But we wish not to urge them. We would rather forget them. We shall naturally forget them. It is easy for us to efface the impression they have made, and think of them no more. This momentary excitement will pass away. You will be satisfied that we mean well, and that you have nothing to fear from the views we entertain on church matters. And we shall be satisfied that you never intended to injure us or the Seminary, but are indeed and in truth our best friend and the best friend of the institution. You will coöperate with us in this great work; you will excite us to diligence and fidelity; and your approbation will be among our best earthly comforts. We *must* have a near and confidential friendship with you while life lasts.

"I have now said all that is in my heart, though briefly. I have only to make one request. Remember that our situation is responsible and trying to a high degree. All the force of opposition against orthodoxy, from Unitarians, Arminians, and semi-Calvinists, is directed against us. We have perpetual trials and difficulties with some of those who are the legal guardians of the Seminary. We have every day weighty and difficult duties to perform. We are constantly borne down, and ready to be exhausted; and must wear out very fast. Do think of us kindly; forgive us when we have done wrong; rebuke us when we go astray; love us, and visit us, and pray for us. And may the God of Abraham bless you and yours evermore.

"Yours, with dutiful affection and esteem,
"LEONARD WOODS.
"Rev. Dr. SPRING."

On the subject of the last letter, Dr. Woods certainly has the advantage of my father; while it must be obvious that in regard to the subject of *theology*, he found no small embarrassment in pursuing a course that conciliated the Hopkinsians and the Calvinists. This was his object, and it was adroitly and successfully pursued. That his views sustained a change in favor of the Calvinism of the Westminster Assembly, the later classes under his care can testify; but that he differed from my father, as has been publicly affirmed, when he was appointed to his professorship, is a misconception and misstatement.

The coalition between the Calvinists and the Hopkinsians of New England was, by many persons, regarded as of bright augury to the church of God. Dr. Joseph Emerson, a disciple of Dr. Emmons, in a treatise upon the Millennium, regards it as one of the auspicious preliminaries of that promised day. Whether the character of the Andover Seminary has retained its integrity or not, I have not sufficient means and opportunity of forming a judgment. My father took a deep interest in the appointment of Dr. Griffin, Mr. Stuart, and Dr. Porter, to their respective chairs; but he was deeply wounded at the appointment of Dr

Murdock. He frankly told Dr. Woods and Mr. Bartlett, that he could not conscientiously, and never would, consent to it. To the objection, that if he did not consent to it, the donation for the support of the professorship would be lost, he replied, "The money had better sink in the bottom of the sea, than the wrong man go there." On the nomination of Mr. Stuart as the Professor of Sacred Literature, my father visited New Haven with the view of satisfying his own mind as to the qualifications of the candidate, and influencing his suffrage in the matter. He called on President Dwight, among others, for his opinion of Mr. Stuart. "He is the very man for the place," said Dr. Dwight, "but we cannot spare him." "Sir," replied my father, "we do not want a man *that can be spared.*" Mr. Stuart received the appointment, and his name will long be honored as the most distinguished pioneer in the cause of sacred literature in the American churches.

It would be too much to say that my father had no anxiety in relation to Andover, during the last months of his life. At my last interview with my mother, in March, 1819, she informed me that he had great fears as to the steadfastness of Andover in the faith; and that about three weeks before his death, he wrote to the Professors, expressing his fears. He told them that he expected soon to die, and felt that he must faithfully give them this his dying admonition. He was very much displeased with a sermon of Dr. Woods', from the text, "He had respect unto the recompense of the reward." It was the last sermon my father heard from him, and was especially displeasing because it elicited the commendation of some in the congregation who had uniformly expressed marked dislike to what they deemed my father's rigid advocacy of a disinterested piety. There were a few among his hearers who, notwithstanding all their affection and reverence for the man and the minister, could not disguise their partiality for a more lax and soothing theology. He could not look with complacency upon any that countenanced, even though it were through misconstruction, their opposition to the truth. His interview with Dr. Woods, a few days before his death, was most solemn and affecting.

CHAPTER XIV.

AMERICAN BIBLE SOCIETY.

It is a melancholy yet a marvellous fact, that since the art of printing there should have been such a scarcity of Bibles. We cannot account for it on any other principle, than that "light is come into the world, but men have loved darkness rather than light." The diffusion of truth naturally arises from the love of truth. The noble men of the 17th century gave no greater evidence of their high-born Christianity than their service and their sufferings to disseminate the word of God.

The great reformation from Popery, and the revivals of religion in these United States, were distinguished, not more for the organization of the great missionary enterprise, than for associations for the circulation of the Holy Scriptures.

Old England has no brighter jewel in her crown than the British and Foreign Bible Society; nor did Lord Teignmouth and the Bishop of London ever wreathe a fairer laurel for their own or their country's honor, than when they identified them with the Bible cause.

It has more than once been affirmed that the United States have never, as a nation, publicly recognized the supremacy of the God of heaven. But it should be remembered that, as early as the year 1777, the want of Bibles was the subject of solemn discussion in Congress, and that body appointed a committee to advise as to the expediency of publishing an edition of thirty thousand copies of the sacred Scriptures.

This Government rests upon Protestant Christianity. Its corner-stone is the Bible: its strength and its hopes lie in disseminating the knowledge of God among all classes. This it has done; this it is doing; and this, under God, it will do, through those associated efforts which are the peculiarity and glory of the age.

The American Bible Society was formed by a convention of various local societies, held in the city of New York, May 11, 1816. It was my privilege, as a delegate from the New York Bible Society, to be a member of that convention; and it has been my privilege, as one of the directors, and associated with one of its standing committees, to attend the meetings of its Board of Managers with punctuality, to acquaint myself with all the important measures it has adopted, and to aid its progress.

My honored father was present as a representative of the Merrimack Bible Society: it was the first and the last time that the father and the son occupied the floor of the same deliberative body. The men who formed that convention, and who were first appointed the officers and managers of that society, were among the most reverend and revered in the church, and the most honorable and honored in the state.

There are three epochs in the history of this society which cannot, in historic verity, be severed from these personal reminiscences. The first is distinguished by the memorable *Baptist Discussion* in relation to the translation of the Scriptures into foreign languages. In regard to our English Bible, the constitution declares that "the only copies in the English language to be circulated by the society, shall be of the version now in common use." The Board of *Managers* consists of thirty-six laymen; but every *minister of the Gospel*, who is a member of the society, is entitled "to meet and vote with the Board of Managers," and is possessed of the same power as a manager himself.

The Board of Managers and Directors, therefore, comprised all religious denominations, including the *Baptists*, who for a series of years cordially coöperated in the extensive circulation of the English Bible, though instead of *translating* the Greek word *BAΠTIZΩ*, they *transferred* it, and gave the English form of *baptize*. In the year 1835, application was made to the society for aid in printing the Scriptures in the Bengalee language. It had previously been made to the British and Foreign Bible Society, and had been rejected, on the ground that the Bengalee translation had rendered the Greek word βαπτίζω *immerse*, instead of *baptize*, and the cognates of this word to correspond with this interpretation. The British and Foreign Bible Society recommended the applicants to the American Society, intimating that the latter institution "had not hesitated in times past to make appropriations for translations of this character." In this way, the fact first came to the knowledge of the Board that they had made any such appropriations. Thus brought to the notice of the Board, the matter was referred to the *Committee on Distribution*, who on the 3d of September, 1835, reported that "they do not deem it expedient to recommend an appropriation to aid in printing the Bengalee Scriptures until the Board settle a principle in relation to the translation of the Greek word βαπτίζω.

This report was referred to a special committee consisting of *one* from each religious denomination in the Board, to consider and report on the subject. On the 1st of October, 1835, the committee made a report recommending the adoption of certain resolutions, and the Rev. Spencer H. Cone, of the Baptist persuasion, submitted a minority report; and the consideration of both reports was postponed until the next meeting. On the 5th of the following November, both resolutions were freely discussed, and during the discussion, a resolution transmitted to the Rev. Dr. Milnor, from President Wayland, of Brown University, together with a series of resolutions offered by Dr. Milnor, as a substitute for those presented by the majority of the committee, were referred back to the same committee to consider and report at the next meeting.

On the 19th of the same month, this committee withdrew their former report on the particular case, and presented for the consideration of the Board the following *general principles:*

Adverting to the fact that the constitution of the society was evidently designed to harmonize all religious denominations, and in conformity with its obvious spirit, they recommend the adoption of the following resolution as the rule of their conduct in making appropriations for the circulation of the Scriptures in foreign tongues:

"Resolved, That in appropriating money for the translating, printing, and distribution of the sacred Scriptures in foreign languages, the managers feel at liberty to encourage only such versions as conform, in the principles of their translation, to the common English version,—at least so far that all religious denominations represented in this society can consistently use and circulate them in their several schools and communities;" and that Missionary Boards be informed that "the versions they propose to circulate," receiving aid from this society, must be executed in accordance with the above principles.

At the same meeting, the Rev. Dr. Cone presented his counter report, alleging that the "Baptist Board of Foreign Missions have not been under the impression that the American Bible Society was organized upon the neutral principle that $\beta\alpha\pi\tau\iota\zeta\omega$ and its cognates are never to be translated, but always transferred in all versions of the Scriptures patronized by them;" that had it been so understood and acted upon, the Baptists would not have solicited aid for translations made by their missionaries; that as "liberal bequests and donations had been made by Baptists, and made in the full confidence that the society could constitutionally assist their own denomination," he proposed that the society appropriate and pay $——— to the Baptist General Convention for missionary purposes, and to aid them in the work of supplying the perishing millions of the East with the sacred Scriptures.

At a meeting on the 3d of December, the first resolution of the Committee came up for consideration, when it was laid upon the table, in order to consider a proposition made by Hon. Mr. Jay; when, after some discussion, the whole subject was laid upon the table. On the 4th of February, 1836, the subject came up again, and was postponed to a special meeting appointed for this particular object. At the special meeting, on the 17th of February, the whole subject was fully discussed, and after full consideration, the preamble and resolutions contained in the report of the Committee, presented November 19th, 1835, were adopted, *thirty* voting in their favor, and *fourteen* against them. On the 3d of March, the Rev. Dr. Maclay gave notice of a "remonstrance of the Baptist members of the Board" in this matter. On the 7th of April, Dr. Cone presented a Protest against the proceedings of the Board, and on the 21st of the same month, the Board decided that "it was inexpedient to receive any protest from a minority on a question which had been decided by yeas and nays recorded." On the 5th of May, 1836, a communication was received from the Secretary of the Baptist General Convention for Foreign Missions, declining the offer of a grant of $5,000, to aid in printing the Burman Scriptures, as they could not conform to the principles of translation required by the Board; and on the 19th of May, a letter was received from the Rev. Dr. Cone, resigning his office as one of the Society's Corresponding Secretaries, and his resignation was accepted.

I was no listless auditor to these discussions, and no idle spectator. The Christian public throughout the land were awake to them, and were prepared for the result. The line was drawn, and henceforth the Baptists could no longer unite with the church of God even in the circulation of his Word, " without note or comment." They went out from us and formed a Baptist Society, more anxious, I fear, to make Baptists than to make Christians.

Looking back now, through the vista of thirty years, I am thankful that the American Bible Society stood firm, and only wonder at the folly of my Baptist brethren. I cannot deny myself the pleasure of expressing the high gratification afforded me by the course of the Committee to whom the subject was referred. I was not more instructed and confirmed by the luminous and unanswerable train of argument pursued in this discussion, than delighted by the inward prompting which constrained my brethren and my betters to take the bold and manly stand they took against the enormous assumptions of that most sectarian of all sects. The more I think of it, the less calmly do I look on and see a body of professedly Christian men perpetrating the most grievous outrage upon the principle which enters into the very life of the church of Christ. I cannot see that the pretensions of Papacy are a whit more abhorrent to the spirit and genius of the Gospel, or more offensive to its Divine Author, than those of the modern Baptists. The basis on which they build themselves as a sect is utterly at war with that charity, sympathy, fellowship, and coöperation which are the native product of the spirit of grace and the glory of Christ's religion. Their claims involve a ruthless rending of the Lord's spiritual body, and a fulminating exclusion from the pale of the church of those whom Christ has received, whom he loves, whom he sanctifies, whom he crowns in heaven. What fouler schism is on the record of the past, than the Baptist secession from the national Bible Society?

I feel that it is due to the offenders themselves, by the law of Christ, to rebuke strongly their sin. The question of the *subjects* and *mode* of baptism is quite subordinate to that of the *moral bearings and results* of the system.

Upon this the controversy hitherto has never sufficiently hinged itself. A vaulting fire may break down their ramparts of prepositions, their *intos* and their *out ofs;* but the citadel of their *uncharitableness* and their *injuries* and *wrongs* to the members of Christ's body, must be stormed and consumed with a fire of holy zeal which " many waters " cannot quench.

The Baptist position is one that in effect forbids any other church in Christendom to celebrate the Lord's Supper. For certainly, if, while I am admitted to be a Christian, I am not at liberty to partake of the sacrament in a Baptist church, it is impossible I can be at liberty to go into a Presbyterian church and do it.

Here, then, we behold the issue. Christ says to me, and my conscience and heart respond, " Do this in remembrance of me." My Baptist teacher says, " Do it at your peril." Can it be! You will not give a Bible to the perishing that does not say, "Go immerse all nations." Shall not these Baptist brethren finally be ashamed into the avowal of their altar-building tribes at the banks of the Jordan—"God forbid that we should rebel against the Lord, to build an altar for burnt offerings, for meat offerings, or for sacrifices, beside the altar of the Lord our God which is before the tabernacle."

The next subject which agitated and embarrassed the managers and directors of the society, relates to THE OPENING OF *its anniversaries with prayer*.

It seems unaccountable to us that such a question should be attended with any embarrassment. But when it is considered that the society comprised many persons of the Episcopal denomination, and some of Friends' Meeting, it is not difficult to account for that embarrassment. Outside of the Board, the subject was fully discussed, and it was concluded that, rather than wound the feelings of the Episcopalians and Quakers, and as a matter of compromise, the monthly meetings of the Board, and the annual meetings of the society, should be opened simply by *reading a chapter from the Bible*. This was the practice for thirty-four years, submitted to for the sake of peace, rather than cheerfully acquiesced in.

At the anniversary of the society in May, 1850, the following resolution was introduced by the Rev. Dr. Carrol, of Newburgh, and referred to the Board. "Resolved, That it be a by-law of the society, that, in addition to the reading of the Scriptures, the meetings of the society shall be opened with prayer." On the 6th of June the resolution was taken up by the board, when, " on motion of the Rev. Dr. Spring, it was referred to a select committee of *seven*, representing the different denominational interests in the Board, to be appointed by the Chair, and announced at the next meeting of the Board." The select committee appointed at the next meeting was increased to *nine*, and consisted of the Rev. Dr. Spring, Rev. R. S. Storrs, jr., Rev. Dr. Vermilye, Rev. Dr. Stone, Rev. Dr. Peck, Rev. A. D. Smith, and Rev. D. Bigler. On the 7th of the following November, the chairman of this committee made the following report: " The committee to whom was referred the subject of religious exercises at the opening of the society's meetings, beg leave to submit, as their report, the following statement and resolutions. When the American Bible Society was formed, in 1816, the union of Christians of different names, for promoting a common religious object, was a novel event. Fear was entertained by many as to the effect of such a measure, and care was observed to exclude from their doings, as far as possible, all denominational features. Hence prayer was omitted at their meetings, save as it was uttered in the portion of the Scriptures which was read. Since the time of the above organization, and by its harmonious action, a wider charity has been diffused. Other associations have been formed, for the circulation of evangelical tracts, for promoting Sunday schools, and the welfare of seamen, and for the advancement of temperance, and other useful objects. The latter associations, although composed essentially of the same mixed elements as the Bible Society, have, by mutual consent, opened their meetings with prayer, and apparently with satisfaction to all. It is found, too, that the local Bible associations which once read the Scriptures merely at their meetings, now have generally the additional exercises of prayer, and with no observable detriment to any denominational interest. In the change of circumstances and of practice, a very natural desire has arisen with many, that the members of the parent institution might, in some distinct form, implore the blessing of the Lord when gathered in their great annual assembly. The committee, after carefully weighing these facts, feel that the friends of the society, while they have heretofore, by a devout reading of the Scriptures at their meetings, acknowledged God in their ways, and that he has directed their paths, may now, in altered circumstances, unite their supplications in a more formal way for the Divine guidance. They, therefore, recommend to the Board the adoption of the following resolutions: 1. Resolved, That the anniversary meetings of the society be hereafter opened with prayer, in addition to the usual reading of the Scriptures. 2. That the manner of carrying the above resolution into effect be left at the discretion of the president, in connection with the anniversary committee."

After much discussion, the further consideration of the report was deferred to the next meeting. The discussion was animated and sharp. The Quakers contended that mental prayer was all that was necessary, and the Episcopalians that the "holding forth" of Methodists and others was not suited to their taste.

On the part of some of the Episcopalians there was a high tone of remonstrance, and even menace; so that even our lamented friend, the Rev. Dr. Bethune, opposed the adoption of the resolution, on the ground that "we could not afford to lose our Episcopalian brethren." Out of doors, also, the discussion waxed warm, and the chairman of the committee was assailed as sowing discord among brethren, and as lending himself to a disruption of the society. On the 5th of December, the Board resumed the consideration of the report. The meeting was one of great interest; the discussion was extended and able; the younger members of the Board nobly confronted the arrogant position of Episcopacy, and the *report was adopted without amendment.*

At the next meeting, Mr. Pelatiah Perit moved a reconsideration of the whole subject; but, after some discussion, the Board adjourned without taking the question. At the following meeting, in February, the subject was resumed, and without taking the question, the Board appointed a *special* meeting, three weeks in advance, for further considering Mr. Perit's motion. At the appointed time, on the 27th of February, 1851, the discussion was resumed, and, without taking the question, the Board adjourned until the next day. The next day, at an unusually large meeting, the motion to reconsider was adopted, by a vote of twenty-nine to twenty; and at the next regular meeting, and while the reconsideration was under discussion, the Rev. Dr. Vermilye moved, that as there has been no legislation on this report, and that, as such legislative authorities seem inexpedient, "The Board recommend that arrangements for religious exercises at the anniversary meetings be left to the discretion of the presiding officer at each anniversary, with full liberty in the matter." This resolution was adopted as the report of the Board to the society, and adopted *unanimously;* and after manifestations of gratitude and mutual respect and esteem, and some minutes of silent prayer, the Board adjourned.

The result of this prolonged and excited discussion is, that not only the anniversary meetings of the society, but the monthly meetings of the Board, are *now opened with prayer and the reading of the Scriptures;* no man, Quaker or Episcopalian, forbidding it. "If thine eye be single, thy whole body shall be full of light." My memory lingers on these scenes with mingled wonder and delight; wonder, that Christian men should need to traverse so circuitous a path, in order to find a place of prayer, when their own hearts instinctively told them that He who is a spirit must everywhere be worshipped in spirit and truth; delight, because I had new evidence that Christianity is superior to sectarianism, and the Bible more reverenced than the Book of Common Prayer.

Is it not a goodly sight, yon Bible House, hallowed by the incense of so many mingled supplications, and sending from its teeming presses the Word of God to millions of the perishing! The Bible Society must look higher than denominational distinctions. It must have a nobler object to dispread its desires upon, and discovers and enjoys it wherever the Word of God has free course and is glorified.

The remaining subject of deep interest to the harmonious coöperation of the friends of the Bible in this land, relates to the *collation of the English Scriptures*, and *the new version*. I was led to pursue a course in this matter which induced some animadversion, if not obloquy; but which my own conscience and subsequent events fully justified. On the 7th of October, 1847, the *Committee on Versions* suggested to the Board of Managers the importance of collating the Scriptures in the English language, and at the same meeting the Board referred the subject to that committee, with directions to have the necessary collation made, and report the result to the Board.

At the next meeting of the Board, in September, 1848, the rules established by the committee in the execution of their trust were read to the Board, and the whole matter was referred to that committee, with powers.

The committee consisted of Rev. Gardiner Spring, Thomas Cock, M.D., Rev. Samuel H. Turner, D.D., Rev. Edward Robinson, D.D., L.L.D., Rev. Thomas E. Vermilye, D.D., Rev. John McClintock, and Rev. Richard S. Storrs, jr., embracing one from each religious denomination.

This committee employed the Rev. James W. McLane, D.D., to perform the laborious work of the collation under the direction of the committee, and to receive $1,500 for his labor. On the 1st of May, 1851, the committee presented a very able report of their labors, drawn up by Dr. Robinson, which was adopted by the Board, and one thousand copies of it were ordered to be printed in pamphlet form. As a suitable token of their regard for the services of this committee, the Board, at a subsequent meeting, presented to each of its members a copy of the imperial quarto Bible. I have no hesitation in affirming that the edition of the English Bible thus collated, is the best edition in the language; yet serious objections were made to it from individuals, from ecclesiastical bodies, and from auxiliary societies—not on the ground that the edition was not the best extant, but that the Board had transcended its powers, and "had issued a Bible as a standard, not in accordance with the version in common use, as required by the society's constitution."

It was urged, that if the society departed from this restriction in one instance, the precedent might lead to liberties which would be subversive of all confidence and coöperation. That they had departed in some cases was a conceded fact. The question was a serious one, and was seriously considered. It was referred to the Committee on Versions; and on the 12th of November the Board held a special meeting, to consider the report of that committee. That report, submitted by Dr. Vermilye on behalf of the committee, made a statement of the indefatigable toil of the committee, in this collation; of their efforts to circulate the report of their proceedings, and draw the attention of the public to the subject; that, for three years and a half, the action of the Board in this matter had been of public notoriety; that from the beginning of the work to the present time, a period of nine years, for full six of which the revised Bibles had been in the hands of the community, no word of objection to it had ever been uttered, but, on the other hand, many words of approbation; that recently, however, the subject had been taken up with warmth, and that misconceptions and misstatements had become current, and, as the natural result, much uneasiness has been felt in various quarters; that the discussion which had been had on the subject, had thrown light on the public mind, and greatly relieved the honest fears of many of the patrons of the society; that, after diligent inquiry, the committee have reason to believe that a very large proportion of the friends of the society are satisfied with what has been done, and desire no change; that, in restricting the society to the "version in common use," the constitution has not precluded the common-sense right, by careful collation and revision, of making their issues of the version as perfect as possible; that the objectors themselves have distinctly and candidly admitted that, in their opinion, our standard edition of the text is the *best* extant; that, as to the *accessories*, the case is different—they form no part of God's Word, but are the work of man, have been altered by men, are various in various editions, and that the Board are not required by the constitution to use them at all, or any part of them; that while the Board pay the utmost deference to the opinions of others, they ought not to infringe upon principle or right; that the old English Bible, "the version in common use," is still given by the society in its integrity.

The report is a long one, nor can I do justice to it in these pages. It closes with five resolutions; and upon the motion to adopt it, and after a prolonged, able, and very interesting discussion, though I gave it my cordial approbation, yet, speaking as a member of the Board, and not as a member of the Committee of Versions, and in order to quiet the public mind, I was ready to undo all that had been done, and well done, in making our standard Bible. I then submitted the following preamble and resolutions : " While the Board have strong convictions of the excellence of their recently revised edition of the Holy Scriptures, and are persuaded that the time is not far distant when the emendations there adopted, if not others of equal and greater importance, will be required by the intelligent readers of the sacred volume, yet, in view of the doubts expressed by numerous individuals, by some of their own auxiliaries, and by several ecclesiastical bodies, as to the constitutional power of the Board to make any such emendations, therefore, Resolved, That while the Board retains the text and its accessories, with the correction of the discrepancies in different editions of the English Bibles, referred to in the report of the Committee on Versions, they do hereby adopt its own royal-octavo edition of the English Bible of 1839, with accessories collated with the standard edition of Cambridge, Oxford, and London, as the standard edition of the text and its accessories, to which all future copies from the press of the society shall be conformed ; hoping by this amicable arrangement to strengthen the confidence and perpetuate the coöperation of all the friends of God's revealed truth."

This resolution, together with a paper submitted by the Rev. Dr. Turner, showing the various changes which have been made in the numerous editions of the Bible since 1611, and the many improvements adopted by the society in collating their standard copy, were referred to the Committee on Versions. At a subsequent meeting of the Board, on the 9th of November, 1857, the subject was resumed; when the chairman of the committee stated that the committee were unable to agree upon a report, and were constrained to return the whole subject to the decision of the Board. Whereupon he submitted the following preamble and resolution: " While the Managers of the American Bible Society have a preference for their recently revised edition of the Holy Scriptures, yet, in view of the doubts from various quarters as to the constitutional power of the Board concerning many of the emendations in that edition; therefore, Resolved, 1st, That in all future issues from the press of the society, the standard edition be the recently revised edition so far, and so far only, as it regards the collation of the text, and the correction of discrepancies in different editions of the English Bible in common use. Resolved, 2d, That the accessories of the text, that is, the use of italic words, capital letters, compound words, punctuation, parentheses, brackets, contents of chapters, running heads of columns, marginal notes, and references of the version in common use, be restored; and that they be subjected only to collation, with a view to the correction of those errors and mistakes which are manifest, and those changes which are required by the progress of the English language. Resolved, 3d, That it be referred to the Committee on Versions to carry out the provisions of the above resolutions, and that, in all cases where changes shall be introduced by them in the accessories of the text, these changes be submitted to the Board for their further approval."

The Rev. Dr. Vermilye then presented a series of resolutions, expressive of different views from the foregoing, and supported them with marked ability. I cannot introduce them here. They will be found at length in the minutes of the Board, vol. 8, p. 434. The Rev. Dr. Bedell and the Rev. Dr. Muhlenberg remarked that there was a wide-spread uneasiness in the Episcopal church in regard to the collated Bible. The Rev. S. I. Prime, D.D., also read the resolutions of the Synod of Pittsburgh, disapproving of the work of revision. After a long discussion, the Rev. Dr. Tyng moved that the whole subject be again referred to the Committee on Versions; which proposal he withdrew in favor of a motion of Rev. Dr. Storrs, referring the subject to a select committee of nine. Dr. Storrs' motion was adopted. This committee consisted of Rev. Dr. Storrs, Rev. William B. Sprague, Rev. Sherman De Witt, Rev. Bishop Janes, Rev. William Adams, Rev. Dr. Bedell, Hon. John McLean, Hon. Walter Lowrey, and Charles Tracy, Esq. On the 14th of January, the Board met and received the report of the committee of nine. The Rev. Dr. Storrs presented a minority report, offering other resolutions; when James Lenox, Esq., for himself and Rev. Dr. Boardman, presented a paper expressing the view that, while they did not entirely agree with the report of the majority of the committee, they would not oppose it. After a protracted discussion, the Board adjourned for two weeks, when, at an unusually large meeting, they took up the report of the majority of the committee and adopted it by a large majority, and which decided, in substance, that the alterations in the collated edition "are a *departure from the principles which should govern the society,*" and that it may "not adopt any change in the version upon ground ever so obvious to its managers or committee, but must confine itself strictly to the great trust committed to it by the constitution."

The Board, therefore, directed the Committee on Versions so to correct the present collated edition as to render it conformable to previous editions published by this society, or by the authorized British presses. At the next meeting, the Rev. Dr. Robinson presented a protest of the Committee on Versions against the action of the Board, which was accepted, and ordered to be placed in file. The Rev. Dr. Turner, Rev. Dr. Robinson, Rev. Dr. Vermilye, Rev. Dr. Floy, Rev. Dr. Storrs, and Thomas Cock, M.D., then offered their resignations as members of the Committee on Versions, which, after many expressions of confidence in that committee, and strenuous efforts to induce them to withdraw their resignations, were ultimately accepted. The Rev. Dr. Spring was the only member of that committee who did not resign his place; and for not so doing, he has been strongly commended and sharply censured. You ask me why, and I will tell you. In few words, I say, we, as a committee, transcended the limits of our authority; the Christian public saw it, and laid their hands upon us, and they did right. It was no part of our business to alter and amend the version in common use, but to present that version in the best form. We did more, and in doing so we were not justified. The Board might have adopted the revised edition without any change whatever. Or they might have rejected it, and returned to the edition of 1816, when the society was formed. I would have done this rather than peril harmony.

It was not a perfect edition, nor is our revision perfect; yet I would have adopted it if there were not "a more excellent way," and that is, to make such changes in the revised edition as shall render it more conformed to the old edition, and especially in restoring the Christology of the Old Testament. And this is what the Board has done. The time had not come for such a revision as the Committee on Versions had made. The cry was echoed and re-echoed, that the Board had been making alterations in the old English Bible! Nor could the Christian public be disabused of their alarm. My sober conviction was that the changes were premature; good as they are, they are not worth contending for, against the consciences of our friends who oppose them. My object was union in the Bible cause. In a day of division and rebuke, when Rome is girded for battle against the Word of God, it was of more importance that American Protestants should agree in adopting a standard edition of the English Bible, than that that edition itself should, in all respects, be unexceptionable. I therefore conscientiously relinquished our emendations. It was a grief of heart to me to grieve my beloved and honored brethren of the Version Committee in this matter.

Be it so, that they accuse me of fickleness; it was

not personal dignity that I contended for in this discussion : it was for the American Bible Society, fast anchored upon the Bible " in common use, without note or comment."

I am happy that the course I was directed by a kind Providence to pursue, received the approbation of the friends of the society throughout the churches, especially of my own denomination. My co-presbyters congratulated me, and the members of my own pastoral charge congratulated me. I hope I may be allowed, without the implication of vanity, to record the following communication.

"New York, *Feb.* 16, 1858.

" Rev. Dr. Spring :

" My honored Pastor : It was with no ordinary feelings of gratification and thankfulness, that I perused in the last number of the New York Observer, the truly Christian and conservative thoughts you were permitted to express so beautifully before the American Bible Society. I can well estimate the courage and self-denying firmness which the case called for on your part, as an advocate of that excellent committee, in whose labors you were so long associated, and whose individual resignations were then still ringing in the ears of the Board of Managers.

" This innovation may work this substantial good, that hereafter sacrilegious hands may be deterred from touching the Ark. May the self-denying brotherly kindness, so beautifully manifested in your appeal to the Board, have a tendency to soften the acerbity which such a position would naturally tend to produce in the other members of the committee. That you, dear pastor, may long remain to pour on the oil of kindness and courtesy, and to give to the Christian world the benefit of your judgment and experience, is the humble desire of

"Yours, S. N."

A beloved daughter has also preserved the following record of the views of the late Rev. Dr. Potts, of this city:—" The morning after the meeting of the Bible Society, at which the members of the Version Committee had all tendered their resignations except my father, I met the Rev. Dr. Potts. He stopped me to inquire whether he should find my father at home; and then spoke of the interest he had taken in the late action of the Bible Society. 'I was much gratified,' he said, ' at the course taken by your good father. Never did he act more in character as a Christian gentleman. It is not easy to *take the back track;* but those of us who have been associated for years with your father in Presbytery and Synod, know that for *him* it is a very hard thing indeed. But last night he did it, and did it handsomely. I was proud of him.' "

I am ashamed to have written this entire chapter almost wholly in self-defence. But the harmony which has distinguished the American Bible Society, and the vigorous and successful prosecution of its great work, if they do not show that in this vexed question " wisdom is justified of her children," at least show that there is no wisdom in " sowing discord among brethren."

END OF VOLUME I.

www.ingramcontent.com/pod-product-compliance
Ingram Content Group UK Ltd.
Pitfield, Milton Keynes, MK11 3LW, UK
UKHW021301180426
11947UKWH00015B/960